Hesse-Hanau Order Books, a Diary and Rosters

A Collection of Items Concerning the Hesse-Hanau Contingent of "Hessians" Fighting Against the American Colonists in the Revolutionary War

Translated by
Bruce E. Burgoyne

HERITAGE BOOKS
2006

HERITAGE BOOKS
AN IMPRINT OF HERITAGE BOOKS, INC.

Books, CDs, and more—Worldwide

For our listing of thousands of titles see our website at
www.HeritageBooks.com

Published 2006 by
HERITAGE BOOKS, INC.
Publishing Division
65 East Main Street
Westminster, Maryland 21157-5026

Copyright © 2003 Bruce E. Burgoyne

All rights reserved. No part of this book may be reproduced or transmitted in any form or by any means, electronic or mechanical, including photocopying, recording or by any information storage and retrieval system without written permission from the author, except for the inclusion of brief quotations in a review.

International Standard Book Number: 978-0-7884-2461-0

CONTENTS

Introduction	i
Anonymous Hesse-Hanau Diary	1
Brigadier (Colonel) von Gall's Order Book	32
Order Book of the Hesse-Hanau Hereditary Prince Infantry Regiment	78
Rosters of the Hesse-Hanau Hereditary Prince Infantry Regiment, Captain Pausch's Artillery Company, Jaeger Corps, and Hesse-Cassel Recruits	228

Introduction

This volume contains miscellaneous items concerning the Heese-Hanau contingent of "Hessians" who fought against the American colonists during the Revolutionary War.

Although the order books are not complete, they contain considerable information which is of importance concerning the American Revolution. The documents are:

1) *An Anonymous Diary,* believed to have been written by Paul Wihelm Schefer, Auditor of the Hesse-Hanau Hereditary Prince Regiment. I can not remember the source of the document, but believe the document from which I worked, had been printed in a German magazine.

2) *Order Book of General von Gall,* Colonel and Commandant of the Hesse-Hanau troops serving in Canada. Upon his arrival in Canada, he was named a brigadier by the English General Guy Carleton, the Governor of Canada. Von Gall accompanied General John Burgoyne on his 1777 movement toward Albany. The document from which I translated was Part 2, of Tom IX, of the Lidgerwood Collection in the Morristown National Historical Park (NHP), at Morristown, New Jersey.

The Lidgerwood Collection contains a number of "Hessian" documents, which have been translated previously by other translators, including Part I of the von Gall Order Book.

3) *Order Book of the Hesse-Hanau (*Hereditary Prince*) Regiment/* A translation in the Lidgerwood Collection, also.

4*)* Rosters of the Hesse-Hanau Infantry Regiment and the Jaeger Corps, are not translations, but lists prepared by Colonel Charles Rainsford, English Commissary Officer in Holland. The Rainsford Papers (Vols. 23644-23680) are in the British Museum, in London, England, and also can be found in *The New York Historical Society Collections for the Year 1879,* Vol. XII.

Bruce E. Burgoyne
Dover, DE - 2002

An Anonymous Diary

Possibly written
By
Paul Wilhelm Schefer
Auditor of the
Hesse-Hanau Hereditary Prince Regiment

Anonymous Hesse-Hanau Diary

Journal - Commencing 15 March 1776
When the Hesse-Hanau Regiment Departed for America

1. The Journey from Kesselstadt to Portsmouth

In 1776, on the 15th of March, the Hesse-Hanau Hereditary Prince received orders, after having been sold into English service on 1 January 1776, to assemble on the usual parade ground. And, after being reviewed by the gracious ruler, the mentioned regiment marched to the Rhine River above Kesselstadt, where seven transport ships and two yachts were already standing, waiting to be boarded. After the soldiers had boarded the above mentioned ships, they immediately sailed as far as Offenbach, where we anchored and spent the night.

On 16 March, early in the morning, we resumed our journey, and had the unbelievable good fortune to have our gracious prince and the court marshal von Gall accompany us as far as Frankfurt am Main, where they took their sad farewell from the troops, and returned to Hanau.

On 17 March we set sail at five o'clock in the morning, stopping on land at Rheinfels and St. Goar at midday and halting for the night on the Rhine River between Coblenz and Ehrenbreitstein.

On 18 March, we resumed our journey, stopping at Andernach at noon, passing the residence city of

Anonymous Hesse-Hanau Diary

Bonn, and arriving at Cologne, where we anchored for the fourth night, at about six o'clock in the evening.

On 19 March, the anchor was raised at five o'clock in the morning. We passed Duesseldorf at about three-thirty, and Kaiserwerth at five o'clock, arriving at Uerdingen, where we anchored and remained overnight. Because of indisposition I slept in the small city during the night.

On 20 March, we did not resume our journey until two o'clock in the afternoon, due to storms and rain, and arrived not far from Orsoy, in Prussian territory, at seven o'clock in the evening, where we anchored and remained overnight.

On 21 March, at six o'clock in the morning, we sailed on, passing Wesel at about nine o'clock, and Rees at noon, after which we arrived near to Emmerich at two o'clock, and anchored at once. The soldiers received both pay and bread here. Also, it was necessary to pay two English bank notes of 200 pounds sterling for the exorbitant Prussian customs, which in our money amounted to 420 ducats, 3 guilder, 3 schillings before receiving a Prussian permit to continue our voyage.

On 22 March, we resumed our voyage with the rising sun, passing the so-called "Schenkenschwanze" at noon, and arriving happily at Nijmegen toward evening, where we anchored. We received orders to debark at once, in order to be mustered at the parade

Anonymous Hesse-Hanau Diary

ground in Nijmegen, which was carried out by the English Colonel [Charles] Rainsford. After this we returned to our ships, and spent the night therein. All the regimental officers dined this evening with the Dutch commandant, van der Hoope..

On 23 March, we left our ships, and the entire regiment, by companies, took the oath of allegiance to the King of England. Afterward we entered on the twelve Dutch ships and three yachts, and immediately set sail, passing Tiel an hour and one-half later, and arrived at Bonnel at about five-thirty in the evening. We spent this night on the Waal River.

On 24 March, the anchor was raised at five o'clock in the morning. We passed the city of Duercken at seven-thirty, Serkendam at nine o'clock, Gliedrecht at eleven o'clock, and Dordrecht, a beautiful Dutch city through which many canals pass, at about twelve-thirty. At that place, an arm of the Waal River goes off to the right toward Rotterdam. Four hours [about ten miles] from Dordrecht lies the beautiful village of Zwinnrecht. Here we saw our first three-masted ships and after traveling a little farther, a much larger view of the water, on which we noticed a few storms. This was where we ended our trip.

On the 25th of March, at about three o'clock, the three yachts, but not the above mentioned transports carrying the regiment, arrived at the harbor at Willenstadt, where the four transport ships assigned to

Anonymous Hesse-Hanau Diary

carry us to our destination, lay at anchor. Here we also met the English Ambassador to the Hague, [Joseph] Yorke, who had come here to see the regiment. All the officers, who had arrived on the yachts, had the honor to dine with him this evening. Willemstadt is small, with a harbor, and a Scottish regiment as a garrison.

On 26 March, the regiment arrived, having been delayed by contrary winds on the 25th and 26th, as well as the yachts of the English transport ships, whose names were: 1. *Three Sisters,* Captain Mueller, on which were the Leib]Body] Company, and half the Gredadier Company; 2. *Margaritha,* Captain Preston, on which were the Lieutenant Colonel's Company, and the other half of the Grenadier Company; 3. *Content,* Captain Bell, on which were the Major's Company, and the other half of the Grenadier Company [?] and 4. *Staggs,* Captain Sanders, on which was Passern's Company. We were immediately engaged with the movement of men and equipment, so that by four o'clock in the afternoon, everything was in order, and the mentioned English ambassador, accompanied by Colonel Rainsford, came aboard the ships to visit the troops, and to wish the ships' captains well. Following this they returned to their yacht, in order to sail for the Hague, and were given a salute by the cannons aboard the four ships.

On 27 March, we set sail at about ten o'clock in

Anonymous Hesse-Hanau Diary

the morning, passing Hellevoetsluis, a small Dutch city on the sea, with a large harbor, where after anchoring several times, we entered a part of the open sea, which is called La Manche, or Les Pas de Calais, and where

On 28 March, we had stormy weather, which set the ships into constant movement. The sails were taken in at once, and in general everyone became seasick.

On 29 March, we became aware of the coasts of England and France during the early morning hours, and after a short time, they were clearly visible. We then anchored eighteen miles from Portsmouth, and remained there overnight.

On 30 March, we set sail at eight o'clock in the morning, but due to poor winds, only arrived at Portsmouth at six o'clock in the evening, where we met the first division of Brunswick troops, who had been lying there in the harbor for some days, and were to proceed with us to America. The English harbor women [Hockenweiber] came aboard our ships as soon as we arrived, and brought us white bread, English beer, oranges, lemons, and many mor3e items, which were for sale.

On 31 March, I went into the city of Portsmouth with several other officers, in part from curiosity to see the city, in part to buy provisions for aboard ship, as well as to get something to eat there, for which we

Anonymous Hesse-Hanau Diary

had to pay dearly, however. A single noon meal ordered by one of us, consisting of a bowl of the host's soup, a dish full of half-cooked potatoes, a good ragout of chicken, and a good roast veal, cost three and one-half schillings. The city is rather large, has pleasant, but also rather low houses, built of bricks, and of no less importance, regular streets. The inhabitants are mostly seamen or sailors, as well as pitiful women, or *Filles de la bonne Fortune*, of whom far too many live here. The large harbor divides the city into two parts. In the main city there is a very fine armory, where rigging is spun , and on which an unimaginable number of cannons are to be found, all of which were poured in this country. They are very fine pieces, and provided with very much ammunition. Opposite the city there is a very fine hospital, which appears from a distance as one of the most beautiful castles, and is responsible for the care of the sailors and marines. Having seen all that, we returned to our ship, where we remained until

2 April, peacefully, going into the city occasionally to observe the ship building and other activations. Here we found several warships, including one of the line, called *Brtittannia*, which was being built. On the forward part of the ship stood Neptune with his trident and the royal coat of arms, and the description *Dieu et mon droit.* There were three levels of cabins, one above the other. The entire

Anonymous Hesse-Hanau Diary

construction was very splendid, kitchen and cellar, and all else so well laid out that it could not be forgotten. The length of the ship, considering the interior, was about 186 English feet; the width, 52 feet, five inches. I did not understand the height too the main deck. Its foremast was nine feet in diameter, the mainmast, ten and one-half feet, and the missenmast, the same as the foremast. The height of the mainmast to the tip, was seventy feet, and set 28 feet deep into the lowest bilge. Ir carried 112 cannons, from 12 to 64 pounders. The beds consisted solely of hammocks. In the academy we also saw a verse in French, written about the conquest of Quebec by General [James] Wolfe and Admiral Saunders. After that we returned to our ship, in a small boat, or shell.

Anonymous Hesse-Hanau Diary

The Voyage across the Atlantic Ocean
To the Coast of Canada

On 4 April, we sailed from Portsmouth under the leadership of General [John] Burgoyne, in the following order: First, His Excellency, the Commanding General Burgoyne, led on the frigate *Blonde*, 28 cannons and the appropriate number of marines. Next, sailed some English artillery; the Brunswick 1st Division, consisting of 1) Breymann Grenadier Battalion, 2) the Riedesel Dragoon Regiment, commanded by Colonel (Friedrich] Baum, 3) the Prince Friedrich Regiment, commanded by Colonel Praetorius, 4) the Riedesell Regiment, commanded by Colonel Spaeth, then our regiment, commanded by Colonel von Gall, and Major General [William] Phillips of the English artillery on the frigate *Juno*, 18 cannons. The entire fleet amounted to two frigates and 37 transport ships. But we anchored almost at once, departing again an hour later, under a cannonade fired by the warships, which was in part a signal to set sail, in part a show of honor to the general. We sailed for about an hour, and then, because of unfavorable winds, again lay at anchor, until finally, during the afternoon, we again set sail.

On 5 April, we continued to advance, but slowly, toward noon, when we had to tack constantly due to the contrary winds. During this time, we had a constant view of the English coast.

Anonymous Hesse-Hanau Diary

On 6 April, we sailed onward, slowly, with the still unfavorable winds. We had completely lost sight of the coast of England, however, and only the water could be seen on all sides. Toward noon, a very tired lark landed on our ship, and received nourishment in the form of some oats.

On 7 April, a storm arose during the night, which caused our ship to move violently. Toward morning, the sea was again quite calm. Also, a frigate from our escort, departed for Portsmouth to escort the remaining warships and transports of the second division, lying there. Toward ten o'clock in the morning, the frigate was saluted with a bombardment of cannons. We cruised steadily along the English coast, and not far from Plymouth, noticed a rock formation in the water, on which a lighthouse stood, in which three people live in order to keep a lantern burning therein at night, so that ships will not run aground. The wind was so strong all day that waves beat over the deck. At eleven o'clock, seven ships carrying Scots, came out of Plymouth to join us, and we then continued our voyager to America, with God's help. This evening, such a strong storm arose, that chairs, tables, rum, brandy, bottles, and everything mixed together, bounced around in the cabin, and broke, including the not yet secured medicine cabinet, cheese, bread, butter, plums, and sugar, all mixed up with a number of articles of clothing, so that it made a

Anonymous Hesse-Hanau Diary

real mess, and because of the exciting disturbance, no one could sleep during the entire night.

On 8 April, we continued to sail with rather good wind, but noticed that one of our ships, with two masts, had raised a red flag a short time before. What was wrong with it, as this is a danger signal, is still unknown to us

On 9 April, the stormy weather continued and the seasickness again became general, from which Colonel von Gall and I were least affected. The rest of the time I felt quite well, however, toward evening the storm abated. We went to bed and slept very well during the night, and the wind could not have been better for our voyage.

On 10 April, we sailed with rather favorable winds, and because of the nice weather, remained on deck almost the entire day.

On 11 April, the wind was still good, but very weak, and the weather indicated several consecutive days of being not so good., but not so rainy.

On 12 April, we sailed onward with a steady wind, but dark and foreboding weather.

On 13 April, we had favorable winds and very fine weather, which caused me, as everything seemed so peaceful, to make a few entries about our situation, and the food on board the ship. Above all, the food, although not that to which a German stomach is accustomed, is very good and consisted of the

Anonymous Hesse-Hanau Diary

following: 1) of salted beef, 2) zweiback, 3) salted pork, 4) flour, 5) peas and raisins, 6) butter, 7) cheese, 8) rum, 9) beer, etc., always changing as to amount and manner, but limited. But this was not the only reason to be careful, because our stomachs could not always tolerate these items, especially the rum, hard bread, and the sickening peas and grout soup made from the unappetizing ship's rations, which those who became sick occasionally received. But what was there to do? When the need exists, learning is quick, especially for soldiers. For the officers, however, it was fortunate that they, like myself had obtained everything in Portsmouth, otherwise they would have had no advantage except for the wine, which His Highness had provided as a gift, so that all the officers who were on the colonel's ship, could have a few bottles. The others received nothing except that which they had provided for themselves. Our ship had, counting all sailors and soldiers, about 380 persons on board. Our ship's captain was a rather coarse and solid man, as are most English, and seamen. He had supplied himself with many necessities, such as wine, coffee, 'sugar, tea, and beer, and also clothing items, which were very expensive, however, and were sold to us at a very great profit.

On 14 April, the fine weather and winds continued, but later were very weak, and we sailed only sixty English miles in a day.

Anonymous Hesser-Hanau Diary

On 15 April, another storm arose, which would have cleared everything from our cabin, if we had not secured it well before hand. It rained all day, but the wind remained favorable, so that we sailed fifteen miles in an hour, or 300 English miles in 24 hours. Again, in the afternoon, a strong storm arose, so that it was nearly impossible to sleep,

On 16 April, the storm still continued, but not as strong. However, it was impossible to stand, and no one was able to cook. Toward evening it appeared as if the storm would abate, but

On 17 April, when we awoke, although the sun was shining, this did not last long, and was soon followed by wind and rain. During the afternoon, it became so bright that everyone went on deck, even though the sea was restless, and the waves beat over the deck

On 18 April this continued.

On 19 April, we had such contrary wind, that we made almost no headway.

On 20 April, the wind was more favorable, and we sailed very well. Soon we were joined by a fleet from Ireland, consisting of 41 transport ships, and some frigates, on which were four artillery companies, and the 9th, 57th, 47th, 20th, 21st, 62nd, 29th, 34th, and 42nd Regiments, a grenadier battalion, and light infantry from England, who were also to sail to America with us. Our ships were given the signal to halt so the two

Anonymous Hesser-Hanau Diary

commanders could speak together. As the new fleet sailed amidst our fleet, one of their ships unfortunately rammed one of ours, but without serious injury, and this fleet continued onward with us, as I have mentioned above. However, we followed behind it at a great distance. During the night, a great storm arose at about ten o'clock, which however, did not last long. Still the ocean was very restless, and carried us a great distance forward.

On 21 April, the Irish fleet still sailed on our right. We had fair weather, but strong winds.

On 22 April, we had a full west wind, with heavy rain. This continued all day, and caused severe problems in our cabin.

On 23 April, we had wind-borne rain in the morning, and a pleasant afternoon, but without wind.

On 24 April, after a good night, we had rather favorable southeast wind, so that we sailed swiftly. We met a packet-boat coming from America, which halted near the admiral's ship, delivered an order, and continued sailing toward England.

On 25 April, we encountered another severe storm, which was much stronger than all the earlier ones had been. It made the previous night very unpleasant, and on the following night,

On 26 April, it was much worse, as a severe storm struck, which threw the ship back and forth, so that the water remained only seven inches below the main

Anonymous Hesser-Hanau Diary

deck. This was followed by a very bright, but cold morning, and the entire day was tolerable. However, nine of our ships were missing, as well as a warship, including the transport ship *Margarithe Mathias*, on board which was our Colonel's Company, and one-half of the Grenadier Company. This caused us some problems.

On 27 April, we had a very bright morning, after having had a much better night's sleep than on the previous night, and such a good wind, that we sailed eight English miles in an hour.

On 28 April, another storm arose with considerable rain, but the wind was favorable for our journey, and after the storm we enjoyed a very pleasant evening.

On 29 April, we had a rather good wind, but at the same time, it was so cold that no one could remain on deck. At this point, the ship's captain assured us that in two days the coast of Newfoundland would be seen, which was very pleasant news for us. [A note states that it took another fourteen days before land was seen.]

On 30 April, the wind was contrary, and we tacked the entire day.

On 1 May, the wind was favorable, but weak, the weather tolerable, but with thick fog so that the ships had to signal all day with cannon shots to prevent colliding with one another.

Anonymous Hesser-Hanau Diary

On 2 May, the wind was weak, and as usual in this region, very foggy. We saw many sea ducks.

On 3 May, the wind was still favorable, but the fog continued. At six o'clock in the morning, a French and a Dutch ship sailed among us, in order to catch fish near the Grand Bank. The first was about 85 miles from Cape Breton. Therefore, we had sailed quite a long distance to this sand bank, where we lay-to for a time in order to fish, catching eleven cod in a short time. We then sailed on with the best of winds.

On 4 May, we sailed a long stretch during the night with a very favorable wind, but because of the constant fog were unable to see land.

On 5 May, the sun shone brightly. Toward evening we saw a very large fish, which shot water as high as two men, into the air, and its head could occasionally be seen. The captain said it must be some type of whale, weighing from four to five thousand pounds, which came from Greenland.

On 6 May, we had almost no wind. Toward evening it became contrary, and it snowed.

On 7 May, the weather was as on the previous day, and with extremely cold weather, we had no chance of seeing land.

On 8 May, the weather was fine, but without wind, and we still had to sail one hundred miles to the closest island.

On 9 May, wind and weather were as on the

Anonymous Hesser-Hanau Diary

previous day. Toward noon, a fairly good wind arose which brought rain, however, and about five o'clock it developed into a storm, which caused the captain to fear the nearby sandbanks and rocks, as well as the coast of Newfoundland, but the storm abated about eleven o'clock in the morning. On the other hand, the sailors rose up in anger against the captain and his officers, and fought them, so that most had bloody faces.

On 10 May, a long-smoldering hatred broke out among the sailors against their captain, who was more than an infamous ruffian, so that they called him all possible bad names, to his face, and really would have thrown him overboard, if he had not been protected by the colonel and all the other officers, who forbid them from laying hands on him anymore. Therefore, he called to the man-of-war for help. The warship at once lowered a boat, and a marine officer came to our ship, and settled the matter at once. He took two of our best sailors back to the frigate with him, which meant the most severe punishment for them. Even the captain of a merchant ship, as long as it is in royal service, is accountable to a man-of-war, or a warship. Not to forget the weather, we had completely dull and windless weather. Toward evening a storm and wind and rain arose, which continued

On 11 May, until noon, when we, as well as three other ships of our fleet, became aware [of something

Anonymous Hesser-Hanau Diary

in the distance to the north. There appears to be a printing error of some sort at this point.] It was very cold, with contrary wind.

On 12 May, we again had a strong wind during the night, which not only continued all the next day, but also drove us from the fleet, and almost no one was able to remain on deck, due to the strong wind and continuous cold weather.

On 13 May, an east wind filled the sails so that we traveled seven English miles in an hour. About nine o'clock, the mate brought us the good news, that the coast of Cape Breton, or Newfoundland, where Louisburg is the capital city, could be seen. Pleased with this news, we hurried on deck to gaze at it in wonder. Some of the sailors even risked climbing the three masts in order to see. Toward noon we left the coast, and sailed directly for the St. Lawrence River.

On 15 May, the weather was beautiful, but there was no wind.

On 16 May, we had almost no wind, and it was very foggy, which resulted in a special situation arising, which fortunately did not cause serious damage. About nine o'clock one of our transport ships collided with ours, and their bow crashed into the window just behind the right side of our cabin, where Lieutenant Sartorius had his bed, which was not disturbed. At once, on both ships, efforts were employed to separate the ships. On the other ship,

Anonymous Hesser-Hanau Diary

more than twenty people, part from the English Artillery on board, part sailors with bare feet and only a shirt, worked at this. Our loss was a window, and the glass therein, and so we were separated. Toward noon, the wind strengthened but we could only profit from part of it. As soon as darkness began to descend, we again caught sight of land, part Anticosti Island. We were sailing rather swiftly, and had a better night than the previous evening, when we were rather close together.

On 17 May, we caught sight of land on the left side, rather more clearly, as we were 27 miles from the Gulf of St. Lawrence. The cold was very strong, and we sailed toward the northeast, full of hope of entering the river. We passed Anticosti Island which remained always on our right side, at about noon, but with a steadily contrary wind. At six o'clock, a better wind developed. We enjoyed one of the most pleasant evenings, with Anticosti always in sight to our right. The night was very restful, and we had

On 18 May, a very clear morning. Soon it became dull and at noon, during a complete calm, a heavy snow began to fall. The evening remained calm, but during the night we had a better wind, so that we sailed a long stretch.

Anonymous Hesse-Hanau Diary

The Voyage in the Gulf of St. Lawrence
And the St. Lawrence River to Quebec

On 19 May, as on a very bright and beautiful day, we could make out the above mentioned island. But even more clearly to our left, we could see the coast of Canada, and the red foot hills called Cape Rouge. We sailed rather swiftly. Toward evening the wind abated, and during a near clam, we spent a peaceful night.

On 20 May, although we had the finest weather, we made almost no headway due to a near calm. The evening was very pleasant and quiet. Still, a favorable wind gradually arose to help our trip, and we had the good fortune, about eight o'clock in the evening, to sail from the gulf into the St. Lawrence River, with the best of winds, and at a frightfully rapid pace.

On 21 May, we lost our good wind, and after much rain the wind became unfavorable. About nine o'clock in the morning, we met a frigate from Quebec with orders to cruise in this area, to prevent the entrance of enemy ships. After halting for a time beside our escorting frigate, it sailed on. Toward three o'clock in the afternoon, we received a good wind, which died out completely during the following night.

On 23 May, we made almost no headway due to contrary winds, and as a result had to tack back and forth. Not only that, but the wind drove us twelve miles backward. It continued like this

On 24 May, for almost the entire day, and the

Anonymous Hesse-Hanau Diary

contrary wind would not let us advance. Toward evening the wind abated so that until the following morning, we made little headway.

On 25 May, a very favorable wind arose, which became so strong by ten o'clock in the morning, that we sailed six and one-half in the sea, and three and one-half miles an hour in the strong St. Lawrence current. But this wind not only continued, but increased in strength. During the evening, because of the many rocks in the area, we anchored between the solid ground and the Isle of Bic, lying to our left. Unfortunately, we also lost our favorable wind until the following evening, which made it necessary for us on this evening, and

On 26 May, the first Whitsuntide, to remain at anchor. It was especially noticeable here, that while in Germany, the east wind seldom, but the south and west winds generally bring pleasant weather. At least we had time enough to enjoy the surroundings here, as we had to lay at anchor all day, due to contrary wind. On our right, lay the mentioned Isle of Bic, which is uninhabited, but grown over with many fir and oak trees. On our left however, lay a stretch of land covered with hills, rocks, and forests. It is said many Indians live therein, who are large and strong, brown complexioned, and with long black hair. Their homes are made with opposing poles, interlaced with wood, and covered over with moss, which they first here, and

Anonymous Hesse-Hanau Diary

then there, set up. They carry on a limited agriculture on this side of the coast, and nourish themselves with hunting and fishing, which they take to Quebec to trade for rum, flints, powder, and lead. The wind swung about nine o'clock in the evening, and became favorable so that the anchor was raised about eleven-thirty. When we awoke

On 27 May, we had sailed so far that we found ourselves in a completely different region, and were aware of several small houses and people on the coast to our left. These were civilized colonists who lived from fishing, and had their cultivated ground and low-built homes made of wood, near the coast.

28 May, the wind was still favorable, but the anchor was not raised until near eight o'clock. After sailing only a few hours, near the Isle of Courdes, we encountered a calm, and found ourselves at the same time, at one of the most dangerous parts of the river. With difficulty we anchored where the flood and ebb tides are most noticeable. The mentioned island lies about 150 English miles from Quebec, the capital of Canada. It is about ten miles in circumference, and inhabited by sixty families, who are mostly royal pilots, and much more polite and friendly than many other polished people. The commander gave the signal to raise anchor, as a severe storm appeared in the offing, during which the wind would blow very strongly. Therefore, we sailed backward a short

Anonymous Hesse-Hanau Diary

distance and again dropped anchor. At this point, an English transport ship, which had several officers dressed in green uniforms on board, came down the river. We were unable to learn if they were captured rebels. Toward evening a small ship, with one mast, approached from the north side, which had sailed from Quebec, and had 41 pilots meant for us on board. Each transport ship was assigned one as a guide, because of the dangerous voyage. The pilots had hardly come on board the ship, before everyone's curiosity to see and speak with this first Canadian arose, not only to hear the news of the recapture of Quebec from the rebel hands, but also to learn the situation inland, all of which he reported completely and truthfully. With a good wind, we sailed onward and passed the Isle de Havre, an island some seven or eight miles long, in the middle of the river.

On 29 May, the wind, which arose during the night, blew frightfully against us, so that we were forced to lie at anchor all day. Toward eleven o'clock at night, the anchor was raised and we sailed a distance past a dangerous place, until

On 30 May, when the ebb tide set in, and we had to anchor again. About ten o'clock the flood tide came, and by tacking we sailed on. The weather was fine, but as cold as in Germany in March. The banks on the right and left were built-up and occupied, and the individual farms were separated by trees.

Anonymous Hesse-Hanau Diary

Generally, the farther into the St. Lawrence that we sailed, the more beautifully the banks and islands were built-up and occupied. We anchored about six o'clock, and a boatload of Brunswickers went on land to buy food. We sailed on at eleven o'clock at night, but

On 31 May, at six o'clock in the morning we anchored again because of the ebb tide, and waited until twelve o'clock when we again sailed with the flood tide. Already at this place, the land is no longer so hilly, and is a pleasant region near the Isle Madame, where several of our pilots lived. The English landed not far from there in 1759, during the last war, near an old church. At the new one, which stands here in a better manner, the second transport ship had dropped anchor and landed, which resulted in the ship's captain finding our old Jew, who had set his ship on fire, and sent it up in smoke, although the people were saved.

[The abrupt change of subject matter would seem to indicate an omission of part of the German text at this point, by the type-setter.] This entire stretch, it is to be noted, is also called "Landslide", and justifiably so. At three o'clock at night, we sailed on and continued until

On 1 June, at noon, we again halted between beautiful regions, only two hours from Quebec, near the Isle d'Orleans. It is a beautiful island, about sixteen miles long, whose end is only a few miles from

Anonymous Hesse-Hanau Diary

Quebec, and it has only seven parishes, or small villages. Here, a boat was sent on land, and we enjoyed the first fresh food. Toward evening we sailed on, and had the good fortune to arrive at Quebec at six-thirty. We anchored at once, and to our joy and great astonishment, met our lone-lost transport ship, *Margaritha Mathias,* on board which was our colonel, his company, and half of the Grenadier Company, as well as many other war and transport ships. They had arrived two days previous, and told us that they had not only visited the Governor and General [Guy] Carleton, but that already ships with troops, had been sent to the second-most important city, Montreal, as well as an equal number to Three Rivers. The colonel and the major immediately went ashore to pay their compliments to the governor.

Anonymous Hesse-Hanau Diary

In Quebec

On 2 June, Sunday, I went in company with, or more correctly, socially into the city of Quebec with several officers, where we ate our noon meal, and saw the sites. Quebec is the capital city and the seat of government for the government of all Canada, and was founded in 1668. It is divided into an upper and a lower city. The lower part lies on the water, and the inhabitants are mostly fishermen and sailors. The upper part lies on a mountain and cliffs, and is therefore not only defended by artificial means, but by nature also. The streets are irregular, crooked, and narrow, also dirty, and unpaved. Still, there are fine buildings here, including several churches, a Jesuit, Franciscan, and a cloister for nuns, as well as a seminary. The above mentioned nunnery, or Ursaline Cloister, lies a quarter of an hour outside the city, and is really a very beautiful building, which is well furnished. What the city has to offer in addition, is that it is of medium size, fortified, and has two suburbs, one of which is called St. Jean. I forget the other name. They were both burned down during the recent siege, and are completely in ruins.

As I had the good fortune to become acquainted with some Canadians, I learned the situation of the recent siege, which merits being noted here. Canada has enjoyed complete peace and quiet since the conclusion of the last peace treaty, but this was greatly

Anonymous Hesse-Hanau Diary

disturbed by the arrival of a corps of American rebels, six thousand strong. They approached over the fortress Carillon on Lake Champlain, captured Fort St. John, and also Fort Chambly, making two regiments, including the 71st Regiment, prisoners of war. These were the only troops in Canada at that time, and therefore, the rebels had the opportunity of moving so far inland, that they were able to take Montreal, and then marched on Quebec, where they arrived on 4 September 1775.

General [Richard] Montgomery, as the commander of the six thousand rebels, at once called upon the city to surrender, which however, the then Commandant and Colonel, [Francis] Maclean, a very good soldier, absolutely refused. At the time, General Carleton was not in Quebec, but in Montreal, from which place he was daily awaited, and to which place because of the swiftness of the rebels' approach, he had secretly fled. On the 10th, the Americans began to fire into the city, and on the 19th, General Carleton quietly arrived. The first order which he gave, was that everyone who wished, could leave the city if not inclined to help with the defense. Many merchants and inhabitants still had good opinions of the Americans, and as can be imagined, left Quebec. Furthermore, he took every opportunity to prepare a good defense, although he had only a few regular soldiers, including men from Maclean's newly raised corps, consisting only of

Anonymous Hesse-Hanau Diary

artillery.

Although it was terribly cold, the Americans continued their siege, with which they seemed relatively quiet, until the night of the New Year, 31 December 1775 to 1 January 1776, when General Montgomery had determined to take the city by storm. However, this did not succeed, fortunately, as will be seen in the following account.

I have not meant to neglect the cloister, which lies a half hour outside Quebec, in which the rebels had their hospital, and among the nuns were two sisters of General Carleton, who, as I will explain, had an important influence on the restoration of freedom to Quebec. They promised their brother, the Governor and General Carleton, above all, to give news of what the rebels were preparing to undertake, and by means of a certain sign, ringing of a bell which was in the tower of the cloister, and whose peal was very familiar to the inhabitants of the city. They actually did this, and on the day when the Americans planned their attack, there was dark and unfriendly weather. The inhabitants also anticipated an attack, so that everyone felt that if this warning were not received, the city would surely be taken by the Americans. Therefore, the two sisters gave the general the appropriate signal at the right time, so that the inhabitants took up their weapons, and were placed in a defensive condition.

About two o'clock in the afternoon, General

Anonymous Hesse-Hanau Diary

Montgomery attacked on one side, and Brigadier [Benedict] Arnold, a former horse-handler, on the other side of the city. They were at once beaten back, and Montgomery remained, as he was about to climb a wall, on the spot, while his brigadier, Arnold, barely had time to retreat with his command.

During this affair, General Carleton captured about 400 Americans

When General Montgomery was found dead the next morning, on the place where he had fallen, the governor had him buried with full military honors.

Although the Americans now saw their advantage lost, they were still determined not to leave Quebec. General Arnold changed the siege into a blockade, remaining in place until 6 May 1776, when to the great joy of all the inhabitants of Quebec, the frigate, *Surprise*, entered the harbor at Quebec, from England. This joy was doubled on 8 May, when Commander Douglas also entered here with the warship *Thio*, 54 cannons, bringing some fresh troops, who immediately put ashore. The same day, General Carleton undertook a sortie, without meeting any resistance, because the Americans, after hearing the news that three ships had arrived in the harbor, experienced such a shock, that on the 8th, they took flight without losing any time, and hurried on to Point au Tremble, arriving at two o'clock in the morning. Cannons, as well as ammunition, gun carriages, and other wagons, and

Anonymous Hesse-Hanau Diary

more of the same, were all left standing.

How pleased the inhabitants of Quebec saw themselves, suddenly freed from the six-month siege, and unrest. General Carleton received the greatest praise, as he had done everything necessary.

This is the full story of the defeat of the rebels, and since then, until our arrival, everything has remained quiet.

After such a story, we again returned to our ships, and slept very peacefully on this night.

On 3 June, we again went into the city, not only to eat, but also to visit the captured officers. With the appropriate permission of General Carleton, we went in. They sat in the seminary, all together in one room, which was very large and spacious, and in which at that time, there were 37 men, some of whom had permission to walk in the seminary gardens. Among these was an artillery adventurer, named [Daniel?] Morgan, and a Lieutenant Riebeck, who was still in Danish service. His regiment lay on one of the islands, belonging to Denmark, in North America, from which he had obtained leave to New England, to pick up an inheritance from an uncle, and then decided to take service with the Americans. After we had visited these officers in the room, we went into the garden, from which place we could see all the ships that entered the harbor. The garden itself was nicely and uniformly laid out.

Anonymous Hesse-Hanau Diary

The Bishop of Quebec often comes here for a change of scenery, as he is considered a very civil man. In the treaty between England and France, there is provision that after his death, France may appoint his replacement, to whom the diocese will belong.

Now the Brunswick Dragoons and the Prince Friedrich Regiment from Brunswick have received orders to land and will be garrisoned in Quebec. Having received this news, we returned aboard ship in the hope of soon learning where we are being assigned.

On 4 June, the birthday of the King of England was celebrated by firing three salvos from the cannons in the fort, and on the ships. Also, all the staff officers dined with Governor Carleton.

[The diary of the anonymous Hesse-Hanau writer ends here.]

Brigadier (Colonel) von Gall's Order Book

von Gall Order Book

Crown Point, 28 October 1776

His Excellency, General [Sir Guy] Carleton, has approved 165 days' forage money for the entire army, on the same basis as the 200 days' forage money which was previously paid. Those troops which have not yet received equipment money, nor the 200 days' forage money, are to receive both the equipment and the 365 days' forage money. As soon as I arrive at Three Rivers, the regiments are to send their regimental quartermasters to Three Rivers, in order to arrange the lists with Chief Cashier [Johann Conrad] Goedecke, who must also be present at headquarters for this purpose. (Brigadier General [Wilhelm Rudolph] von Gall is not to take his place as colonel of the regiment, but will serve on the staff with his brigade major.)

Colonel [Johann Friedrich] von Specht is announced as a brigadier general with the army. He commands the 1st Brigade of German troops, consisting of the von Rhets and Specht Regiments. Brigadier General von Gall commands the 2nd Brigade, consisting of the Prince Frederick and the Hesse-Hanau Regiments. As the von Riedesel Regiment lies in general quarters, it will stand alone this winter, but is to come under the orders of Brigadier General Specht, eventually. The Dragoons, Grenadiers, and Light Infantry, also, remain

von Gall Order Book

unassigned and at the disposition of His Excellency, General Carleton. All regiments and companies are to maintain rough copies [of muster reports ?], so that when notified by Captain [Edward] Foy, as many clean copies as are desired, can be made at once. It is highly recommended that a format be developed. Captain Foy will provide the format for the muster lists. If these differ from those provided by Colonel [William] Faucitt, it will be necessary to change the rough format to make it like the earlier one.

So as not to unnecessarily fatigue the regiment, Captain Foy is to muster the companies in their separate quarters' areas, and if it is cold, the troops may wear their winter uniforms.

Therefore, it is necessary to provide convenient night quarters in each quarters' area, and everyone who thus assists him on his tour, will earn my gratitude.

The chief or commander of each regiment is to be present during the mustering of all companies of his battalion. It is worth mentioning that all French noblemen, priests, and the captains of militia, are free of the obligation of providing winter quarters, and one or two quarters must be left unoccupied in each parish, in order to provide convenient quarters to officers traveling in the King's service, whether English or German. Otherwise, the regiments are to be spread as evenly as possible, and it is wished that men can be

von Gall Order Book

assigned one or two together. As soon as each regiment has entered its winter quarters, a list is to be sent to me as to which it occupies, which companies are in each parish, how many inhabitable houses each parish has, and how many men are in each. Each company is to provide a proportionate number for the guard at the captain's quarters, and a staff guard for the battalion commander; the first can be relieved by a guard mount every 24 hours, the latter every 48 hours.

Each company chief is to rotate inspection of his company with his officers every 48 hours, and the battalion commander is to do likewise, every 4 weeks. They are to insure that the troops conduct themselves properly in their quarters, and check the uniforms and small clothing, weapons, and leather equipment. That in need of repair, which belongs to the company, is to be repaired as quickly as possible. All those who are sick are to be sent to the hospital at Three Rivers, and the company medics must attend the troops frequently. General Carleton's expressed order is that the soldiers cut their own firewood for the winter. The local residents however, are to deliver it to the houses. It is also ordered herewith, that all the soldiers establish wood supplies before the severe winter, and with the strongest, solid wood, so that there is no shortage of firewood during the winter. The generals, brigadiers, staff, and other officers require from their subordinate troops such numbers as are needed for fatigue details,

von Gall Order Book

to cut the necessary firewood, and the host or captains of militia must insure that it is delivered to the respective quarters. A similar activity is needed to supply wood for the guards.

General Carleton requests that the commander of the quarters' area carefully observe the conduct of the local residents, because it is possible that they might go to the rebels, through the forest, and take intelligence to them.

Also, when strangers or suspicious persons enter the quarters, the companies are to report such to their battalion chiefs, those to their brigadier generals, and they are to report to me. If very suspicious persons appear in the quarters, or if local residents are encountered under suspicious circumstances, they are to be arrested, and after receipt of the report, such actions as may be necessary will follow. In addition, General Carleton wants and requests each regimental commander to determine, with the help of the local residents and captains of militia, which subjects in each respective parish were good Royalists during the previous winter, or which were inclined toward the rebels, and each regimental commander eventually is to send a list of the evil-intentioned in his area, directly to me. This is difficult, of course, but on the other hand, the well-intentioned inhabitants are to be helped in every situation, and earn General Carleton's beneficences. [There is an obvious copying error at

von Gall Order Book

this point, but the meaning appears to be as I have given it.] The evil-intentioned individuals are to be closely watched and burdened with guidance and work. The report and accompanying lists required by this instruction must be submitted once each week to the brigadiers, and sent to me so as to arrive for me at Three Rivers on Sunday evening, without fail. From the regiments not assigned to brigades, in the same manner, all reports are to be sent directly to me. All reports and announcements are to be sent by orderlies from parish to parish, to Three Rivers, and on the other hand, all orders must be expedited from place to place, with the greatest speed. The subsistence of the soldiers is to be determined later. Until then, each regiment is to receive provisions from the closest magazine. I am still deciding how to equalize the quarters' areas according to the strength of the regiments.

Riedesel,
Major General

In Winter Quarters, Three Rivers
13 November 1776

To improve the movement of orders and dispatches, commanders are to keep a coach and horse ready, within their parish. These are the only ones which need not be paid for. All others must be paid. The brigadiers and battalion chiefs are to pass this

von Gall Order Book

order to their subordinate commanders and brigades, in the parishes.

Julius Ludwig August von Poellnitz
Brigade Major

- - - - - - -

Three Rivers, 16 November 1776
Order of Major General von Riedesel

As has always been the case, whenever orders are given, those orders, reports, and letters pertaining to duty, which are carried by non-commissioned officers, or orderlies, from parish to parish, and to a designated place, always arrive exceptionally dirty, and when it contains large packages of correspondence, the covers are completely torn, so that it must be feared that some of the letters and papers could be lost from the packets. Therefore, it is necessary to wrap such letters in an extra heavy wrapper, and to direct the orderlies to keep them clean, and in every case, to wrap them in their handkerchiefs. The officers in the parishes who dispatch the orderlies can improve the situation, if they are directed to order the new orderlies, who are sent on with the dispatches or letters, to be as careful in this regard, as possible, as otherwise they are to be held responsible.

[Friedrich Christian] Cleve
Aide-de-camp

- - - - - - -

von Gall Order Book

Three Rivers, 18 November 1776

His Excellency, General Carleton, has required an exact list of how many bateaux each regiment has received, how many have been lost, how many are completely unusable, how many of those can be repaired, and through what manner the bateaux were lost, or made unserviceable. Therefore, each regiment is to be informed of a standard format by which the lists are to be submitted. It is therefore strongly recommended that they take the very best care of their bateaux, so that during the coming campaign, every regiment will have the greatest advantage of the bateaux being maintained in the best condition. Therefore, it is strongly recommended to beach them with their oars, before the St. Lawrence River freezes, so that during the bad season, no damage can occur to them.

Brigadier von Gall is to make this order known to the regiments in his subordinate brigade, insure the format of the lists, as required, when submitted, and personally send them to me.

Riedesel, Major General

- - - - - - -

Three Rivers, 20 November 1776

His Excellency, General Carleton, has learned that the regimental surgeons send soldiers to the general hospital when their illness is not in the least serious.

von Gall Order Book

However, as this is against the intention of His Excellency, he orders those regimental surgeons never to send anyone to the hospital, except those who are very sick. In case someone is sent to the hospital, suffering from venereal disease, the regimental surgeon is to submit a written report each time, as to how long the man has had the disease, and how much mercury has been administer. In the future, those who are ill are to be escorted to the hospital administrator by a non-commissioned officer, who is to hand the hospital administrator a list, signed by the company chief, of all the possessions and weapons which the sick individuals take to the hospital.

William Barr, Lg. C. of His
Majesty's Hospitals in Canada
Riedesel, Major General

- - - - - - -

Three Rivers, 20 November 1776

As is well-known, the parishes of the government of Three Rivers do not bring the least amount of foodstuff to the city, and that which is brought to the city, sells at such enormous prices, that it can not be paid for. I have found it necessary, not only to prevent a food shortage, but also to maintain cheap prices, to publish the following order:

Based on reports we have received, that the inhabitants of the government of Three Rivers ruthlessly, and because they chose to use the time

von Gall Order Book

when the King's troops are entering winter quarters, at the start of bad weather, to raise the prices of foodstuffs, so that it can no longer be afforded, and without reason, and by the evil example, mislead those evil-intentioned inhabitants of the city, who rather than serving the best interest in general, cause an excessive expense on all the foodstuffs brought in from the surrounding area, we have found it necessary to prevent this, and to control all sales by those who have surplus food, to order markets to be held twice a week, on Mondays and Fridays, from 8 in the morning until 12 o'clock noon, on the Place d'Arms.

In order to insure compliance, we have placed a small tax on the foodstuffs necessary for human subsistence, and to insure that it will be exactly complied with, those who oppose it, are to be punished initially with imprisonment on bread and water. The second offense against it, however, will cause far more severe punishment.

Taxes on foodstuffs, which take effect immediately upon publication:

    1 pound of fresh beef - 6 coppers
    1 pound of fresh pork - 6 coppers
    1 sheep, over 1 year old - 7 shillings (Halifax)
    1 sheep, under 1 year old - 5 shillings (Halifax)
    1 pound of butter - 12 coppers
    1 dozen eggs - 10 coppers
    100 heads of cabbage - 8 shillings

von Gall Order Book

100 onions - 1 and ½ shillings
1 minot (39 liters) potatoes - 15 coppers
1 minot beans or peas - 2 and ½ shillings
1 pair lean turkeys - 2 and ½ shillings
1 pair fat turkeys - 3 and ½ shillings
1 pair lean poultry - 20 coppers
1 pair fat poultry - 30 coppers

The colonel also orders, herewith, of the military government of Three Rivers, that all militia captains order their departments to give close attention, that the present directive be adhered to, and a written report is to be completed for each parish of their department, and the warning circulated, that all those who secretly sell foodstuffs outside the several prescribed markets, but the buyer and the seller, are to be severely punished, and the foodstuffs are to be confiscated for the use of the army.

We want and demand the Grand Curate of the government of Three Rivers to disseminate to all priests of his department, that the present directive is to be read next Sunday, from the chancel, after the benediction. Therefore, however, the congregation is to be strictly warned to adhere to this order and to obey it exactly, and finally, the said order is to be fastened on the church door.

L. S. von Riedesel, Major General

- - - - - - -

von Gall Order Book

Three Rivers, 24 November 1776

As Captain Corbin, who has the overall responsibility for all the bateaux from General Carleton, has made an inspection of the regiments on the Sorel River, and at Berthier, personally, has found that some regiments, when taking their bateaux out of the water, and wishing to protect them during the winter, have tipped them over, and turned them over, which however, is the incorrect method of protecting the bateaux, because the weight of the frequent snowfalls lies on the flat side of the bateaux, so that what snow gets in it, can not clear away, but causes rot in the soil, and makes [the bateaux] unserviceable. Therefore, the mentioned captain has made the following suggestions as to how the bateaux can best be protected during the winter, from moisture, snow, and cold. When the bateaux can no longer be of service in the water, they are pulled up on land at a somewhat elevated place, where there is no damp, swampy ground. Three pieces of wood are then cut for each bateau, as wide as it is, and at least three-fourths of a foot thick in diameter, which are placed so that both ends and the middle of the bateau sets on the ground, on the three pieces of wood, as it sits in the water, and it is left this way, because in this way the bateau sits high, so that neither frost nor cold can damage it. However, when snow falls, it is necessary to take the precautions of carefully tipping the bateau

von Gall Order Book

briefly, to allow the water from the melting snow to run out. Then the bateau is returned to its former position. All the bateaux of each company are to be kept together, so that a sentry can keep watch over them.

Riedesel, Major General

General Orders, Three Rivers, 7 December 1776
General Orders from Headquarters, dated Quebec,
2 December 1776

The soldiers' field equipment is to be inspected and put in order, so that the individuals can move out immediately, and a report on this is to be submitted to Aide-Major-General Captain Foy. The men are to be ready, after receiving this order, to march at once.

An assembly point is to be assigned for the regiments, and likewise for the brigades. The regiments are then to assemble at their designated locations, and if time permits, at the place for the brigades

Snowshoes are to be made for the troops, which are to be sent to them, so they can practice walking on snow.

The regiments and brigades of German troops are to inform Major General von Riedesel about the place they have chosen to assemble, and are to submit a report thereon to him. A report

von Gall Order Book

concerning bateaux, is to be sent to the quartermaster general at Montreal, as to the number the regiments have with them. They are also to note their condition, also, and whether oars, sails, or other items are missing. If it happens that there is a march after a freeze, and if their bateaux can not be used, a detail is to remain with the heavy baggage, pending further orders. However, if the water is open, the serviceable bateaux are to be taken and used during the march, to transport the necessary equipment and baggage, and in that case, the heavy equipment is to be sent to Three River. The damaged bateaux are to be turned over to the respective captains of militia for guarding, in exchange for a receipt. As soon as the respective regiments have received snowshoes, all the commanders are to insure that the soldiers practice diligently walking on the snow with the snowshoes, so that if the army is to provide details on snowshoes, the Germans can march equally well with the other troops. As the German troops quickly learned how to paddle [the bateaux], I do not doubt but that they will also become proficient with snowshoes.

    Those regiments which have had changes, because of their bateaux, or who have not yet sent in their report, are to submit it, so that the necessary bateaux can be supplied, and the

von Gall Order Book

complete bateaux list can be sent to the quartermaster general at Montreal, by Lieutenant Colonel Carleton.

Riedesel, Major General

- - - - - - - -

General Quarters, Three Rivers,
16 December 1776

As a great many mistakes have been found in the lists, which the hospital at Montreal sends here, concerning the sick and convalescent, so that even the correct name of the regiments and companies are never noted, and it has often been reported that the convalescents have not had all their uniform items, which they took with them, returned to them, therefore in the future, when a sick individual is sent to the hospital, a list of his uniform items is to be submitted, according to the accompanying format. This list is to be delivered to the hospital administrator at that place, by the non-commissioned officer escorting the sick individual, and in return he is to obtain a receipt from the administrator that the listed items are actually there. This receipt, when the sick individual is again discharged from the hospital, must be exchanged with the hospital administrator for the list which he has held so long, so that it can be seen from the noted uniform items, that nothing is missing.

von Poellnits, Brigade Major

von Gall Order Book

General Order in Headquarters, Quebec,
16 December 1776

Negotiations in London have provided a sum of money for the soldiers wounded or killed in the service of the King, in America, specifically, ten talers for a wounded individual, and for the widow of one killed, five pounds, which they will receive upon presentation of an attestation, by an officer under whom her husband served, and the wounded are to be paid by the Receiver-General of the Province, Mr. Dunn. The regiments and corps however, are to have previously submitted a list of the names of the wounded and the widows to Mr. Dunn.

von Poellnitz, Brigade Major

Three Rivers, 22 December 1776

On orders of His Excellency, General Carleton, a thanksgiving celebration is to be held on the 31st of this month, in honor of the liberation of Canada. The regiments which have chaplains, are to conduct church services on that day, and the chaplains are to preach on this subject.

von Poellnitz, Brigade Major

General Quarters, Berthier,
27 December 1776

His Excellency, General Carleton, orders that all those individuals who have served as a volunteer in

von Gall Order Book

the Company of Captalin Monin during this campaign, are to be free of all requirements to provide quarters, but also the captains of militia are ordered, that those men are also free of all guide, orderly, or other military service.

Captain Monin is to submit a name list to the brigades, and the brigades to the regiments, and all those mentioned volunteers, according to this list, are to be fully released. On the other hand, the soldiers are to be quartered on others, and especially with such residents as are known to be against the King, and who are on the conduct list. Furthermore, it is of no consequence if such evil-intentioned individuals are burdened more than others, and required to billet four or five soldiers in their houses.

Brigadier General von Gall orders that the assignment of soldiers to quarters, after receipt of the mentioned list of volunteers, is to closely conform thereto. Nevertheless, the captains of militia must be instructed to free from all fatigue duties and details, which might be assigned those volunteers, whom they know. As soon as this order has been carried out, the regiments are to report to the brigade.

Riedesel, Major General

General Quarters, Berthier, 4 January 1777
Order of Brigadier General von Gall
Commanders in the parishes are to order the

von Gall Order Book

captains of militia to have the local residents bring the required men to their magazines, as well as the necessary grain to be ground, without any objection, and no one is to be excused from all fatigue details, by the order of His Excellence, General Carleton.

- - - - - - - -

General Quarters, Berthier, 3 February 1777
Order of Brigadier General von Gall

The provisions are to be transported from Quebec to Sorel and St. Jean on sleds, on orders of His Excellence, General Carleton, and the orders for the necessar6y transportation are to be given by Lieutenant Governor Cramahe in the Quebec district; Colonel of Militia Tonnecourt in the district from Quebec to Three Rivers, and from there to and including Berthier; and excluding Berthier, but on to Montreal, by Major of Militia Pree. Therefore, the brigadier orders the regimental commanders, as well as those commanding in the parishes, and his subordinate officers in the parishes, not to hinder the carrying out of this order, but in every instance, to lend assistance, even when the captains of militia are negligent in ordering the transport for which they have been made responsible. The commanders are to provide the best possible assistance to the captains of militia, when the local residents make it difficult for them to carry out the order by resisting.

Riedesel, Major General

von Gall Order Book

General Quarters, Berthier,
18 February 1777

As it has been learned that 4 rebels, 2 of whom speak German, have plotted to enter the quarters of the German troops, to spread rumors against His Majesty, and where they are able to enter, to try to get our soldiers to desert, His Excellency, General Carleton, orders all regiments to remain especially alert against the above mentioned individuals, and if possible, to apprehend them, but to be especially vigilant, and when strangers, suspiciously or talking in a suspicious manner, are to be arrested at once, and placed in the custody of the regimental staff. Next, the individuals are to be interrogated, not only to their origin, condition, and business, but also, specifically about the suspicious speech which they have been accused of. After a detailed investigation, a record and a report by the commander is to be sent to Major General von Riedesel for further disposal. The individuals in arrest are to be held at the guard of the regimental staff, pending further orders, supplied with provisions, and a special receipt for those provisions is to be prepared, containing their names and where they were from.

Riedesel, Major General

- - - - - - -

von Gall Order Book

General Headquarters, Berthier,
18 February 1777

As Commissary General Day has noted that sentries have not been provided at some locations for royal magazines, it is necessary to issue the following general order so that no one, as long as we are here in America, might misunderstand, everywhere where there is a royal magazine, or a house filled with royal property, immediately after a battalion, company, or any other command enters quarters, or camp near such location, a post, and if necessary for security, as many more as the commander finds necessary, after careful consideration, is to be established, and it is to be carefully instructed, that it is to allow as few individuals into the magazine during the day as at night, if they do not belong there, and also, because of the danger of fire, to be attentive and take all necessary precautions. Above all however, the commissary must be afforded full cooperation by the commander of the place, under all circumstances. Also, every regimental commander is to grant every non-commissioned officer to be assigned, as an assistant commissary, and paid extra by the commissary, upon the request of the senior commissary of a magazine, for his assigned magazines.

Riedesel, Major General

- - - - - - -

von Gall Order Book

General Order, Quebec, 24 February 1777

It is the order of His Excellence-in-Chief, that all troops are to be held in readiness to march on the shortest notice.

General von Riedeel makes this known to the regiments, so that if any field equipment, or anything else is missing, it can be replaced as quickly as possible.

Otherwise, everything remains as it was pending further orders.

Berthier, 1 March 1777
von Poellnitz, Brigade Major

General Orders, Berthier, 24 March 1777

It is announced to the regiments that His Excellence, General Carleton, has named Captain von Poellnitz as Aide-Major General to Major General von Riedesel. Therefore, all regimental commanders and other officers are to obey the orders of the mentioned Adjutant General in the name of General von Riedesel, oral or in writing, as if they came from the general himself.

von Poellnitz

General Quarters, Berthier, 9 April 1777

His Excellence, General Carleton, in consideration of the necessity after we cross the lake and enter the region of New England, where various governments

von Gall Order Book

are in close proximity, and where every officer must be made aware of how he is to conduct himself toward the governors, lieutenant governors, presidents, and presidents of council, orders the accompanying directive to all the German troops, to be published. The lieutenant colonels are ordered to publish this for all their subordinate companies, to enter into the company order books, to provide a copy to every officer for his information and compliance, and finally, in applicable cases, to comply with the order exactly.

                                Riedesel, Major General

----

von Gall Order Book

Extract of the Instructions
Of His Majesty

The generals and commanders in chief of troops actually in America, concerning the rank and order which the commanders, chiefs, and others of His Majesty's troops are to observe, as well as the governors, lieutenant governors, and others in His Majesty's colonies.

As we have found it necessary to establish certain rules, which are herewith issued, which the commanders, chiefs, generals, and other officers among our troops in America are to observe concerning rank and precedence, and which apply to the governors, presidents of councils, in the various provinces and colonies, therefore it is our will and desire that steps be taken to insure that this rule be observed at every opportunity, in all places, and that it be publicly announced for this purpose, posted, and where it is found necessary, distributed in America.

Copy of the Rules and Instructions Concerning
Rights and Privileges in America,
Signed by the King and Countersigned
By His Staff Secretary
George, Rex

As our grandfather of blessed memory established certain rules concerning the rank and privileges, which were to be observed by the commanders-in-chief, generals, and other

von Gall Order Book

officers of our troops in America, and also concerning the governors, lieutenant governors, presidents of councils of the various provinces and colonies, we have found it advisable to prevent all causes of strife, to establish and declare certain rules concerning the privileges and rank among the commander-in-chief, etc., and the governors, etc., and it is our desire that the said rules concerning the above mentioned individuals be exactly adhered to and followed in their rank, in the following manner:

NB

1) The commander-in-chief of our troops, who is confirmed under the great seal of Great Britain

2) The generals and governors-in-chief of our provinces and colonies, if they have been confirmed in their positions by a patent with the great seal and are presently there

3) General officers

4) The commanders and generals of our provinces and colonies present within their respective governments

5) The lieutenant governors and presidents of council, if they are the commander-in-chief of a province or colony and present in their government

von Gall Order Book

6) The colonel

7) The lieutenant governors and presidents of council, if they are the commander-in-chief of a province or colony, and outside their respective government

8) The lieutenant governors of our provinces and colonies, if they are not the commanders-in-chief, and present in their government

9) The lieutenant governors of our provinces and colonies, if they are the commanders-in-chief, and are outside their respective government

10) The governors of colonies, who are confirmed by a patent in their respective colony

11) The lieutenant colonels and majors

12) The lieutenant governors in their own government, who find themselves outside their respective government

13) The governors of colonies confirmed by a patent, who find themselves outside their respective government

Among the generals and governors-in-chief, the rank is to be determined by the oldest date of their patent. A similar situation applies to the lieutenant governors of provinces, governors in their own government,

von Gall Order Book

and also the governors of colonies, confirmed by patents. These are to take precedence according to the oldest date of their patent.
Given at St. James, in the first year of our reign, signed by order of the King
William Pitt

- - - - - - -

Copy of His Majesty's order concerning the power and authority of the civil government over His Majesty's troops in the various provinces, as they were sent to the commanders-in-chief in America, in a letter of 9 February 1765, by the Secretary of State.

It is His Majesty's intention that the orders to the commanders-in-chief and the brigadiers, who serve under them in the several southern and northern parts, are to be exactly obeyed in consideration of the military situation of the troops, just as those are applicable which are from the governments on them, here in America.

In case either the commander-in-chief or the commanding officer in a district has not issued a specific order, the civil government in council can. In cases in which they are not in agreement, the civil government, on its own, can, if to the advantage of the government, order troops to march, supply others, send out detachments, provide safeguards, and exercise other military authority within its government, and the commanding officers of the troops commanded, is to give the order, that these orders are to be exactly carried out, assuming he could have received them from the commander-in-chief or the commanding general of the district. The commanding officer is to make a report from time to time, to the commander-in-chief or the general, on the orders he has received from the civil governor.

The civil governor is to issue the password in the localities of his province, except when the commander-in-chief or brigadier is also present in those localities.

The report as to the condition of the troops at the magazines and the defensive positions must be submitted to the civil governor, also, as well as to the commander-in-chief and brigadiers.

The civil government is not to interfere in the military discipline of a regiment, but the reports on such are to be made to the commanding officer, who must submit a full report to the civil governor. If the commander-in-chief or brigadier is present, all reports are to be submitted only to him.

- - - - - - -

von Gall Order Book

Honors

1) The commander-in-chief, if not a general - present arms, three drum rolls, and saluted. If a general - instead of three drum rolls, a march is to be beaten

2) His Majesty's admirals and governors-in-chief are to receive honors according to their rank

3) For the generals and governors-in-chief in their own province - present arms and two drum rolls

4) General officers of the staff, according to rank

5) General officers and commanders-in-chief outside their own province - present arms and one drum roll

6) Lieutenant governors and presidents of council, if they are commanders in their own provinces and in their government - present arms and one drum roll

7) Colonels and staff officers, if occupying a garrison command position - present arms

8) Lieutenant governors and presidents of council, outside their government - present arms

9) Lieutenant governors in their own province and in their own government -

von Gall Order Book

present arms

E. Foy, Deputy Adjutant General

NB

There are three types of governments in America. The royal, which are so called because they are directly subordinate to the King and the proprietor. Its council and all public officials are appointed by him. The people, on the other hand, are his representatives. These are the proprietorships of Virginia and New York.

The privileged governments, charter governments, are those with a privileged society whose authority is held by this group, and have that type of government which they established as most satisfactory to themselves, assuming they are not against English law. Rhode Island and Connecticut.

The third type is a private government, in which the King has transferred possession of a colony to a person. Maryland and Pennsylvania are the only private governments in America.

These three types of government are indicated by the following signs, for each type, which are:

von Gall Order Book

The royal governments by an "a",
The privileged governments by a "b",
The private governments by a "c".

- - - - - - - -

Three Rivers, 10 May 1777

The following promotions in the brigade have been announced by Major General von Riedesel: His Serene Highness, as of 18 January 1777, has named Ensign [Ernst Christian Heinrich] Brandes, of the von Riedesel Regiment, a 2nd lieutenant, and he is transferred to the Leib Company of the regiment. On the other hand, Lieutenant [Christian Theodor] von Pincier, of that company, is transferred to Captain von Poellnitz' Company.

Flag Bearer [Friedrich Ludwig] Denecke, is promoted to ensign, as of 20 October 1777, and assigned to Major General von Riedesel's Leib Company. Standard Bearer Count von Rantzow, according to his ensign's patent of 18 February 1776, is assigned this rank, and transferred to the von Barner Light Infantry Regiment.

The Flag Bearer von Hille, of the Prince Friedrich Regiment, according to his ensign's patent of 8 January 1776, is assigned to that regiment as an ensign.

Standard Bearer von Foerstner, is promoted to ensign, as of 20 January 1777, and transferred to Captain von Poellnitz' Company of the von Riedesel

von Gall Order Book

Regiment.

von Poellnitz, Deputy Adjutant General

- - - - - - -

Berthier, 12 May 1777

The following promotions have been announced to the brigade by Brigadier General von Gall:

His Serene Highness, the Hereditary Prince of Hesse-Cassel, has promoted the previously Captain von Passern to major; Staff Captain [Carl August] Scheel receives the Vacant Major's Company; 2nd Lieutenant [Friedrich] von Geyling is promoted to 1st lieutenant; and Ensign [Ludwig] von Hohorst is promoted to 2nd lieutenant; all as of 25 November 1777.

- - - - - - -

von Gall Order Book

General Quarters, Berthier,
31 May 1777
March Disposition of the German Troops
to the General Rendezvous
at Cumberland Head with the Entire Army

After the brigades and regiments have received the orders given by General [John] Burgoyne for the army to march, the following order from Major General von Riedesel is added.:

Major von Barner is to draw his battalion together so that it is assembled at Sorel by 2 June, and is to take his quarters there, so that the quarters of the 62nd Regiment and the detail from the 33rd Regiment remain vacant, and, if the Breymann Grenadier Battalion should enter Sorel the same day, the necessary houses must be kept vacant for it. If the troops must be quartered in barns and not in houses, as may be necessary, each company is to receive two barns, and a house for their company officers.

Major von Barner is to schedule his march so as to arrive in Chambly on the 6th of the month, and fulfill every condition in General Burgoyne's order so as to arrive with his battalion at Cumberland Head, where the army rendezvous is. If his battalion has not yet been provided with sufficient provisions, because the time is too short to get more from Three Rivers, it must get them along the march, wherever it can, from magazines established, so that the battalion can have enough until it reaches Cumberland Head. At the same time, the battalion has to determine where it can acquire the missing ammunition, at Sorel, St. Jean, or Chambly, according to the list which the battalion itself prepared.

The bateaux, which the battalion is to return, are to be employed to transport the baggage, ammunition, etc., which the battalion has with it, and as many men as the bateaux can carry. The troops, which can not fit into the bateaux, must march along the shore, with officers and non-commissioned officers in proportion, until the additional authorized bateaux are received, which is to take place at Sorel, St. Jean, or Chambly.

All heavy equipment which the regiment does not need to take across the lake, is to be sent to Three Rivers, for which purpose the battalion is to supply one non-commissioned officer, and each company two men, who are trustworthy, and from the entire corps, one officer is to be assigned, who is to come from the Specht Regiment. The baggage, of which the non-commissioned officer of each regiment has charge, must be arranged by companies, and is to be guarded here, apparently on the barracks' grounds. To insure that the heavy baggage arrives here in a proper condition, it is to be escorted here by an officer from each regiment, delivered to the officer detailed to do so for the entire corps, so that it is kept separated and well-guarded, so when everything is in proper order, he is to follow the battalion. The regiments, which lie back beyond Three Rivers, are to deposit their heavy baggage at Three Rivers, and supply themselves with provisions. A situation exists with the sick, all of whom are to be brought to the hospital, and one surgeon from the regiments, who is to be an officer, is to remain to care for the sick.

All regiments and battalions are to obtain an attestation from their vacated quarters that there has been no claim for provisions, or any complaints, as, if these remain, the troops' quarters, where they were cantoned, are not to be vacated without obtaining such attestation.

On the march, the best discipline is recommended, so that not the least excess occurs, for which each regimental commander must take responsibility, just as we have done for the entire army this winter.

The von Breymann Grenadier Battalion is to report as soon as it receives this order, whether it can arrive at Sorel in one day. If so, fine, but if it requires night quarters between St. Suplice and Berthier, which necessitates the Hesse-Hanau Regiment vacating their quarters, and crossing the St. Lawrence River the next day, it can occupy the quarters which the von Barner Battalion has had. It can then follow that battalion on the march to the general rendezvous at Cumberland Head, and observe what it encountered on the march, concerning other arrangements as noted above.

Prince Friedrich Regiment is to follow the Grenadier Battalion. It is to move out from its quarters on 2 June, take quarters between Maskinonge and the post house for Berthier, and cross the St. Lawrence River, on the fourth, behind the Grenadiers.

The Hesse-Hanau Regiment is to vacate its quarters on the second, then go from the mouth of the Berthier River to behind Guigy's house, leaving their quarters vacant for passing troops, as also the parishes of la Valtrie Norde and Dautre. Brigadier von Gall is responsible that this regiment also is quartered in two barns per company.

The von Riedesel Infantry Regiment is to march to Maskinonge on the third, to Berthier on the fourth, cross the water on the fifth, and then follow the route of the first troops, as explained above. The Dragoons are to march to Riviere aux Loups on the fourth, to Berthier on the fifth, and if possible, cross the St. Lawrence River on that day, otherwise on the morning of the sixth, arriving at St. Denis that day, and so on.

The Specht Regiment is to assemble the three companies together at Cape Magdalaine on the third. One company is to move into the barracks here on the morning of the second. The Specht Regiment is to march to Machichi on the fourth, to Maskinonge on the fifth, Berthier on the sixth, cross the St. Lawrence River the seventh, and so on to its destination

The von Rhetz Regiment is to assemble at Champlain on the third, march to Point du Lac on the fourth, to Riviere aux Loups on the fifth, Maskinonge on the sixth, cross the St. Lawrence River on the seventh, and then follow the march of the Specht

Regiment.

All companies of the Riedesel, Specht, and Rhetz Regiments, which lie on the south side, are to march with their cannons parallel to the opposite shore, so as to arrive at Sorel at the same time. If their respective regiments come together, they are to remain, but immediately upon receipt of this order, they are to send their baggage to the regimental staff, or if it is convenient, to Three Rivers, so that it can be stored with the rest of the heavy equipment. General von Riedesel will pass the regiments on the march, so it will not be necessary to send reports to their rear, but to him, as he passes the first troops.

Riedesel, Major General

- - - - - - -

General Quarters, Berthier,
31 May 1777
Plan for Assembling the Army

Friday, 30 May -The corps of the brigadier is to move out and plan its march so as to arrive at Point au Fer, on 3 June. The 9th and 47th Regiments are to cross the St. Lawrence River, and the 9th is to canton at Boucherville, and the 47th at Longueuil.

Monday, 2 June - Major General von Riedesel is to order the first German troops to cross the St. Lawrence River and canton, so as not to disturb the quarters of the 62nd Regiment, nor the detail of the English 33rd Regiment.

Thursday, 3 June - The first troops of the Germans

are to continue their march along the Sorel River. The following German troops are to cross the St. Lawrence River, enter the quarters which the first ones vacated, and plan their outward march daily, until all arrive at Chambly. Major General von Riedesel is to make preparations so that the head of the German troops have arrived at Chambly, by 6 June.

As the regiments still do not have enough bateaux for their troops and equipment to cross the river, when they arrive at the St. Lawrence River, first they will take the baggage across and to Sorel. When it is then unloaded at a convenient place, the bateaux will be sent back and the rest of the regimental troops picked up and transferred across. Then they can continue their march, all baggage and provisions by water, and the men of the regiment, who can not fit into the bateaux, by land. No vehicles are to be requested for transporting the baggage on the Sorel River, because all are to be used at the portage at the passage of the rapids. The bateaux of the German troops are to cross the portage near Chambly, as the divisions arrive, and should there be enough vehicles to carry all the baggage and provisions of the troops across, the troops are to continue their march, without stopping more than one night in Chambly, then continue on so as to enter the camp at St. Theresa the following day. However, if there are not enough vehicles, the bateaux are to be moved across first, and then the baggage and provisions are to follow, so that during the time the bateaux which have been damaged, can be repaired. The 9th and 47th Regiments, which have halted at Boucherville and Longueuil until now, so that the carts used by Fraser's Brigade have time to return, are to continue their march to Chambly, and on the same day, the 53rd Regiment is to enter the camp at St. Theresa.

Wednesday, 9 June - The 53rd Regiment is to follow the 9th and 47th Regiments.

It is hoped that there will be enough water so that the bateaux with the troops and baggage can pass the second rapids between Chambly and St. Jean, and in every case, each regiment must help itself and use every means to pass those rapids.

When each regiment and division has its canoes ready at St. Jean, including those which are now missing, they are to continue their route as previously, but not less than a single regiment to Cumberland Head on Lake Champlain, which passage is adequately covered. Cumberland Head is the general rendezvous for the advanced fleet and the corps which have already moved ahead.

General [William] Phillips is to make all arrangements for the artillery. All troops are to carry sufficient provisions with them to reach the general rendezvous, and halt as seldom underway at the depots which are encountered, so as not to delay their march.

von Gall Order Book

All ships assigned to transport necessities are to be loaded during this time, and everything arranged so that 200 tons, without fail, arrive on 8 June at Cumberland Head.

Riedesel, Major General

- - - - - - - -

Notification as to What Most Individuals Can take Across the Lake

The regiments are herewith notified how much baggage they can take with them in the bateaux. For staff officers, nothing is prohibited, and they can take such items for preparing meals as are needed, but within limits.

A captain is to take 1 tent, 1 bed, 1 suitcase with clothing, and as many items of small clothes as are needed by half the company, 1 pair of canteens, 1 or 2 baskets for foodstuffs, and 2 saddlebags.

A subaltern officer, 1 tent, 1 bed, 1 suitcase, 1 basket with foodstuffs, 1 pair of canteens; and persons of the middle staff, the same.

Riedesel, Major General

- - - - - - -

Chambly, 7 June 1777
Order of Major General von Riedesel

That the Hesse-Hanau Infantry Regiment, upon receipt of this order, is to send out at once, its quartermaster to arrange quarters for the regiment in houses and barns, which lie on the other side of Fort

von Gall Order Book

Chambly, where General Carleton had his headquarters in the previous summer, and where the von Barner Light Infantry Battalion now lies. The houses designated for the general staff are to be occupied.

The Hesse-Hanau Infantry Regiment must march out so that it enters the cantonment quarters here, about one o'clock in the afternoon, and so that it will be possible to begin transporting the bateaux and baggage over the rapids. Therefore, Lieutenant Colonel [Johann Christoph] Lentz must inform Captain Corbin, who is responsible for moving the bateaux overland at the portage, when the regiment will arrive.

In accordance with the order received, Lieutenant Colonel [Christian Julius] Praetorius is to determine and continue his march, so as to arrive here at Fort Chambly with the Grenadier Battalion tomorrow afternoon or evening.

The regimental quartermaster of the Prince Friedrich Regiment can report to Captain von Poellnitz, who will assign the quarters' area. If the Prince Friedrich Regiment can not reach Chambly, tomorrow, which is still hoped, they may continue until they can make the rendezvous, and arrive here early the next day. Lieutenant Colonel Praetorius is also to inform Captain Corbin of his arrival, so that arrangements can be made for crossing the portage.

von Gall Order Book

Riedesel, Major General

Chambly, 9 June 1777
Order of Major General von Riedesel
Parole - St. George and Crown Point

In the future, the parole is to be announced at the general's quarters at eleven o'clock, and at that definite time, all reports are to be made by the regiments lying here in general quarters. There must always be a non-commissioned officer for each brigade and regiment at the general's quarters, so that orders for the regiments can thus be expedited. From now on, every week, on Saturday, a weekly report, according to the format which each regiment now possesses, is to be submitted.

The Prince Friedrich Regiment is to relieve all detachments from the Hesse-Hanau Regiment, consisting of 1 officer, 1 non-commissioned officer, 1 drummer, and 30 privates, at the portage; 1 non-commissioned officer and 18 privates in the fort; and 1 non-commissioned officer and 6 privates at the guard for General von Riedesel. The brigade is to provide a non-commissioned officer orderly to General von Riedesel, and today he is to be from the Prince Friedrich Regiment. General Riedesel orders that the house of Mons. Montzambere, in which 40 privates of the Prince Friedrich Regiment are quartered, is to be vacated, and these can be replaced by several officers.

von Gall Order Book

[Friedrich] Geismar, Brigade Major

- - - - - - -

General Quarters, Three Rivers
1 June 1777

As a detail of 1 staff officer, 6 captains, 12 officers, 48 non-commissioned officers, and 60 [sic - should be 600] privates, is to remain behind here in Canada, the Hesse-Hanau Regiment is to provide 1 captain, 2 officers, 7 non-commissioned officers, and 96 privates for that detail.

The detail, initially, is to remain at Berthier, and the captain is to submit his report to Lieutenant Colonel [Johann Gustav] von Ehrenkrook, who has command of the detail here at Three Rivers, and the mentioned captain will then receive more specific orders from him.

For this detail, those people can be selected who are sickly, and who can not march well. The detail required here, by the previous order, for the heavy baggage, consists of 1 officer (provided by the Specht Regiment) and per company, 1 non-commissioned officer, and per company, 2 men, may also be included in the total required by this order, and taken from the 96 privates.

von Poellnitz, Deputy Adjutant General

- - - - - - -

General Order, Cumberland Head,
18 June 1777

von Gall Order Book

Parole - St. Helene and Montreal
General Disposition of the Army

To the advance corps of the army, under the command of General [Simon] Fraser, are assigned the companies of Monin, Boucherville, the detachment of Captain [Alexander] Fraser, and a corps of Indians.

The Grenadiers, Jaegers, and Light Infantry, under the command of Lieutenant Colonel Breymann, are to form the reserve corps, and never camp in the line. The Riedesel Dragoon Regiment is also to remain outside the line, and is assigned for the present to cover the headquarters. Also, the corps of Peters and Joseph remain outside the line. The recruits from the 63rd Regiment, under the command of Lieutenant Nut, for the present are to serve aboard the fleet.

After the initial movement, the army is to camp in the following order, and until ordered otherwise, the same order is to be constantly maintained.

Left Wing - 1st Brigade, commanded by Brigadier Specht - Rhetz, Specht, and Riedesel Regiments; 2nd Brigade, commanded by Brigadier von Gall - Prince Friedrich and Hesse-Hanau Regiments.

Right Wing - 2nd Brigade, commanded by Brigadier [Gustavus] Hamilton - 21st, 69th, and 20th Regiments; 1st Brigade, commanded by Brigadier [Henry] Powell - 47th, 53rd, and 9th Regiments.

When necessary, two lines are to be formed in the following manner: the 2nd English Brigade behind the

von Gall Order Book

1st, and the 2nd German Brigade behind the 1st, also. The brigadiers are to camp with their brigades at all times.

General Burgoyne will troop the line at seven o'clock tomorrow morning, at which time the regiments are to be under arms. The Dragoon Regiment, Specht, and Rhetz Regiments are excluded, however, as the general has already inspected them at St. Jean. At this time, a collective report of the strength of the German corps is to be presented to the general.

The Hesse-Hanau Regiment is to provide a non-commissioned officer orderly for General Burgoyne today, and the same is to be provided by Prince Friedrich Regiment tomorrow. If no changes have taken place since the last weekly reports by the regiments, no additional reports are necessary today. However, if something has occurred, the report is to be submitted at once. The adjutants of the regiments, of the brigade under Brigadier von Gall, are to receive orders daily at twelve o'clock, in the future, in the camp of the Hesse-Hanau Regiment.

Parole for the 19th - St. Theresa and Longueuil

The army is to receive provisions upon to and inclusive of the thirteenth. The 47th Regiment will be first, as it has the greatest need. It is to be followed by the first regiment of the 1st English Brigade, and these

von Gall Order Book

by the German brigades. As soon as the provisions have been received, they are to be loaded aboard the bateaux, and each regiment is to post a guard there. All provisions are to be received today, and the regimental quartermasters are to report therefore to Captain [Heinrich] Gerlach. Tomorrow the army is to begin its move. Instead of reveille, general march is to be beaten, and the quartermaster sergeants and guards, and the carpenters from the grenadiers, are to embark at once, and sail ahead. They are to assemble with their bateaux on the right wing of the 9th Regiment, where the vice-quartermaster general will receive them and direct them onward. At the same time, the tents are to be struck and the baggage loaded as quickly as possible. Assembly is to be beaten one hour after general march, and each regiment is to embark. As soon as General Burgoyne believes the regiments can be ready to sail, a cannon shot is to be fired from the ship *Marie*, and the sails on the forward-most mast unfurled. Then all the regiments are to aline themselves in their bateaux in the following manner, and hold their positions. First, the von Barner Jaeger Battallion and the Grenadiers, under the command of Lieutenant Colonel Breymann, form the advance guard. These are to take position on the right wing of the army. Next follows the Dragoon Regiment. The 1st English Brigade moves into line 200 yards behind the Dragoons. Finally, the German

von Gall Order Book

brigades follow in order. Each corps is to form a column with a four-bateaux front. Those battalions on each flank must try to hold position in the middlemost place. As soon as everyone is alined, two cannon shots are to be fired from the *Marie,* and a flag raised on the forward- most mast. Then everyone is to begin the march, and each battalion is to employ as much sail and oars as necessary, to maintain its position.

ORDER BOOK
Of the Hesse-Hanau Hereditary Prince Infantry Regiment

Hesse-Hanau Order Book

Headquarters, Berthier, 13 April 1777
Password - St.Sterent   Countersign - Pennsylvania
Watch - 1 Ensign [Friedrich Ludwig] Kempfer; 2 non-commissioned officers, 1 drummer, and 29 privates of the Leib Regiment
Tomorrow, the fourteenth of this month, Ensign von Richtersleben goes to Bayonne, where Ensign [Jacob] Heerwagon has been quartered, and Lieutenant Bischhausen is to inspect the quarters at Maicon.

Headquarters, Berthier, 14 April 1777
Password - St.Michael   Countersign - Maryland
Watch -

Headquarters, Berthier, 15 April 1777
Password - St. Joseph   Countersign - Virginia
Watch - 1 Lieutenant Trott; 2 non-commissioned officers, 1 drummer, and 29 privates of the Colonel's Company
In arrest - 1 drummer [Joseph Philipp] Wissenbach of the Colonel's Company
` From the survey of the 13th of this month, it is noted that a great amount of ammunition is missing, and that the balls delivered were not alike. The brigadier has ordered that on the 17th, the captains and company commanders reply to the lieutenant colonel in writing, as to where the missing ammunition and

missing balls are. Otherwise, the brigadier will charge the companies for the missing ammunition. Provisions are to be received from the staff each day, for the following day, so that on the day when they are to be issued to the troops, they can be given out during the morning The drill is to be held on the day of issue, this can be delayed until after the drill, and provisions for the 27th can then be issued also.

The regiment is notified that Ensign Heerwagon has the duty as adjutant.

The winter uniforms are to be discontinued. The brigadier also hopes that the leggings are in good serviceable condition.

Headquarters, Berthier, 16 April 1777
Password - St. Christopher   Countersign - Carolina
Watch -

Headquarters, Berthier, 17 April 1777
Password - St. Augustine   Countersign - Georgia
Watch - Ensign [Ludwig] von Hohorst; 2 non-commissioned officers, 1 drummer, and 29 privates

----

Headquarters, Berthier, 18 April 1777
Password - St. Simon   Countersign - Florida
Watch -

The Drummer Wissenbach of the Lieutenant Colonel's Company released from arrest.

Hesse-Hanau Order Book

Headquarters, Berthier, 19 April 17777
Password - St. Francis   Countersign - Mexico
Watch - 1 Lieutenant [Maurice] von Buttlar; 2 non-commissioned officers, 1 drummer, and 29 privates of Captain von Passern's Company

On order of Brigadier [Wilhelm Rudolph] von Gall, the winter uniforms are to be discontinued on the 24th of this month, and the yellow breeches and leggings worn. Each individual is to write his name on a piece of paper and sew it into his breeches. The caps and gloves are to be fastened onto the breeches, and the company commanders are to see that the winter uniforms are collected from the individuals and properly accounted for, so that they can be reissued next winter.

Church services are to be held on the 20th of the month in Berthier.

- - - - - - -

Headquarters, Berthier, 20 April 1777
Password - St. Lazerus   Countersign - Chile
Watch -

- - - - - - -

Headquarters, Berthier, 21 April 1777
Password - St. James   Countersign - Peru
Watch - 1 Lieutenant [Christian] von Eschwege; 2 non-commissioned officers, 1 drumme4r, and 29 privates from the Grenadier Company

1 Lieutenant von Buttlar in arrest.

Hesse-Hanau Order Book

On orders from headquarters, Lieutenant von Buttlar released from arrest this evening.

Headquarters, Berthier, 22 April 1777
Password - Julian   Countersign - Newfoundland
Watch -
One arrested brought from Sorel by a detachment, has been escort to St. Culpear by one non-commissioned officer and four privates.

Headquarters, Berthier, 23 April 1777
Password - St. Denis   Countersign - Labrador
Watch - 1 Ensign [Heinrich] Siebert; 2 non-commissioned officers, 1 drummer, and 29 privates from the Leib Company.

Headquarters, Berthier, 24 April 1777
Password - St. Gregory   Countersign - Patagonia
Watch -

Headquarters, Berthier, 25 April 1777
Password - St. Ignatius   Countersign - Brazil
Watch - 1 Lieutenant Count von Puckler; 2 non-commissioned officers, 1 drummer, and 29 privates of the Colonel's Company.
On orders of Brigadier Gall, Lieutenant Bischhausen is released from his arrest.

Hesse-Hanau Order Book

Headquarters, Berthier, 26 April 1777
Password - St. Benedict   Countersign - Tobago
Watch - 1 Ensign von Richtersleben; 2 non-commissioned officers, 1 drummer, and 29 privates from Captain von Passern's Company

On orders of Brigadier von Gall, as of today, all watch and orderly formations are discontinued. The new drummers are to report to headquarter tomorrow, with all their luggage and bedding in order to learn to play the drums.

On the 3rd of next month, the companies are to report the number of usable white breeches which they have or can be made to the lieutenant colonel.

As the brigadier has ordered that no battalion be formed when the regiment drills together, or moves out, but that the companies are to be divided into two platoons, so that the battalion has ten platoons. Therefore, when the captains and company commanders drill their companies, they are to divide them into two files each time, with the captain on the right wing, and the next senior officer in the middle, so that the troops will become accustomed to the officers commanding the battalion, as well as the officers commanding the two files of each company, even at a distance. The companies must also practice this alignment so that the spacing is maintained. The turning movement must be made with a longer step, but not running, otherwise the troops bunch up. On paydays drill is not to be conducted until further orders. When marching according to the above prescribed manner, with the weapons by the feet, held out, or shouldered [There is obviously a copying error in the German text at this point.] high on the right arm, and on the reverse shoulder, on the command to load. It must be strictly observed that the troops, according to regulation, command, remove the hammerstall cover. Load, close, and place it behind the strap, and not, as has happened previously, close the hammerstall prematurely. It is obvious that when the companies are arranged in two files, if the second file moves out, that the section steps off with the right foot, as the third file has done previously. For the Grenadier Company, the senior officer remains on the left flank, and the others divide, the same for the Colonel's Company, the captains on the left flank, the senior officer on the right, and the junior divides the company.

Captain [Friedrich Ludwig] von Schoell, by the end of April, is to render the company accounts.

- - - - - - -

Headquarters, Berthier, 30 April
Password - Athernasinus   Countersign - Bermuda
Watch -

In arrest, 1 Private Halaschka of Captain von Passern's Company

- - - - - - -

Hesse-Hanau Order Book

Headquarters, Berthier, 1 May 1777
Password - St. Anton   Countersign - Brunswick
Watch - 1 Lieutenant [Friedrich] von Geyling; 2 non-commissioned officers, 1 drummer, and 20 privates from the Grenadier Company
In arrest 1 Ensign von Richterleben.

Headquarters, Berthier, 2 May 1777
Password - St. Judith   Countersign - Bristol
Watch -
1 Ensign von Richtersleben, 1 Private Halaschka of Captain von Passern's Company, on orders from headquarters, are released from their arrest.

Headquarters, Berthier, 3 May 1777
Password - St. Vincent   Countersign - Isle aux Noix
Watch - 1 Lieutenant Bischhausen; 2 non-commissioned officers, 1 drummer, and 20 privates from the Leib Company

----

Headquarters, Berthier, 4 May 1777
Password - St. Simon   Countersign - Biv
Watch -
In arrest, 1 Surgeon's Mate Weiss

Hesse-Hanau Order Book

Headquarters, Berthier, 5May 1777
Password - St.. Joseph   Countersign - Coudres
Watch - 1 Ensign [Ernst] von Weyhers; 2 non-commissioned officers, 1 drummer, and 20 privates from the Colonel's Company
    Surgeon's Mate Weiss is to be locked up for 48 hours on the orders of Brigadier von Gall.

- - - - - - -

Headquarters, Berthier, 6 May 1777
Password - St. Christoph   Countersign - Quebec
Watch -

- - - - - - -

Headquarters, Berthier, 7May 1777
Password - St. Anthony   Countersign - Sorel
Watch - 1 Lieutenant Sieffert; 2 non-commissioned officers, 1 drummer, and 20 privates from the Lieutenant Colonel's Company
    Surgeon's Mate Weiss, on orders from headquarters, is released from his arrest.

- - - - - - -

Headquarters, Berthier, 8 May 1777
Password - St. Jacob   Countersign - Montreal
Watch - 1 Ensign Kempfer, 2 non-commissioned officers, 1 drummer, and 20 privates from Captain

Hesse-Hanau Order Book

Passern's Company

- - - - - - -

Headquarters, Berthier, 9 May 1777

Password - St. Benedict Countersign - Yamaska

Watch -

The following promotions have been announced for the brigade, by Major General [Frierdrich Adolph] von Riedesel.

As of 18 January 1777, His Highness named Ensign Brandes, of the von Riedesel Regiment, to be 2nd lieutenant, and transferred him to the Leib Company of this regiment. At the same time, Lieutenant Pincer of that company, was transferred to Captain von Poelnitz' Company. Captain-at-arms Demcke was promoted to ensign on 20 October 1776, and assigned to Major General von Riedesel's Leib Company. Flag-bearer Count von Rantzow, according to his patent as ensign, dated 18 February 1776, was promoted to that position and assigned to the von Barner Light Infantry Regiment. Captain-at-arms Hille, of the Prince Friedrich Regiment, according to his patent as ensign in 1776, was assigned to the regiment as an ensign. Flag-bearer von Forstner was promoted to ensign on 20 January 1777, and assigned

Hesse-Hanau Order Book

to Captain von Poelnitz' Company of the regiment.

*[This and subsequent paragraphs, followed by an asterisk, are also contained in Tom IX of the Lidgerwood Collection in the Morristown National Historical Park archives, in the same or nearly identical words.]

The following promotions for the regiment have been announced by Brigadier General von Gall. His Serene Highness, the Hereditary Prince, has the pleasure on 25 November, to promote Captain [Ludwig Wilhelm] von Passern to major; Staff Captain [Carl August] Scheel, of the Vacant Company, has been confirmed in that position; 2nd Lieutenant von Geyling was promoted to 1st lieutenant; and Ensign von Hohorst to 2nd lieutenant.

Captain von Schoell is assigned with Major von Passern. However, he is to assume command of the Vacant Company. 2nd Lieutenant von Hohorst, of the Colonel's Company, the Vacant Company, Captain Schoell, 1st Lieutenant von Geyling, and Ensign von Heerwagon. [There is obviously a copying error near the end of this paragraph.]

- - - - - - -

Hesse-Hanau Order Book

Headquarters, Berthier, 11 May 1777
Password - St. Martha   Countersign - La Chine
Watch - 1 Lieutenant von Trott; 2 non-commissioned officers, 1 drummer, and 20 privates from the Grenadier Company

- - - - - - -

Headquarters, Berthier, 12 May 1777
Password - Charles   Countersign - Pointe aux Tremble
Watch -
Brigadier von Gall orders the companies to drill tomorrow morning, from seven to eight o'clock.

On Thursday, a list which is to be prepared at once, is to be submitted of the number of troops who wish to take communion with the Reformed [chaplain] on Sunday. The troops must be here in Berthier by Saturday evening, provided with provisions for three days.

- - - - - - -

Headquarters, Berthier, 13 May 1777
Password - St. Thomas   Countersign - Cape Sante
Watch - 1 Lieutenant von Buttlar; 2 non-commissioned officers, 1 drummer, and 21 privates from the Leib Company

- - - - - - -

Hesse-Hanau Order Book

Headquarters, Berthier, 14 May 1777
Password - St. Phillip   Countersign - Three Rivers
Watch -
In arrest, one Private List of the Major's Company

- - - - - - - -

Headquarters, Berthier, 15 May 1777
Password - Quintini   Countersign - Sillery
Watch - 1 Ensign Siebert; 2 non-commissioned officers, 1 drummer, and 21 privates from the Colonel's Company
Musketeer List of the Major's Company, is released from arrest on orders from headquarters.

- - - - - - - -

Headquarters, Berthier, 16 May 1777
Password - St. Catherine   Countersign - Vallery
Watch -

- - - - - - - -

Headquarters, Berthier, 17 May 1777
Password - St. Paul   Countersign - Point Levy
Watch - 1 Lieutenant von Puckler; 2 non-commissioned officers, 1 drummer, and 21 privates from the Colonel's Company

- - - - - - - -

Hesse-Hanau Order Book

Headquarters, Berthier, 18 May 1777
Password - St. Magdalene   Countersign - Cape Rouge
Watch -

On the morning of the 18th of this month, church is to be held before the colonel's quarters, when the Leib Company, the Colonel's Company, and the Major's Company, as well as the Grenadiers and the Lieutenant Colonel's Company, are to assemble. Lieutenant von Eschwege ordered herewith, tomorrow, the 19th of this month, to report with sixty Canadians, to receive the bateaux for the regiment, at Maschaische. At the same time, the Senior Corporal Vaupel, of the Leib Company, is also ordered to be here.

- - - - - - - -

Headquarters, Berthier, 19 May 1777
Password - St. Mary   Countersign - Eclaire
Watch - 1 Ensign von Richtersleben; 2 non-commissioned officers, 1 drummer, and 21 privates

- - - - - - -

Headquarters, Berthier, 20 May 1777
Password - St. Agnes   Countersign - Berthier
Watch -

- - - - - - -

Hesse-Hanau Order Book

Headquarters, Berthier, 21 May 1777
Password - St. Lucia   Countersign - Maschaische
Watch - 1 Lieutenant von Geyling; 2 non-commissioned officers, 1 drummer, and 21 privates from the Grenadier Company
In arrest, 1 Grenadier Kalbfleisch

Headquarters, Berthier, 22 May 1777
Password - St. Christine   Countersign - Verscheure
Watch -
On orders of the lieutenant Colonel, Grenadier Kalbfleisch is released from his arrest.

Headquarters, Berthier, 23 May 1777
Password - St. Sophia   Countersign - Varenne
Watch - 1 Lieutenant von Eschwege; 2 non-commissioned officers, 1 drummer, and 21 privates from the Leib Company
On the orders of Brigadier von Gall, the clumsy troops, on drill days, are to be drilled from two to four o'clock, by an officer, when it is cool. However, when it is warmer, they are to be drilled from five to seven o'clock.

Headquarters, Berthier, 24 May 1777
Password - St. Ann   Countersign - Longueuil
Watch -

Hesse-Hanau Order Book

Headquarters,, Berthier, 25 May 1777
Password - St. Eliza   Countersign - La Prairie
Watch - 1 Lieutenant von Lindau; 2 non-commissioned officers, 1 drummer, and 21 privates from the Colonel's Company

- - - - - - -

Headquarters, Berthier, 26 May 1777
Password - St. Agat4ha   Countersign - Isle au Jesus
Watch -

- - - - - - -

Headquarters, Berthier, 27 May 1777
Password - St. Laurentia   Countersign - Chambly
Watch - 1 Ensign Weyhers; 2 non-commissioned officers, 1 drummer, and 21 privates from Lieutenant Colonel Lentz' Company

- - - - - - -

Headquarters, Berthier, 28 May 1777
Password - St. Charlotte   Countersign - Beauport
Watch -
In arrest, 1 Private [Martin] Voltz from Captain Scheel's Company

- - - - - - -

Headquarters, Berthier, 29 May 1777
Password - St. Margarete   Countersign - Laurette
Watch - 1 Lieutenant Bischhausen; 2 non-commissioned officers, 1 drummer, and 21 privates from the Major's Company

- - - - - - -

Hesse-Hanau Order Book

Headquarters, Berthier, 30 May 1777
Password - St. Ruth   Countersign - Isle d'Orleans
Watch -
In arrest, Ensign Weyhers. Corporal [Andreas] Koch, of the Lieutenant Colonel's Company, is to be locked up in close arrest, on orders of Brigadier von Gall.

- - - - - - -

Headquarters, Berthier, 31 May 1777
Passwords - St. Helena and Chinoi
Watch - Lieutenant von Sieffert; 2 non-commissioned officers, 1 drummer, and 21 privates
Ensign von Weyhers and Corporal Koch are released from their arrest, on orders of Brigadier von Gall. Tomorrow, being the 1st of June, church services are to be held at Brigadier von Gall's quarters, where the Colonel's and Major's Companies, as well as the nearby Grenadier and Leib Companies, are to assemble.

- - - - - - -

Order from General Headquarters,
Three Rivers, 21 May 1777
March Dispositions for the German Troops
As far as the General Rendezvous,
At Cumberland Head, for the Entire Army

Hesse-Hanau Order Book

After the brigades and regiments of General [John] Burgoyne have received the order to march, the following orders issued by Major General von Riedesel are to take effect.*

1) Major [Ferdinand Albrecht] von Barner is to draw his battalion together, so that punctually on 2 June, he will be at Sorel, and establish his headquarters there, leaving the quarters of the 62nd Regiment and the detachment of the 33rd Regiment empty. Also, if the Breymann Grenadier Battalion enters Sorel on the designated day, the necessary houses must be available. If the troops can not be quartered in houses, but must enter barns, insure that there are enough, so that every company has two barns, and one house for the company officers.*

Major Barner is to conduct his march, so as to arrive at Chambly on the 6th of next month, and above all else, carry out the orders received from General Burgoyne, so that he arrives at Cumberland Head, where the army is to rendezvous, with his battalion. If this battalion has not been provided with sufficient provisions, he must, because the time is so short, obtain them at Three Rivers, where they are available during the march, in sufficient time, so that he arrives at Cumberland Head on schedule. At the same time, the battalion must report as to where it can receive any shortage of ammunition, at Sorel, St. Jean, or Chambly, according to the lists submitted by the

Hesse-Hanau Order Book

battalion.*

The bateaux, which the battalion already has, are to be used to transport the baggage, ammunition, and anything else which the battalion has, and as many men as the bateaux can carry. The troops who can not go in the bateaux, must march on land with the required officers and non-commissioned officers until the battalion receives the number of bateaux, which will be at Sorel, Chambly, or St. Jean.*

All heavy equipment, which the regiments do not carry across the lake at this time, is to be sent to Three Rivers, where each battalion is to detach one non-commissioned officer and two men, who are dependable, from each company, and for the entire corps, one officer from the Specht Regiment, The baggage, for which a non-commissioned officer has been designated from each regiment, must be separated by companies, and is to be guarded here on the barracks' grounds. To insure that the heavy baggage arrives here on time, the officer from each regiment is to accompany it here, deliver it to the officer commanded to tend it for the entire corps, so that it is properly placed and guarded, and when everything has been put in order, return to his battalion. The regiments which lie beyond Three Rivers, are to deposit their heavy baggage at Three Rivers, and acquire their provisions at that place. The same handling of the sick, who are to be brought here

Hesse-Hanau Order Book

to the hospital, is to be made, and one surgeon's mate from the regiment, is to care for the sick, under the officer already assigned.*

All regiments and battalions are to obtain certificates from the quarters they are leaving, that no provisions have been advanced to their troops, and that there are no complaints, as, if these remain, the troop quarters, where they were cantoned, are not to be vacated without obtaining such a certificate.*

During the march, the best discipline is to be maintained, so that not the least excess occurs, for which each regimental commander is responsible, and in such a manner as to insure the same approval which they had from the entire army during this winter.*

2) The Breymann Grenadier Battalion is to move out upon receipt of this order. It will be good if it can reach Sorel in one day, otherwise it is to take night quarters between St. Sulpice and Berthier, for which reason, the Hesse-Hanau Regiment is to vacate their quarters, and cross the St. Lawrence River the next day, and occupy the quarters which have been occupied by the von Barner Battalion, follow that battalion to the general rendezvous at Cumberland Head, and see that the march and all other arrangements comply with the above order.*

3) The Grenadier Battalion is to be followed by the Prince Friedrich Regiment. That regiment is to move out of quarters on 2 June, and take new quarters

Hesse-Hanau Order Book

between Maskinonge and the Post House of Berthier, and cross the St. Lawrence River on the 4th, after the Grenadiers.*

4) The Hesse-Hanau Regiment is to vacate its quarters on 2 June, and move to the Berthier River, behind the Guigy House, so as to leave the quarters for the use of the troops passing through the parishes of Valerie, Norei, and Dautre, and Brigadier Gall is to insure that the regiment has two barns for each company.*

5) The von Riedesel Infantry Regiment is to march on the 3rd to Maskinonge, on the 4th to Berthier, to cross the water on the 5th, and then follow the route of the first troops. The Dragoons are to march on the 4th to Riviere du Loups, and on the 5th to Berthier. If it is not possible to cross the St. Lawrence River that day, they are to cross on the 6th, proceed to St. Denis, and so onward. The Specht Regiment is to pull the companies together at Cape Magdelene on the 3rd, with one company entering the barracks there on the morning of the 2nd. The Specht Regiment is to march to Maschische on the 4th, to Maskinonge on the 5th, to Berthier on the 6th, cross the St. Lawrence on the 7th, and then continue to its destination. The Rhetz Regiment is to assemble on the 3rd. It is to march to Pointe du Lac on the 4th, Riviere du Loups on the 5th, Maskianonge on the 6th, cross the St. Lawrence River on the 7th, and then follow the march route of the

Hesse-Hanau Order Book

Specht Regiment.*

6. All companies of the Riedesel, Specht, and Rhetz Regiments lying on the south side, are to march along the shore with their bateaux parallel with their regiments, so as to arrive at the same time as their respective regiments, in order to join together. At the time of receiving this order, they are to forward their heavy baggage to the regimental headquarters, or if not convenient, to Three Rivers, so that all the heavy equipment is collected together.*

General Riedesel will pass the regiments while on the march, so that it will not be necessary to send reports back, but they may be given to him as he passes the first troops.*

Hesse-Hanau Order Book

Orders from Headquarters, Three Rivers, 31 May 1777
Plan for Assembling the Army. Friday, 20 May*

The corps of Brigadier [Simon] Fraser is to be set in motion, and direct its march so as to arrive at Pointe au Fer on 3 June.*

Sunday, 1 June: The 9th and 47th Regiments are to cross the St. Lawrence River and the 9th is to enter camp at Boucherville, and the 47th at Longueuil.*

Monday, 2 June: Major General von Riedesel is to order the first German troops to cross the St. Lawrence River, and enter camp, so as not to disturb the quarters of the 62nd Regiment, nor the detachment of the English 33rd Regiment.*

Tuesday, 3 June: The first German troops are to continue their march on the Sorel River. The following German troops are to cross the St. Lawrence River, and enter the quarters which the first have vacated, and continue their daily marches, until they arrive at Chambly. Major General Riedesel is to make arrangements, so that the first of the German troops arrive at Chambly on 6 June.*

As the regiments do not have enough bateaux to proceed with the men and equipment, on the river, when they reach the St. Lawrence River, they are to send the baggage across to Sorel first, and when that has been unloaded at a convenient place, send the bateaux back pick up the remaining people from the regiment, and take them across, so that they can continue their march with all baggage and provisions by water, and such troops as the bateaux can not hold, on land. At no time is anyone to use vehicles to transport baggage to the Sorel River, because all of them are to be used to portage around the rapids. The bateaux of the German troops are to pass the portage at Chambly as a division arrives, and if the vehicles are sufficient to transport the baggage and provisions across, the troops may halt their march at Chambly, but not for more than one night, in order to continue their march and enter the camp at St. Therese the next day. If there are insufficient vehicles however, the bateaux are to be transported across first, and then the baggage and provisions, so that during the intervening time the damaged bateaux can be repaired. The 9th and 47th Regiments, which have halted at Boucherville and Longueuil in the meantime, so as to give the wheeled vehicles, which were used by Fraser's Brigade time to return, are to continue their march to Chambly, and the same day the 53rd Regiment is to enter the camp at St. Therese.*

    Wednesday, 4 June: The 53rd Regiment is to follow the 9th and 47th Regiments. It is hoped that there will be water enough, to allow the bateaux with troops and baggage, to pass the second rapids, which are between Chambly and St. Jean, and each regiment, in any case, must help itself and use every means to pass the rapids. When each regiment and division has

Hesse-Hanau Order Book

its bateaux ready at St. Jean, as well as those which are now lacking, they are to continue their route as designated, but not less than one regiment at a time, until they reach Cumberland Head on Lake Champlain, which passage is adequately protected. The general rendezvous is at the fleet and previously advanced corps at Cumberland Head.*

General [William] Phillips is responsible for all arrangements for the artillery. All the troops are to take sufficient provisions to last, as far as the general rendezvous, and to stop as seldom on the march, at depots on their route, as will prevent delays. All ships used to carry necessities are to be loaded during the time of this movement in such a manner, that when they arrive at Cumberland Head on 8 June, each will, without fail, have 200 tons on board.*

- - - - - - - -

Announcement as to What each Officer
is Permitted to take Across the Lake*

The regiments are notified herewith as to the amount of baggage, which they can take in the bateaux.*

For staff officers, there is no limit, and they can take necessary cooking and serving items, but only as needed*

A captain can take a tent, bed, and pack with such small clothing items as are needed for half of the campaign, one pair of canteens, one or two baskets

Hesse-Hanau Order Book

with foodstuffs, and two saddlebags.*

A junior officer, can take a tent, bed, and a pack, one basket of foodstuffs, one pair of canteens, and for persons of the middle staff, the same.*

- - - - - - - -

Headquarters, Berthier, 1 June 1777
Password -

On orders from Brigadier von Gall, all companies are to march tomorrow morning at exactly six o'clock, to the headquarters at Berthier

Quartermaster sergeants and guards must arrange their march in such a manner, as to arrive at Berthier at least two hours before their companies, and report to Regimental Quartermaster [Carl August] Sartorius. The captains of companies must obtain a receipt from the militia captain, that they have no claim for provisions delivered to the German troops. While this is being carried out, the troops are not to vacate the quarters in use, until the receipt is obtained.*

Hesse-Hanau Order Book

Orders from General Headquarters,
Three Rivers, 1 June 1777

As a command of 1 staff officer, 6 captains, 12 subalterns, 48 non-commissioned officers, and [blank] privates is to remain behind in Canada, the Hesse-Hanau Regiment is to provide 1 captain, 2 subalterns, 7 non-commissioned officers, and 96 privates.

Initially, the command is to remain in quarters in Berthier, and the captain is to report to Lieutenant Colonel [Johann Gustav] von Ehrenkrook, (who is to command the detached troops) at Three Rivers, from whom the captain will then receive further orders. Individuals, who are sickly and can not march well, may be designated for this command. The command designated in the previous order for moving the heavy baggage here, which consisted of 1 officer from the Specht Regiment, 1 non-commissioned officer per regiment, and 2 men per company, is included in the total for men of this order, and are to be taken from the 96 privates. To more quickly allow compliance with this order, the Prince Friedrich Regiment has been notified by orders from here.

- - - - - - - -

Headquarters, Berthier, 2 June 1777

Password -

The Leib Company is to provide the watch today, on order of Brigadier von Gall. Each company has 2 barns, before which 1 lance corporal and 3 privates,

Hesse-Hanau Order Book

are to be on watch, so that each company is to provide 2 lance corporals and 6 privates as a watch on the barns. One non-commissioned officer of the day is assigned to this barn watch. At the same time, in each barn, there is to be 1 non-commissioned officer of the day for the entire day, to supervise the troops. He is also to note what they cook, so as to know who has been foraging. Tomorrow, the regiment is to provide 1 officer - Lieutenant von Trott - for the headquarters watch, 1 non-commissioned officer, 1 drummer, and 4 privates from each company, who are to be brought to the brigadier's quarters at eleven o'clock. The barn watches are not to attend the guard mount, but are to be relieved by the company. As orderlies, 1 non-commissioned officer is to serve the brigadier, and 1 orderly each, the lieutenant colonel and major. All other orderlies are to be discontinued from today onward, and all watches are to be relieved every 24 hours. Those sharing tents are to be designated, and kettles, bottles, and axes are to be issued to them. The officers of each company are to be rotated, days as well as nights, to inspect the company barns, so that no complaints arise, in which case, the brigadier, the company commanders, or those in charge, are to be held responsible, and be required to pay for any damages. At the same time, all precautions are to be taken to prevent any complaints, and the troops must be discouraged by punishment of running the gauntlet.

Hesse-Hanau Order Book

No structure is to be burned down. This afternoon the cartridges, which are short, are to be issued, 30 per man, by Ensign Heerwagon, according to the lists which have been turned in, as well as 4 ammunition cases, in which the remaining cartridges, 100 per man, are packed. Attention is to be given to insure that cartridges, and the cases are not damaged due to wet weather. Four poles are to be fastened on the handles, so they can more easily be carried. The heavy baggage is to be brought to Three Rivers at four o'clock tomorrow morning, for which purpose a lieutenant - von Buttlar - 1 non-commissioned officer from the Major's Company and 24 privates are to be assigned.

For the command remaining in Canada, 1 captain - von Schoell, - 1 2nd lieutenant - von Hohort - 1 ensign - Kempner - 7 non-commissioned officers from Schoell's Company, and 96 privates; 16 from each company, are to be assigned. Of these, 1 non-commissioned officer and 12 privates are to be detached to [guard] equipment at Three Rivers.

- - - - - - -

Headquarters, Berthier, 3 June 1777
Passwords - Friedrich and Sorel

On orders of Brigadier von Gall, general march is to be beaten at six o'clock tomorrow morning, and at six-thirty, assembly. The battalion is to fall in, in full marching order, between the lieutenant colonel's and the major's quarters. The Leib Company is to carry the colors. One lieutenant, Sieffert, 1 non-commissioned officer, and 2 privates per company are assigned to the baggage detail. The quartermaster sergeants and quartermaster guards are to depart from here precisely at six o'clock. The detachment commanded by Captain von Schoell, which remains in Canada, is to assemble before the lieutenant colonel's quarters this afternoon, at four o'clock, with tents and all necessary equipment. The watch is to be relieved today by [Schoell's] Company.

In arrest, 1 Corporal Orbig and 1 drummer [Leonhard] Klie, who are to be released after 24 hours of confinement, on orders of the brigadier.

- - - - - - - -

Orders in Camp, Sorel, 4 June 1777

General march is to be beaten at precisely seven o'clock tomorrow morning, and assembly at seven-thirty. The companies are to assemble before their chiefs' and commanders' quarters, until the brigadier arrives with his company. Quartermaster sergeants and their guards are to march at six o'clock tomorrow morning, and as soon as general march is beaten, the Grenadier and Leib Companies are to cross to the other side of the water, leaving their equipment in the bateaux, and the companies are to leave their bateaux before their quarters. One non-commissioned officer and 7 men are to be assigned to row each bateau.

Hesse-Hanau Order Book

Equipment for the middle staff is to be placed in Lieutenant Sartorius' bateau.

On orders of the brigadier, Corporal Orbig and Regimental Quartermaster Klie are released from arrest.

Quartermaster Sergeants [Ludwig] Becker and [Nicolaus] Stopel are to serve as sergeants in the Lieutenant Colonel's and Captain Scheel's Companies. Corporal Kolb is to serve as quartermaster sergeant for the Lieutenant Colonel's Company, and Corporal Vaupel is to serve as quartermaster sergeant for Captain Scheel's Company. The Privates [Peter] Ewald and [Adolf] Zwhner are to serve as corporals for the Leib Company, and the Lieutenant Colonel's Company.

- - - - - - -

Orders, 5 June 1777, in Camp at St. Charles

There will be no march tomorrow, and the officers may have hot meals prepared at noon. The orders not to march are not to be mentioned until tomorrow morning.

- - - - - - -

Orders, 6 June 1777, in Camp at St. Charles

On orders of Brigadier von Gall, the baggage is to be sent away at exactly four o'clock this afternoon to Belle Isle, over the crossing and the equipment is to be unloaded on the other side. One non-commissioned officer and 3 privates from each company, are to remain with the unloaded equipment, and 2 men are to bring back the unloaded bateaux. Then the regiment is to be taken across. As soon as the regiment has passed the crossing, the baggage is to be reloaded in the bateaux, and used for those persons in the detachment who had to march yesterday. At four o'clock, general march is to be beaten, and at exactly four-thirty, assembly. Quartermaster sergeants and guards one hour previously.

- - - - - - - -

Orders, 7 June 1777, in Camp at Belle Isle

There will be no march today. The troops are to clean weapons, and loading facilities. However, general march is to be beaten at five o'clock tomorrow morning, and assembly at five-thirty. Quartermaster sergeants and guards are to move out at five o'clock. All equipment is to be loaded in the bateaux, and sent ahead as soon as general march is beaten.

- - - - - - -

Orders of Major General Riedesel
Chambly, 7 June 1777*1

Upon receipt of this order, the Hesse-Hanau Infantry Regiment is to send out its quartermaster sergeants and guards, to arrange quarters for the regiment in houses and barns, on the far side of Fort Chambly, where General [Guy] Carleton had his headquarters last summer, and where the Barner Light Infantry Battalion is now located. The half [This is an

Hesse-Hanau Order Book

apparent copying error in the German text, and should be house.] allotted to the general staff is to be left unoccupied.*

The Hesse-Hanau Infantry Regiment must move out so as to enter its cantonment quarters here, at about one o'clock in the afternoon, so that during the afternoon it can begin transporting the bateaux and baggage past the rapids. Therefore, Lieutenant Colonel [John Christoph] Lentz must regulate the arrival of the battalion. Upon receipt of this order, Lieutenant Colonel Praetorius is also to move out, and continue his march to Fort Chambly, which the Grenadier Battalion is to enter tomorrow afternoon or evening. The regimental quartermaster of the Prince Friedrich Regiment can ask Captain Poellnitz where the quarters are to be. If the Prince Friedrich Regiment can not reach Chambly tomorrow, which is to be hoped , however, it must continue as far as possible so that on the following day it can join here at an early hour. Lieutenant Colonel Praetorius is to report upon his arrival here to Mr. Corbin, so that the problems of portage can be attended to.*

- - - - - - -

Hesse-Hanau Order Book

Orders in Camp at Chambly, 8 June 1777

At exactly six o'clock tomorrow morning, a fatigue detail of 1 officer, 1 non-commissioned officer, 1 drummer, and 30 privates, commanded by Lieutenant von Geyling, will proceed to the portage and establish a post by the equipment. The field and fire watch for today is to be Friedrich Seibert, 3 non-commissioned officers, 1 drummer, and 39 privates. One-non-commissioned officer, and 18 privates are to go to Fort Chambly and establish a post. For the reception of the bateaux, Lieutenant von Lindau is designated, and is to report to Captain Corbin at the fort. The officers are reminded that the honors to be paid to the generals and brigadiers; to the general, two drum rolls, and to the brigadiers, one drum roll. The field watch for tomorrow is to be 1 Lieutenant von Puckler; 3 non-commissioned officers, 1 drummer, and 39 privates; for the general guard, 1 non-commissioned officer, and 6 privates.

- - - - - - - -

Orders from General Riedesel, Chambly, 9 June 1777*

In the future, the passwords are to be given out at the general's quarters at eleven o'clock, and all regiments which are in the area of the general's quarters, are then to use them at the appropriate time. The brigades or regiments are always to assign an orderly at the general's quarters, to insure receiving

Hesse-Hanau Order Book

the orders as expeditiously as possible. From now on, each week, on Saturday, a weekly report, according to the format which each regiment has, is to be submitted by each regiment. The Prince Friedrich Regiment is to relieve all detachments of the Hesse-Hanau Regiment at once. These detachments consist of the following: 1 officer, 1 non-commissioned officer, 1 drummer, and 30 privates at the portage; 1 officer, and 18 privates in the fort; 1 non-commissioned officer, and 6 privates on guard at General Riedesel's. The brigade is to furnish 1 non-commissioned officer as an orderly at General Riedesel's, and toady the orderly is to be from the Prince Frierdrich Regiment. General Riedesel herewith orders that the house of Monsieur Montzambere, in which 40 privates of the Prince Friedrich Regiment are quartered, is to be vacated and used as quarters for officers.

- - - - - - -

Orders, 9 June 1777, in Camp at Chambly

Today at two o'clock, march is to be commenced, and the troops are to be ready to march at one-thirty. The kettles and bottles are not to be placed on the wagons, but carried. The quartermaster sergeants and guards are to move out at one o'clock.

- - - - - - -

10 June 1777, in Camp at St. Therese

Watch - Ensign von Richtersleben; 3 non-commissioned officers, 1 drummer, and 39 privates

Hesse-Hanau Order Book

General march is to be beaten tomorrow afternoon at two o'clock and assembly at two-thirty. Quartermaster sergeants and guards are to move out at precisely one o'clock, but the baggage at two o'clock.

- - - - - - - -

Orders, 11 June 1777, in Camp at St. Jean
Passwords - St. Luke   Countersign - Montreal
Watch - Lieutenant von Geyling; 3 non-commissioned officers, 1 drummer, and 39 privates

The battalion is to be prepared to embark at exactly nine o'clock tomorrow. On orders of the brigadier, Lieutenant von Buttlar is to convey this order to the Brigadier's Company.

- - - - - - -

Orders, 12 June 1777, in Camp at Riviere la Col
Password - John   Countersign - Quebec
Watch - Lieutenant von Lindau; 3 non-commissioned officers, 1 drummer, and 39 privates

The brigadier announces to the officers, that they are permitted to cook, because the march will not commence until one o'clock tomorrow. Tomorrow, the court-martial is to be held for Musketeer [Maurice] Lehr, of Captain Scheel's Company. Lieutenant von Trott and Ensign Siebert are designated. A non-commissioned officer from the Grenadiers is to observe. The picket is 1 Lieutenant Buttlar; 2 non-commissioned officers, 1 drummer, and 30 privates

- - - - - - -

Hesse-Hanau Order Book

Orders, 13 June 1777, in Camp at Cumberland Head
Password - Nicolaus   Countersign - Three Rivers
Watch - Ensign von Weyhers; 3 non-commissioned officers, 1 drummer, and 39 privates

- - - - - - - -

Orders, 14 June 1777, in Camp at Cumberland Head
Passwords - Charles and Brunswick
Watch - Lieutenant Bischhausen; 3 non-commissioned officers, 1 drummer, and 39 privates

The watch is to assemble at nine o'clock tomorrow morning, and a prayer hour is to be held tomorrow evening.

- - - - - - -

Orders, 15 June 1777, in Camp at Cumberland Head
Password - George   Countersign -
Watch - Lieutenant Seiffert; 3 non-commissioned officers, 1 drummer, and 39 privates

When punishment is being administered by running the gauntlet, no soldier is to leave the camp without permission of his captain or company commander, on orders of the brigadier. This evening at six o'clock, and every evening from now on, when it does not rain, prayer hour is to be held. The soldiers are not to wear long breeches in camp, nor a sword in a shoulder belt, and during the prayer hour, no sash or gorget. Also, during the prayer hour a patrol is to go about in the camp to prevent shooting.

- - - - - - -

Hesse-Hanau Order Book

Orders, 16 June 1777, in Camp at Cumberland Head
Passwords - Heinrich and Cumberland Head
Watch - Lieutenant von Buttlar; 3 non-commissioned officers, 1 drummer, and 39 privates

- - - - - - -

Orders, 17 June 1777, in Camp at Cumberland Head
Password -
Watch - Lieutenant von Trott; 3 non-commissioned officers, 1 drummer, and 39 privates

After parade, a court-martial for the Musketeer Voltz, to which Lieutenant von Bischhausen and Ensign von Weyhers are assigned. (Musketeer Voltz is to be placed in stocks for 48 hours.)

- - - - - - -

General Orders, Cumberland Head, 18 June 1777
Passwords - St. Helene and Montreal
Watch - Lieutenant von Trott; 3 non-commissioned officers, 1 drummer, and 39 privates

General Disposition of the Army

The Monay and Boucherville Companies, Captain [Alexander] Fraser's Detachment, and a corps of Indians are assigned to the advance corps of the army, under the command of General Fraser.

The Grenadiers, Jaegers, and Light Infantry, under the command of Colonel [Heinrich] Breymann, are to form the reserve corps, and never camp in the line. Riedesel's Dragoon Regiment is also to camp outside the lines, and for the time being, is to cover the

Hesse-Hanau Order Book

headquarters. At the same time, the corps of Peters and Joseph are to remain outside the line. The recruits of the 63rd Regiment, under the command of Lieutenant Nutt, are to serve on board the fleet, for the time being.

After the initial movement, the army is to camp in the following order of battle, and until ordered otherwise, the same order is to be maintained.

Left Wing

1st Brigade [on the left, consisting of] Rhetz, Specht, and Riedesel Regiments - Brigadier [Friedrich] Specht in command

2nd Brigade [on the right, consisting of] Prince Friedrich and Hesse-Hanau Regiments - Brigadier von Gall in command

When necessary, two lines are to be formed in the following manner: The 2nd British Brigade behind the 1st, and the 2nd German Brigade is also to move behind the 1st. The brigadiers are also to camp with their brigades at all times. General Burgoyne is to troop the line tomorrow morning at seven o'clock, at which time the regiments are to be under arms. The Dragon Regiment, and Specht and Rhetz Regiments are excused, as the general inspected them previously at St. Jean. At this time, the inclusive report of the strength of the German Corps is to be given to the general. The Hesse-Hanau Regiment is to furnish 1

Hesse-Hanau Order Book

non-commissioned officer, as an orderly for General Burgoyne, and tomorrow the Prince Friedrich Regiment is to furnish the same. If no changes have occurred, since the last weekly report, no additional report will be required today. However, if changes have occurred, this is to be reported at once. In the future, the adjutant of both regiments commanded by Brigadier von Gall are to pick up orders daily, at twelve o'clock, in the camp of the Hesse-Hanau Regiment.

Watch - Ensign Siebert; 3 non-commissioned officers, 1 drummer, and 39 privates

1 Captain [Friedrich] von Germann, 1 non-commissioned officer, and 7 privates are ordered on fatigue detail, at Sorel. Promptly at six-thirty tomorrow morning, the entire regiment is to assemble at the front in full gear.

Orders in Camp at Cumberland Head, 19 June 1777
Passwords - St. Therese and Longueuil
Watch - Lieutenant Count von Puckler; 3 non-commissioned officers, 1 drummer, and 39 privates

The army is to draw provisions to take them through the thirtieth, starting with the 47th Regiment, which has the most pressing need. It is to be followed by the 1st English Brigade, and then the German brigade. As soon as the provisions have been received, they are to be loaded into the bateaux, and each regiment is to provide a guard for the same. All the provisions must be drawn today, and the regimental quartermasters are to present their requirements to Captain Gerlach. Tomorrow the army is to begin its movement, and instead of reveille, general march is to be beaten. At the same time, the quartermasters, guards, and carpenters from the Grenadiers are to embark, and depart. They are to assemble in their bateaux on the right wing of the 9th Regiment, where the vice-quartermaster general is to meet them, and lead them onward. At the same time, tents are to be struck, and the baggage loaded in the swiftest bateau. An hour after general march is sounded, assembly is to be beaten, and each regiment is to embark where the bateaux are standing. As soon as General Burgoyne believes that the regiments can be ready to depart, a cannon shot is to be fired from the ship *Maria*, and the sail on the forward mast unfurled. Then the bateaux of all the regiments are to be arranged in the following order, and remain so: first the Jaegers, then the von Barner Battalion, and the Grenadiers, under the command of Lieutenant Colonel Breymann, are to form the advance guard. They are to be followed by the Dragoon Regiment. The 1st English Brigade is to lead the line, 200 yards behind the Dragoons. The German brigades are then to follow in order. Each corps is to be formed in

Hesse-Hanau Order Book

columns, with a four bateaux front. Each battalion, which is on the flanks, must try to maintain an even distance from the center line. As soon as everyone is in line, two shots are to be fired from the *Maria*, and a flag raised on the forward mast. Then everyone is to begin the march, and the bateaux are to use sails and oars, as necessary, to maintain proper distances.*

- - - - - - -

Orders, in Camp at Point au Sable, 20 June 1777
Passwords - St. Peter and Florence
Watch - Lieutenant von Eschwege; 3 non-commissioned officers, 1 drummer, and 39 privates

His Excellency, General Burgoyne, takes this opportunity, at the assembling of the army, to publicly declare, it being his opinion concerning the troops which His Majesty, the King, has seen fir to place under his command, and who could not give him greater satisfaction, that the troops, having received the recommendation concerning their fame and conduct, will accept these remarks, and so conduct themselves, and he promises to grant them all possible encouragement, which the service can provide for them. On the other hand, the general requires that every officer of the army contribute what he can to maintain a continuous and constantly equal system in adherence to orders. The following orders are to be adhered to, so that it will not be necessary to repeat them in the future.*

Hesse-Hanau Order Book

1) All officers, of whatever rank, sent on command to any post, are to make as secure as conditions permit, and as the terrain will allow, with abatis made with trees, with the points directed outward, palisades erected at churches and houses, breastworks made from dirt and wood. Such manner of defenses can only be made in a short time, but do not require the technical knowledge of an engineer. The defense of all posts, which are useful and necessary under all conditions, are even more necessary in this war, when the enemy is not willing to compete in the open field, and engage in a direct confrontation against the royal troops, who have been instructed in disposition and training over a prolonged period, in conducting warfare. Neither the distance from the enemy, nor the disposition of the corps, which might be hidden by a woods or stream, can be taken as security against an enemy plan. It is also worth noting that a guard position or outpost, should never be established without having a tree or other defense in front, in order to prevent its being overrun by a small detachment. With these precautions being taken, each officer will understand how dependent the general, and his own honor, are in defending a post, or in carrying out a noteworthy retreat. Certainly this last case can only occur when the enemy strength is incomparably greater, than would be necessary to defend oneself with good and capable troops.

Hesse-Hanau Order Book

2) All officers are to exert themselves to bolster the confidence of the private soldiers and rely upon the use of bayonets, because a clumsy and half-trained individual can fire as well as a good soldier, but an attack with bayonet in the hands of motivated troops can not be resisted. The enemy, convinced of this truth, has sought to prevent this by entrenching, and long-barreled rifles. Therefore, it is to our honor as brave soldiers to storm [his defenses].

3) Officers must be attentive to their men at all times, and never worry about their own well-being, and still less, occupy themselves by using their own weapons against the enemy.

4) Loaded weapons are never to be stored in weapons' racks, nor carried loaded upon the march, unless having been so ordered.

5) No group nor individual is to leave the regimental camp unless accompanied by an officer or non-commissioned officer. This is necessary not only to maintain discipline and honor among the troops, but to prevent marauding and plundering. The Indians and the army provost are to be ordered to punish, on the spot, and with the greatest severity, anyone who violates this order.

6) The camp is always to be spread out as much as the terrain allows, to insure cleanliness and good health. But, as there will be times when the place is not large enough for the regiments, they will have to

Hesse-Hanau Order Book

enlarge the site. by chopping down [trees and brush] so each battalion can be granted an equal amount of area by the quartermaster general, and so that each has an equal amount of work required, and this must be the first activity upon entering camp.

7) As it is often necessary in this land to clear an attack place [field of fire] behind, as well as ahead of the army, attention is to be given to insure that they are prepared, so that they can support an advance, as well as a retreat. It will be necessary to clear large areas, which otherwise could serve the enemy purpose, for firing against our troops.

The camp guards are always to be stationed within 100 or 200 yards of the weapons racks. The front is to have a covering defensive position made with dirt or wood.

8) When the camp is laid out with the front on the water, or close to the water, so that this rule can not be applied, the field watch is to be positioned behind the front, and those regiments which camp on the flanks are to take position on the front. When the terrain prevents the officer tents being set up in their normal locations, they must never be placed so as to interfere with the field of fire.

9) All deserters who come in from the enemy, who might possibly be spies, or other persons who appear at the outposts, or who otherwise come in, are to be brought to headquarters as soon as possible, without

Hesse-Hanau Order Book

being delayed for preliminary questioning.

10) All service, by detachments, as well as by each corps, is to be preformed with the required effective strength.

11) When His Excellence, [General Burgoyne], visits an outpost, no honors or weapons' salutes are to be rendered.

12) The *Articles of War* are to be read to the troops of each regiment tomorrow, before tattoo, and then these orders are to be read, also.

The daily tour of duty is to be as follows:

A brigadier of the day is to be designated daily, who is to inspect the outlying posts, and is to have general supervision of the camp. Reports are to be submitted to him, and from him to His Excellence. Should an attack, or other unusual situation arise at one of the other posts, a report is to be submitted to His Excellence.

A brigadier of the day is to assign all commanders for details, and sup[ervise] the breaking of camp.

After the last brigade of the corps has arrived in camp, the pickets are to consist of: 1 staff officer from each wing, 1 captain for each brigade, and from every regiment, 1 subaltern, 2 non-commissioned officers, and 25 privates. The entire picket is to assemble one-half hour before retreat, before the center of the line, and practice drilling, marching, and

Hesse-Hanau Order Book

charging with sloped weapons, under the supervision of the brigadier of the day. Half of the picket is at all times during the night, at a pre-determined distance, on the roads, hidden pass ways, and such routes where the enemy might secretly approach, and the brigadier of the day is to post them himself.

Orders of Major General von Riedesel

Shooting in camp is strictly forbidden. Every regiment is to be alert to the rear, as well as to the front, to insure that such does not happen, and in cases when it does, who went against the order, and whether from our, or our English troops. They are to be arrested and reported to the brigadier under whom they serve. All general orders apply to the corps of Lieutenant Colonel Breymann and the Dragoon Regiment, also. Detachments from the army, such as pickets and similar duties, are not applicable to these two corps. However, Lieutenant Colonel Breymann is to post his picket at his own corps. Each brigade, including the corps of Lieutenant Colonel Breymann and the Dragoon Regiment, is to dispatch 1 non-commissioned officer as an orderly to General von Riedesel, who are to deliver the orders to the various corps. Corps which, separated from the general headquarters by water, must send a non-commissioned officer with a bateau which is to remain at the general headquarters. The front of the camp must be aligned

Hesse-Hanau Order Book

today and tomorrow, not only so the regiments can move out, but so that there is ten to fifteen yards of room to allow access to nearby water.

On orders of Brigadier von Gall, the carpenters from the Grenadiers are to be assigned no duties except those expressly ordered by the regiment.

- - - - - - -

Orders in Camp at Point au Sable, 21 June 1777
Passwords - Burgoyne and Chambly
Watch - Ensign von Richtersleben; 3 non-commissioned officers, 1 drummer, and 39 privates

Major General von Riedesel herewith extends his sincere thanks to the brigadiers and commanders of the corps, and requests at the same time, that a thanks be extended to the regimental commanders, in his name, for the exceptional exactness with which the march out of winter quarters, until today, have been executed, as well as for the exactness with which the orders for the march were adhered to. If everyone conducts himself in a similar manner, all the orders of the commanding general of the army will be executed with the same exactness, and everyone will merit the satisfaction of his ruling sovereign.

As the general is now completely confident that his orders will be carried out in every detail, it is his intent not to burden the troops with excessive orders, and hopes at the same time, that such compliance is to be practiced, and that anyone who fails, will be more closely observed by his superiors.

The orders of the general will always be given to the respective brigadiers and corps commanders, and he relies upon each of them, with his subordinate regiments, to carry them out in the same manner as has been previously practiced.

Should conflict or misunderstanding arise between the English and German troops, it must be reported to the proper brigadiers and commanders of regiments and corps, who can then make recommendations to the general, so that he can make arrangements which will satisfy the situation, because it must be one of the main objectives in this war, to live with the English troops in peaceful harmony.

To prevent future delays in delivering orders, the brigade majors and adjutants from the separate corps, are to report to the headquarters of His Excellence, General Burgoyne, and receive the orders there from Captain Poellnitz, after the general orders have been issued by the commanding general, at which time, General von Riedesel, who is at the headquarters, will issue to the various corps such information as he thinks necessary. If the general is not present in the headquarters, such orders as the general may wish to issue, will be sent to the regiments, in writing, by an orderly assigned to the general headquarters.

Everything pertaining to brigade and regimental lists, is always to be sent to Captain Poellnitz.

Hesse-Hanau Order Book

Everything pertaining to bateaux and such related items, is to be reported to Captain Gerlach, and obtained from him. Such previous and similar items requested by the Specht Brigade, are to be submitted to Adjutant Clarke, by the von Gall Brigade, the corps of Lieutenant Colonel Breymann, and the Dragoon Regiment, to Captain Gerlach.

Although from the side of General von Riedesel all possible efforts are made to meet the requirements directed by the above name person, it is not always possible to act promptly, because often those necessities are lacking, and despite all efforts of higher authorities, they can not be obtained. At the same time, everybody must do his best, considering the circumstances.

The detachment for the bateaux of the general staff, is to be furnished in the future, by the 5th Infantry Regiment., and , although to solve the regular distribution of provisions, when such are issued, 1 officer, and 1 non-commissioned officer from each regiment, are to be present, that detail must remain, at the same time, at its post, by the general's guard.

The day after tomorrow, the army is to move and occupy the place now occupied by General Fraser, and at the same rime, it is to receive orders from General Riedesel. As soon as the morning dispositions have been made, Captain Gerlach is to proceed to the place where the troops are to camp.

Hesse-Hanau Order Book

If the regiments have means, they can be sent ahead, even today, and if building materials are found, they may build bake ovens. The regiment must provide one bateau to carry its men there. Captain Gerlach will, when he passes the regiments about to depart, inform the troops how they are to proceed, in order to depart at once in their bateaux.

- - - - - - -

Hesse-Hanau Order Book

Orders of Brigadier von Gall

The regiment is to provide a guard of 1 non-commissioned officer, and 24 privates as a watch for General Riedesel. It is to be provided with kettles, tents, and canteens [There appears to be a copying error at this point in the German text.] marching on the left flank of the Rhetz Regiment. The *Articles of War* are to be read to the soldiers at six o'clock this evening.

- - - - - - - -

Orders in the Camp at Point au Sable, 22 June 1777
Passwords - Maria and Scotland
Watch - Lieutenant von Geyling; 3 non-commissioned officers, 1 drummer, and 39 privates

The army is to be set in motion tomorrow. Instead of reveille, general march is to be beaten, and the regimental quartermasters, quartermaster sergeants, and guards, are to embark and assemble on the right flank, at the camp of Lieutenant Colonel Breymann. Captain Welan is to be present, in lieu of the vice-quartermaster general, at Lieutenant Colonel Breymenn's Corps, to guide the quartermaster sergeants and their guards to the new site. The tents are to be struck as soon as general march is beaten, and assembly is to be beaten one hour later. After assembly, each regiment is to embark in its bateaux, and take its place in the same order as the regiments came here from Cumberland Head on 19 June, and then hold that position. Lieutenant Colonel Breymann's Corps is to hold its position in the same order before its camp. The Dragoon Regiment, after it is embarked, is to close on the Grenadiers. All the regiments of the army are to close, as they follow, one behind the other. The 9th Regiment of the English Brigade is to lead, and the Rhetz Regiment is the last of the column. As soon as this is accomplished, the Rhetz Regiment, in the bateaux, is to begin to beat march. The other regiments are to do the same, until it reaches the front. As soon as Lieutenant Colonel Breymann hears the 9th Regiment beat march, he is to begin to row, and the mentioned regiments are to use every effort to maintain the previously established position by rowing. The 1st English Brigade is to maintain a constant interval of 100 yards from the advance guard.

Orders in Camp at Point au Sable, 23 June 1777
Passwords - St. George and England
Watch - Lieutenant von Landau; 3 non-commissioned officers, 1 drummer, and 39 privates

As contrary winds and high water do not allow passing the point, the army is to remain lying at bivouac, pending further orders. Tents and all baggage are to remain lying in bateaux. However, the troops may cook, so that they can not only eat here, but also have something cold that they can take with them. As soon as possible, march is to be beaten, one-half hour later, assembly, then everything is to occur as contained in yesterday's orders.

The army may set up tents. However, tomorrow morning, general march is to be beaten instead of reveille, and the tents are to be struck then, but assembly is to be when ordered. General march and assembly are to begin at the Breymann Corps, and proceed from the right to the left flank. In case conditions require general march to be beaten prior to daybreak, loading is to proceed from right to left, also.

- - - - - - - -

Orders in Camp at Riviere au Boquet, 24 June 1777
Passwords - St. Margrete and Chambly
Watch - Ensign von Weyhers; 3 non-commissioned officers, 1 drummer, and 39 privates

His Excellency, General Burgoyne, has seen with pleasure that some regiments have the ability to produce baked goods without using an oven, and as it is as healthy as the best bread, the other regimental chiefs are ordered to let their troops learn how, because at times, the movement of the army may be so swift, that it will not be possible to build ovens. All shooting in camp is strictly forbidden, and to insure that no one goes beyond the outposts, everyone is reminded, and all the regimental commanders are ordered to strictly obey. The regiments are to cook this evening for one day in order to be constantly

Hesse-Hanau Order Book

supplied with one day's food, during the next movement of the army.

- - - - - - -

Order in Camp at Riviere au Boquer, 25 June 1777
Passwords - St. Julian and Lisbon
Watch - Lieutenant Bischhausen; 3 non-commissioned officers, 1 drummer, and 39 privates

The army is to be set in motion today, if the weather permits. Major General von Riedesel is to take over the command. The daily duty, as given out in the orders of the 20th is to commence tomorrow, and the brigadier of the day is Brigadier [Henry] Powell. Captain of the brigade for Brigadier von Gall is from the Prince Friedrich Regiment. Each regiment [is to provide] 1 officer, 2 non-commissioned officers, 1 drummer, and 25 privates. The captains are to alternate. In picket, Lieutenant von Trott.

- - - - - - -

Orders of Major General von Riedesel

General march is to be beaten this afternoon, tents and baggage taken to the bateaux, so that nothing more needs to be done after assembly, which is to be beaten at two o'clock, when the troops are to be embarked in the bateaux. The 1st English Brigade is then to move so far forward with their bateaux, that they arrive before the camp of General [Gustavus] Hamilton's 2nd Brigade, and General Hamilton's Brigade, then is to fall in behind the English 1st

Hesse-Hanau Order Book

Brigade. This is to be followed by Brigadier von Gall's Brigade, and then that of Brigadier von Specht, as was done yesterday. Lieutenant Colonel Breymann's Corps must get underway from its present position, so that at precisely two o'clock, it will be ready with its bateaux, 400 yards from the camp of the 2nd Brigade, and serve as the army's advance guard. The Dragoons are to follow the Grenadier Battalion, otherwise, everything remains the same as contained in the first order, and is to be commenced again by the Rhetz Regiment beating march, which is to proceed up to the advance guard. General march and assembly are to begin being beaten at Brigadier Hamilton's Brigade, followed by the Dragoons, and so through the army from the left to the right wing. Quartermaster sergeants and guards move ahead of the Grenadiers when assembly is beaten, and continue their route under the direction of the vice-quartermaster general.

- - - - - - -

Orders in Camp at Crown Point, 26 June 1777
Passwords - Anthony and Padua
Watch - Lieutenant Seiffert; 3 Non-commissioned officers, 1 drummer, and 39 privates
Picket - Lieutenant von Trott; 2 non-commissioned officers, 1 drummer, and 30 privates

Each company is to submit a list to the adjutant general in which the date of rank of all officers is to be

Hesse-Hanau Order Book

entered, and also, which of those have rank in the army, but not in the regiment. The weekly lists are always to be the first sent in. The English lists are to be sent in according to the printed format. The brigades are to send in their weekly reports at once, and send them in every Monday in the future. Each regiment is to submit a list as to the number of rations needed each day.

When the two wings of the army are separated by a river, it is not necessary for the two pickets to unite. However, they are to assemble wing-wise before the front of their camp, and the staff officer of each wing is to post the detail which moves forward each night. No retreat cannon is to be fired, until so ordered by Lieutenant Twiss, aide-de-camp to Major General Phillips, who is to command the Engineer Corps, and this is to be made known to the army. In case the camp is attacked, the army is to assemble before their camps. If no further orders are received, orders will be given out the next morning at twelve o'clock in the country. Once again, all shooting is strictly forbidden. After the regiments have entered camp, and the troops have finished cooking, in compliance with the orders of the 20th, the front and rear are to be cleared as much as possible, and what can not be done today, is to be continued with the greatest haste tomorrow. Redoubts are to be made ahead of the field watch, and that of the Rhetz Regiment is to be located on the left

Hesse-Hanau Order Book

flank. The field watch of the Specht Regiment is to be located in the space between the Rhetz and Specht Regiments; that of the Riedesel Regiment, a bit left of center; and that of the Prince Friedrich Regiment, ahead of the front. The fire watches are also to have redoubts, and they are to be started as soon as the most advance one for the field watch is finished. The picket moves out according to the orders, and half is to be left as a cover for the left flank and left rear. Lieutenant Colonel [Ernst] Speth, of the Riedesel Regiment, is ordered to inspect the picket and field watches, morning and evening. Brigadier Specht has inspection of the camp and posts today. He, accompanied by Captain Gerlach, is responsible for posting the picket. As an outpost is necessary on the left flank, where the captain's post is to be at night, a subaltern and 24 men are to remain there during the day.

1 lieutenant, von Trott, is ordered to the picket.

At four o'clock tomorrow morning, the English are to send six bateaux, and the German troops, ten bateaux, each with five men, with the necessary commissioned and non-commissioned officers, to Washington. They are to receive their orders from Commissary General Clarke, concerning the dividing and reloading of provisions on land.

Hesse-Hanau Order Book

The English are to send forty men, and the Germans twenty men, with commissioned and non-commissioned officers, to organize the provisions at Chimney Point. That detail is to be ready one-half hour after the first, at four-thirty. The von Gall Brigade is to provide 1 officer, 1 non-commissioned officer, and 15 men, as well as 3 bateaux, for the first detail, and 8 men for the second detail at Chimney Point. NB. - Chimney Point lies 1 lieu [2.76 miles] from here, on this side of the lake. The officer is to be furnished by Hesse-Hanau. Each regiment is to provide 1 non-commissioned officer, the Hanau Hereditary Prince Regiment 12 privates, 4 for the first detail, and 1 non-commissioned officer and 8 privates to the latter; Prince Friedrich Regiment is to provide 1 non-commissioned officer and 11 privates to the first detail. Each regiment is to provide 2 bateaux, and assemble the details after three o'clock in the morning, at the Hesse-Hanau bateaux. 1 lieutenant, Count von Puckler, is ordered on the first detail.

Orders in Camp at Crown Point, 27 June 1777
Passwords - James and Genoa
Watch - Lieutenant von Buttlar; 3 non-commissioned officers, 1 drummer, and 39 privates
Picket - Captain von Schachten; Ensign Siebert; 2 non-commissioned officers, 1 drummer, and 30 privates

Hesse-Hanau Order Book

Major of Brigade - Clerc
Staff Officer - English - Lieutenant Colonel Hill
German - Lieutenant Colonel Praetorius

This afternoon a report is to be given as to how many bateaux are short, and which need repairs. The retreat shot is to be fired this evening on the right wing, and proceed to the left wing. This is to be the practice until the army is pulled together. If the regiments need entrenching tools, they are to turn to each of the Artillery flanks, where they may obtain the same. As soon as the work is completed, they are to be turned in, and the regiments are responsible that none are missing. Lieutenant Robertson of the Engineer Corps is attached to the right wing, and is to receive orders, as appropriate, from Brigadier Powell, and [James] Hamilton, in order to fortify the right wing. Lieutenant Dumfort is attached to the left wing, and for the fortification of the left wing, is to receive orders from General Riedesel. Each wing is to send a non-commissioned officer as an orderly to headquarters, and 1 non-commissioned officer to the brigadier of the day. If he is English, a German non-commissioned officer must be the orderly; but if it is a German brigadier, the non-commissioned officer must be from the English troops.

- - - - - - - -

Orders in Camp at Crown Point, 28 June 1777
Passwords - Beatrix and Dublin

Hesse-Hanau Order Book

Watch - Lieutenant von Trott; 3 non-commissioned officers, 1 drummer, and 39 privates

Picket - Lieutenant von Eschwege; 2 non-commissioned officers, 1 drummer, and 30 privates

    According to General Burgoyne's orders, only half of the pickets are to move out. General von Riedesel orders that in the future, a double roster is to be maintained, that is, an original; [There appears to be a copying error in the German text at this point.] reserve picket, which is to be under Adjutant General von Poellnitz, as long as we are here. So that the brigade of Brigadier von Gall can insure that the captains do not come up short, it is to assign one captain from among the captains of the five regiments, to the picket daily, and 2 officers are to remain with the reserve picket. At the same time, the officers designated by this order, who remain on duty 24 hours, are to be assigned specifically. This arrangement is valid only as long as we are here in camp. All regiments can send their bakers, and wood, and flour to the fort, where the Dragoon baker, Hermann Jaeger, will assign the ovens to them.

Brigadier-of-the-day - General Hamilton, Major Kickman

Staff-officer - English - Lieutenant Colonel Lind
                German - Lieutenant Colonel Lentz

    For the picket moving out, the officers of the Prince Friedrich and Riedesel Regiments, the captain

Hesse-Hanau Order Book

from the Rhetz Regiment. For the reserve picket, the captain from the Riedesel Regiment, 2 officers from the Rhetz Regiment, and 1 from the Specht Regiment. The von Gall Brigade is to provide 21 men for the picket moving out, and the Prince Friedrich Regiment, 11 men, and Hesse-Hanau, 10 privates.

If it becomes necessary for the army to embark quickly, 2 cannon shots are to be fired, from the right wing, and repeated by the left wing. Upon this signal, the soldiers' tents are to be taken down, and taken to the bateaux, together with knapsacks, blankets, provisions, and ammunition. All other baggage is to be left behind. For this purpose, each English regiment is to use 11 bateaux, and each German regiment, 22 bateaux. The remaining bateaux are to be left behind for the officers' tents and baggage, when so ordered. From each English regiment, 1 officer and 20 men, and for each brigade, 1 captain is to be ordered to guard the equipment left behind. If it should be necessary for the army to be set in motion, without embarking, 4 cannon shots are to be fired from the right flank, answered by an equal number from the left. Upon this signal, the regiments are to form as quickly as possible, leaving the tents standing. This order is to be observed throughout the entire campaign. Those regiments which do not have enough powder, lead, and paper, should apply to the Artillery. If, however, the ammunition ship does not

Hesse-Hanau Order Book

arrive soon enough to provide those items, the regiments must make an equal distribution of the ammunition which they have on hand. The brigadier generals are responsible for this action. The cartridges must be well protected; those in the cartridge pouches, as well as those in the cases, and the balls must never be lost nor thrown away. Because it is so difficult to bring new ammunition across the lake, the company chiefs must give special care, although the regimental chiefs are responsible, that this order is carried out.

Commissary Clarke is to be given an orderly bateau with seven men. These are to be relieved alternately by the right and left wings, and are to serve for four days, beginning with the right wing. Tomorrow at daybreak, 1 officer, 2 non-commissioned officers, and 25 men are to be provided for work. An officer from the Engineer Corps is to supervise. They are to rest between eleven and three o'clock, and then continue working until evening. The troops can take their provisions and kettle along each time. The officer is to be from the Specht Brigade, and each brigade is to furnish 1 non-commissioned officer and 5 men. Although, according to the German regulations, when the picket has a redoubt before it, it is to enter therein with closed ranks when they give honors, this is not to occur here. Each time the picket, even if it has a redoubt before it, is to give honors behind the redoubt with open ranks. The outposts are

Hesse-Hanau Order Book

not to give such honors, however. It is noted that if a general posts the guard after tattoo, the picket is to give honors with closed ranks in the redoubt, with shouldered weapons. The same applies for the staff officer of the day, after tattoo.

In arrest, 1 regimental drummer, Klie.

- - - - - - -

Orders for 29 June, in the Camp at Crown Point
Passwords - St. Francis and Cork
Watch - Ensign Siebert; 3 non-commissioned officers, 1 drummer, and 39 privates
Picket - Lieutenant Count von Puckler; 2 non-commissioned officers, 1 drummer, and 30 privates
Brigadier-of-the-day - Brigadier Powell
Brigade Major - Maurice for the right wing
Staff Officer - Major Foster
Brigadier-of-the-day - Brigadier Specht
Brigade Major - Clerc for the left wing
Staff Officer - Major Hille

For the picket moving out - 1 captain from the Specht Regiment, 1 officer each from the Rhetz and Hesse-Hanau Regiments.

For the reserve picket - 1 captain from the Prince Friedrich Regiment, 1 officer each from the Hesse-Hanau and Specht Regiments. Prince Friedrich Regiment is to furnish the non-commissioned orderly for General Burgoyne.

For the picket moving out - 1 Lieutenant von

Hesse-Hanau Order Book

Eschwege,

For the reserve picket - 1 Lieutenant von Buttlar

As long as the two wings of the army are separated, the inspection is to be made by a brigadier from each wing, who is to serve for three days. The brigadier of the left wing is to submit his report to General von Riedesel daily. The reserve corps of the left wing to receive provisions this afternoon for the period through 8 July. The other regiments are to receive theirs for an equally long period. All the bateaux needing repairs are to be sent to Chimney Point, with sufficient troops to guard them. When it is necessary, these troops are to be put to work helping with the rigging. The reserve corps for the German troops is to form a guard consisting of 1 officer and 30 men for the depot at Chimney Point. Commissary General Clerke is to indicate to the officer where the sentries are to be posted. Also, the same corps is to provide a guard of 1 non-commissioned officer, and 12 men, in order to provide the working troops with wood. These are to receive their orders from the Engineer Twiss. Two bateaux with oars are to be sent by each regiment to Chimney Point to be delivered to Mr. Hourt. For this purpose, bateaux can be used which are in need of repair. The pickets are to move out one hour before sunset, in order to establish their posts during daylight. At the same time, all the regiments are to move out in order to practice

Hesse-Hanau Order Book

landings. Two hundred forty-six gallons of beer are to be received today on the right wing, near the German troops, and the regiments are to bring barrels, as the beer is to be accepted during the next few days. This afternoon, at five o'clock, each regiment is to send one private to the Specht Regiment to pick up ten axes. As Lieutenant Colonel Breymann's Corps is to march tomorrow morning, the detachment to be formed by today's orders, consisting of 1 officer, 2 non-commissioned officers, and 30 men, as well as the guard ordered at the same time, consisting of 1 non-commissioned officer and 12 men, which were provided by the mentioned corps, are to be relieved at daybreak tomorrow, by the five infantry regiments

Regimental drummer Klie is released from his arrest.

In arrest, Lieutenant [Michael] Bach, of the Artillery.

- - - - - - -

Hesse-Hanau Order Book

Orders in Camp at Crown Point, 30 June 1777
Passwords - David and Wallis
Picket - Captain von Schachten; Commander - Lieutenant von Trott
Watch - Lieutenant Count von Puckler; 3 non-commissioned officers, 1 drummer, and 30 privates
Work detail - Lieutenant Seiffert, Ensign von Weyhers
Staff officer of the day for the right wing - Lieutenant Colonel [Nicholaus] Southerland
For the left wing - Major Menge
For the picket moving out - 1 captain of Hesse-Hanau, Captain von Schachten, the officers from the Rhetz and Prince Friedrich Regiments
For the reserve picket - 1 captain from the Specht Regiment, the officers from the Rhetz, Prince Friedrich, and Riedesel Regiments
The non-commissioned orderly for General Burgoyne - from the Riedesel Regiment
For the general guard for General Riedesel - from the Specht Regiment, 1 officer from each regiment, 1 non-commissioned officer, and 18 privates

The regiments are to exercise for one-quarter to one-half hour during the evening, before retreat, in stockings and overalls, but at all times in uniform, and use this opportunity to practice charging and making a combined assault. On days when we are marching or entering camp, this is not necessary. If the regiments have empty barrels for provisions, or such, they are to be delivered to the spruce beer brewery. When spruce beer is to be delivered, and an order to march is received, the empty barrels into which the beer would have been received, are to be taken along by the wing which would have received the beer, and upon entering camp, once again delivered to the brewer.

When the corps enter camp, it is just not necessary that the picket be a designated number of paces ahead of the front, and the fire watch so far behind the front, not that they lie just ahead of the regimental center, but that at every opportunity, a height, ravine, or other defensive factor should be considered. The brigadiers should personally oversee how the pickets are placed. Tomorrow the army is to embark. We should fight our best for the royal and British throne, in order to uphold the law and assist the unfortunate. The royal and allied troops will battle with equal ardor for the cause, that is why you have taken up arms. The service, which is desired during this expedition, is very critical. As long as we move forward, we will find many situations in which neither difficulties, work, nor even life itself can be considered. This army must never retreat. Tomorrow morning at daybreak, instead of reveille, general march is to be beaten. The Dragoon Regiment is to form the advance guard, except for those men who are required for the guard for General Burgoyne. Then follows the line. Each wing is to form a line with bateaux as previously

Hesse-Hanau Order Book

ordered.

The left wing remains along the east shore, and the right wing along the west shore. As soon as the army enters camp, it is to form two lines. A detail consisting of 1 staff officer, 2 captains, 4 officers, and the appropriate number of non-commissioned officers, and 200 men is to remain at Chimney Point to guard the magazine. This detail is to be provided by the brigade on the right wing. The 2nd English Brigade is to provide 1 staff officer, who is Lieutenant Colonel [John] Anstruther of the 62nd Regiment, 1 captain, 2 officers, and 100 men; the German Brigade is to provide 1 captain from the Hesse-Hanau Regiment, Captain von Schoell, each regiment 1 officer, Ensign von Richterleben, 3 non-commissioned officers, and each regiment, 50 men. This detail is to be relieved at sunset this evening at Chimney Point. Tomorrow, as soon as the army moves to its new camp, each regiment of the right wing is to provide a fatigue detail consisting of 1 officer and 25 men. They are to assemble before their front, and are to be directed by an engineer of that wing to make defensive positions. The men ordered on that duty are not to row [the bateaux]. At the same time, the left wing is to clear its front for a distance of two rifle shots. A number of the bateaux, which were ordered yesterday, have arrived. Those regiments, which have not yet sent their bateaux, are to do so immediately. When orders are

Hesse-Hanau Order Book

issued, and no specific time is noted, they are to be executed as quickly as possible, and followed exactly. No officer is to go to the advance corps of the army without permission, nor, without special permission of the commander, go beyond that unit's outposts. The captain of the 31st Regiment is designated the general's aide for General Phillips during this campaign. At the same time, from the five regiments in camp here, a detail of 2 non-commissioned officers and 39 men is to be assigned to serve the cannons which belong to the brigade. They are to report to Captain [Georg] Pausch, who commands the Artillery with the left wing, and he is to give them instruction. For this detail, each regiment is to provide 6 men, and each brigade, 1 non-commissioned officer. As this detail is to be permanently assigned to the Artillery, they are to receive their provisions therefrom. Therefore, a competent non-commissioned officer must be designated, who can keep the necessary accounts. Each regiment is to provide the detail with a tent, and pots, and bottles, as this detail is to camp with the Artillery at all times.

    Lieutenant Bach, of the Artillery, is released from arrest.

- - - - - - -

Hesse-Hanau Order Book

Orders in Camp near Carillon, 1 July 1777
Passwords - St. Peter and Westminster
Watch - Lieutenant von Eschwege; 2 non-commissioned officers, 1 drummer, and 39 privates
Picket - Lieutenants von Geyling and von Trott
Staff officer for the right wing - Forster
Staff officer for the left wing - Ehrenkrook
For the picket moving out - a captain from the Specht Brigade, the officers from the Riedesel and Hanau Regiments
For the reserve picket - a captain from the Specht Regiment, the officers from the Hanau and Rhetz Regiments
The non-commissioned orderly for General Burgoyne - from the Hanau Regiment

A communication is to be established between the first and second lines, and from the first line, communication is to be established with Crown Point. Should it be necessary for the advance corps of the army to halt, the 1st Brigade is then to march by land, and the 2nd Brigade by water, and the terrain through which the 1st Brigade passes, is to be thoroughly reconnoitered. The regimental chiefs and brigadiers are to be familiar with the terrain to their front at all times. No trees are to be set on fire at their base, and those left standing, are not to have the bark stripped off, as the communications routes are to be indicated by notching [trees]. Tomorrow morning the regiments

Hesse-Hanau Order Book

of the right flank are to provide a work detail consisting of 1 officer and 25 men. The detail is to receive its orders from the commanding engineer.

- - - - - - - -

Orders in Camp near Carillon, 2 July 1777
Passwords - Theodore and Closter
Watch - Lieutenant von Geyling; 3 non-commissioned officers, 1 drummer, and 39 privates
Picket - Captain von Schachten and Ensign Siebert; 2 non-commissioned officers, 1 drummer, and 30 privates
Brigadier of the right wing - Hamilton
Brigadier of the left wing - von Gall
Staff officer of the right wing - Major Erwin
Staff officer of the left wing - Major von Lucke

As it has been ordered that a post is to be established at Point au Fer, Lieutenant Eikts of the Engineer Corps, and Lieutenant Bechtold of the 24th Regiment are to be sent there to establish the post. At the same time, a detail is to be sent there to cover the workers and to defend the post. However, a problem arose as to whether the officer commanding the detail was to be under the orders of the engineer, if the officer had an earlier date of rank. In order to prevent any doubt in the future, it was announced to the army that the senior officer, according to his date of rank, was to command. Therefore, all engineers and assistant engineers, who are sent to this post by the

Hesse-Hanau Order Book

chief of the army, are also to assume command when they have seniority, according to the commanding engineer. The performance of those officers sent to Point au Fer is very praiseworthy, as they have not allowed themselves to be involved in any situation harmful to the performance of duty. For the reserve picket, the Prince Friedrich Regiment, Hanau, and the Hereditary Prince Regiments are to provide officers. The non-commissioned orderly for General Burgoyne is to be from the Specht Regiment.

Orders of 3 July [1777] in Camp near Carillon
Passwords - St. Honora and Dover
Watch - Lieutenant von Lindau; 3 non-commissioned officers, 1 drummer, and 39 privates
Picket - 2 non-commissioned officers and 30 privates
Staff officer of the right wing - Lieutenant Colonel Hill
Staff officer of the left wing - Major von Passern

As it appears, in spite of being frequently ordered, that cognac is being sold to the Indians, that this nevertheless still happens, therefore, the regimental chiefs are to assemble the sutlers and the women and inform them, that anyone who violates this order in the future, will not only be chased out of the army, but also be subject to running the gauntlet. The officers are to make this order known to their servants at once, and no officer is to protect anyone who violates this

Hesse-Hanau Order Book

order, but is to report them at once. In order to further stress this order, Adjutant General Major Kingston is to pay the individual reporting such violation, ten piasters. A pathway is to be made at once from the camp of the left wing to Lieutenant Colonel Breymann's Corps. The von Gall Brigade is to occupy the camp at Three Mile Point, where General Fraser previously camped. The Quartermaster sergeants and their guards are to cross over at once, and take directions from Captain Valentine. The baggage is to be taken to the Bateaux, but the regiments are not to cross until after dark. They are to bivouac tonight, and be prepared to set up their tents tomorrow morning. The 1st Brigade is to march at once and set up its camp on the left wing of Fraser's Brigade, extending to the ravine. As soon as the 1st Brigade enters camp, the 2nd Brigade is to move back to its camp and be prepared to move forward tomorrow morning. From now on, until ordered otherwise, the regiments are to have two days' cooked provisions on hand. It is well known that there are many people in the rebel army who are loyal to the King, and to the English government. Some of them have been forced into service, others have taken service only in order to surrender to the royal army at the first opportunity. Therefore, it is forbidden for the Indians to shoot at individuals in small detachments, which might be seeking to desert. Such individuals must not be

Hesse-Hanau Order Book

considered as ordinary deserters by the army, but must be treated in the best possible way and manner. Should it unfortunately happen that a soldier of our army falls into enemy hands, it will be his responsibility to make this order known in their army. The hospital is to remain at Three Mile Point pending further orders. A non-commissioned officer and 12 men are to be furnished by each wing as a hospital guard. This detachment is to take all its provisions with it. The hospital is to receive provisions from the commissary general. The commissary general is ordered to provide fresh provisions to the sick as often as possible. As soon as the doctors find it necessary to move sick individuals, they are to report to the adjutant general.

The von Gall Brigade is to provide 5 men for the hospital.

- - - - - - -

Orders in Camp near Carillon, 4 July 1777
Passwords - St. Hillary and Dartmouth
Watch - Ensign von Weyhers; 3 non-commissioned officers, 1 drummer, and 39 privates
Picket - Captain von Schachten and Lieutenant von Bischhausen, 2 non-commissioned officers, 1 drummer, and 30 privates
English staff officer - Major Lucke
[German staff officer] of the day - Lieutenant Colonel Lentz

Hesse-Hanau Order Book

The von Gall Brigade is to provide a work detail on the west side of the lake. An English non-commissioned officer is to remain at the house at Three Mile Point, day and night, pending further orders.

The Dragoons are to occupy the terrain on the height behind Fraser's Brigade, where the headquarters is located. The communications route for the Artillery is to be completed as quickly as possible. No one is to buy horses from the Indians, as they are meant for the King's service.

Orders of Major General von Riedesel

When the adjutant or other officer is sent out to reconnoiter, and has been ordered to take the first guard with him, it is, if time allows, always his responsibility, to report to the officer commanding the corps. If however, the commanding officer is too great a distance, and the time for reconnoitering would be lost, the officer is still authorized to take the first guard along. However, the officer must report to the corps commander through a non-commissioned officer, or lance corporal, at once, so that not only is the officer well-informed, but so that the guard post can be reestablished, also.

- - - - - - -

Orders in Camp near Carillon, 5 July 1777
Passwords - St. Agatha and Dorchester
Watch - Lieutenant Bischhausen; 3 non-commissioned

Hesse-Hanau Order Book

officers, 1 drummer, and 39 privates
Work detail - Lieutenant Count von Puckler; 2 non-commissioned officers, 1 drummer, and 33 privates
Brigadier of the right wing - Powell
Brigadier of the left wing - Muire
Sstaff officer - Major Carl Friedrich Ehrenkrook
Inspection - a captain from the Prince Friedrich Regiment

As the heat is so great, and the men must work so hard, rum is to be issued to the entire army this afternoon. The regimental quartermasters are to go to Three Mile Point this afternoon, where they are to receive the appropriate amount of rum from Commissary Lequinese, a half pint per man. The brigadiers are responsible for having a quantity of water available, and are to announce the time when the rum is to be issued. In addition to the work detail, which is to work on the main route, 400 men are to be provided by the right wing tomorrow evening at sunset to work, and these men are not to be assigned to other details, so as not to be fatigued. They will receive their orders from the engineer general.

-- -- -- -- -- -- --

Orders in Camp at Carillon, 6 July 1777
Watch - Lieutenant Seiffert; 2 non-commissioned officers, 1 drummer, and 39 privates

The brigades are to assemble at once, and sail to Fort Independence. Tents and equipment are to

Hesse-Hanau Order Book

remain in place, and, as previously ordered, the appropriate guard is to remain with them. -- Burgoyne

- - - - - - -

Orders at Fort Carillon, 6 July 1777
Passwords - St. Stephen and Cambridge

The 62nd Regiment is to take a position at Fort Independence at once, and the Prince Friedrich Regiment is to enter Ticonderoga. Brigadier Hamilton is to command both forts. The rest of the army is to commence the march to South Bay at once, in bateaux, and the guard left behind, and the tents are to follow the army as quickly as possible. General Hamilton is responsible that a guard and guard posts are placed on the baggage, and other items left in the fort are to be collected and securely maintained.

- - - - - - -

Orders in Camp at Skenesborough, 7 July 1777
Passwords - St. Martha and Berkshire
Watch -

The regimental quartermasters are to report aboard the frigate *Royal George* at five o'clock this afternoon to receive eight days' provisions. The remaining provisions are to be brought on land tomorrow morning by the 2nd Brigade, under the direction of the civil commissaries. All papers which are found containing intelligence about the rebels, or any reports about them, are to be brought to the adjutant general at once. This order is to be observed at all times in the

Hesse-Hanau Order Book

future. It is very disadvantageous to the King's service to mistreat individuals who are taken captive. Therefore, it is strictly forbidden to rob those persons of the smallest items, and even more so to mistreat them. Therefore, all plundering is to be severely punished. The orders, which were issued some time ago, that all deserters, coming in, are not to be questioned extensively, are not being obeyed in all cases, and therefore are to be stressed again.

Orders in Camp at Skenesborough, 8 July 1777
Passwords - St. Simeon and Exeter
Watch - Lieutenant von Buttlar; 2 non-commissioned officers, 1 drummer, and 29 privates
Picket - Lieutenant Count von Puckler; 2 non-commissioned officers, 1 drummer, and 30 privates

General Burgoyne has established the headquarters on Colonel Skene's property. The brigades are to debark at once and the army is being aligned in the following order of battle: The 1st English Brigade is to place its right wing against the cliffs near the woods so that its left wing meets the burnt out defenses. The Dragoon Regiment is to cover the woods on the height with the right flank. The 2nd British Brigade is to occupy the defenses. The five companies of the 24th Regiment are to form the reserve corps behind the defenses. The von Specht Brigade is to form the field of battle where it stood

Hesse-Hanau Order Book

this morning, keeping the fortified barn before its center. The Hesse-Hanau Regiment is to place its right wing against the von Specht Brigade. The von Specht Brigade and the Hanau Regiment are to provide a picket at the barn. They are to leave a fortified post, containing up to 100 men, on the mountain peak behind the left wing. The terrain leaves no other choice, but that the army camp ahead of the order of battle line. If it must move out, the tents are to be struck and left lying on the ground. It is to be noted that the line is to remain behind the army at all times.

- - - - - - - -

Orders in Camp at Skenesborough, 9 July 1777
Passwords - St. Agnes and Stanford
Watch - Ensign Siebert; 3 non-commissioned officers, 1 drummer, and 29 privates
Work detail - Lieutenant Bischhausen; 2 non-commissioned officers, 1 drummer, and 55 privates
Picket - Lieutenant Seiffert; 1 non-commissioned officers, and 25 privates
Detail on the mountain - Lieutenant von Trott; 2 non-commissioned officers, and 25 privates

All prisoners are to be taken on board the *Royal George* immediately, except those who are wounded.

Hesse-Hanau Order Book

The guard who accompanies them is to return [to his unit] at once. Two hundred men, and officers in proportion, are to be ready to go to work at once, and are to receive their orders from the engineer general. One officer and 20 men from the right wing are to provide a guard at the fort, and are to receive all prisoners sent in. The left wing is to provide 1 officer and 20 men for the same purpose at the barn, in order to guard the prisoners. The work detail of 200 men which was provided today, is to be relieved tomorrow morning by an equal number of men.

- - - - - - -

Orders in Camp at Skenesborough, 10 July 1777
Passwords - St. Eustis and Falmouth
Watch - Lieutenant von Trott; 3 non-commissioned officers, 1 drummer, and 39 privates

6 July - The enemy abandoned Fort Ticonderoga. They were driven out merely by the presence of the army. On one side, they ran beyond Skenesborough, and on the other side, to Hubbardton. They abandoned all their ships, a great amount of ammunition, provisions, and all sorts of baggage.

7 July - Brigadier Fraser, with half of his brigade, but without artillery, encountered 2,000 fortified rebels. He attacked, and chased them away. The rebels lost many officers, 200 dead, even more wounded, and taken captive. Major General von Riedesel, with the advance guard, consisting of the

Hesse-Hanau Order Book

Jaeger Company and Light Infantry, arrived in time to support Brigadier Fraser, and with well-directed orders and the brave conduct with which they were carried out, gained a large share of the honor for the victory for his troops

8 July - Lieutenant Colonel Hill, at the head of the 9th Regiment, was attacked near Fort Anne by the rebels, who were six times stronger, and after withstanding three hours of continuous fire, he drove them out with heavy losses. After this incident, the rebels abandoned Fort Anne, after setting it on fire. A detachment of our army now occupies the area beyond Fort Anne.

This rapid progress, for which Good can not adequately be thanked, gave our troops much honor, the greatest praise is due the Riedesal and Fraser forces, which by their bravery, demonstrated by both officers and men, have done the greatest service to the King, as they have withstood much fatigue and bad weather, and although they have been without bread, they have not shown the least unwillingness to perform their duty.

On the coming Sunday, religious services are to be held ahead of the line, and the advance corps, and at sunset on that day, a *feu de joie* is to be fired with cannons and small arms at Ticonderoga, Crown Point, and in the camp at Skenesborough, and at the camp at Carillon by Lieutenant Breymann's Corps.

Hesse-Hanau Order Book

Each regimental chief is personally to read this order before the front of the regiment. Major General von Riedesel is responsible for sending this order to the detached corps on the left wing, and Brigadier Hamilton is to send it to Crown Point. A list is to be sent to headquarters this afternoon as to the number of wounded officers and men who are in condition to be sent to Ticonderoga.

All the generals are to send a list to Commissary Rousswau as to the number of rations they need for their personnel. A list is to be submitted this afternoon as to how many volunteers they have with their regiment, to include their names, the length of their service, and by whom they are commanded. The German and English brigades of the advance corps, and of the Dragoons, are to complete their 100 cartridges per man, again. Tomorrow morning a list is to be sent to Major General Phillips as to how much balls, powder, and paper each regiment needs to complete the required number of cartridges. As it is difficult to have the ammunition keep up with the army during its rapid march, each regiment must do its best to conserve ammunition.

Orders in Camp at Castleton, 11 July 1777
Passwords - St. Heloise and Italy
Watch - As yesterday

Hesse-Hanau Order Book

Orders in Camp at Castleton, 12 July 1777
Watch - Lieutenant Echwege; 3 non-commissioned officers, 1 drummer, and 39 privates

- - - - - - - -

Orders in Camp at Castleton, 13 July 1777
Passwords - St. Dorothy and Winchester
Staff officer of the day - Major von Ehrenkrook
Watch - Lieutenant von Geyling; 3 non-commissioned officers, 1 drummer, and 39 privates

Each regiment is to try its best to obtain a cart and team of oxen, which each regiment must closely guard behind its front, first as a means of transporting the musketeers' tents, and their officers' most necessary baggage, which however, must be reduced as much as possible, and then for the constant picking up of rations, which still lie in the bateaux. If possible, each regiment is to obtain a wagon, so that during the march, when baggage must be taken to the bateaux, that can be done. So that the oxen can never get away from the cart, a guard must be provided to be alert at the pasture, as well as on the march, and also watch the farmers so that they do not desert. In addition to the wagons, which are to be delivered to the regiments in equal numbers, no vehicle is to be seized, and no regiment is to allow that such be taken from the English, or anyone else, and in case that should happen, it is to be reported to Major General von Riedesel at once. As soon as each regiment has eight or ten tents, it is to set up a proper camp, and the regiments are to try to protect their weapons from the dampness. In case that the corps standing here is attacked, Lieutenant Colonel Breymann is to come for support with the Grenadier Battalion, half of the Jaeger Company, and two companies of Barner's Battalion. The other companies and the half Jaeger Company are to take the most favorable position at their place, so as to defend their position. In the meantime, and if Lieutenant Colonel Breymann is attacked, Brigadier Specht is to go to the support of Breymann's Corps with the two regiments from the left wing. In that case, the camps are to be left standing. As General Burgoyne has issued a proclamation to the population, that they should declare their obedience to the King, the regiments must maintain their best discipline in order to show the best conduct toward those inhabitants in their homes, so that the most distant subjects might be influenced to declare for the King, and bring provisions to the camp. Major General von Riedesel is to issue an order to the inhabitants that each one who has more than one cow, is to deliver them here, so that in so far as possible, the regiments have fresh meat delivered instead of the salted meat. It is to be announced by the commissary, also, that when oxen or cows are available, they are to be collected. Whenever the regiments find ovens, they may be used to bake bread, so that there will be no

Hesse-Hanau Order Book

shortages. An hour before tattoo, a *feu de joie* is to be fired, with three running firings, and after the last running fire, hurrah is to be shouted three times. The Hesse-Hanau Regiment is to provide 1 non-commissioned officer and 40 men for a work detail tomorrow morning at daybreak, in order to repair the bridges which are two miles ahead of the front of the camp, toward the Specht camp. Captain Pausch is to send 1 non-commissioned officer, who will show them what needs to be repaired, so that the troops' equipment can cross over, and if this work can not be completed tomorrow, a similar detail is to be provided the next day.

Orders in Camp near Castleton, 14 July 1777
Passwords - St. Joseph and Durham
Staff officer of the day - Lieutenant Colonel von Speth
Watch - Lieutenant von Lindau; 3 non-commissioned officers, 1 drummer, and 39 privates

As it has been noted, that the orders given to the army concerning officers' baggage has not been obeyed, and that the army has much useless baggage, which it is impossible to transport once the bateaux are left behind, it is once again ordered, that the officers are to take only the most necessary baggage with them, as the bateaux are to be sent back to Ticonderoga. Otherwise, the officers risk leaving the baggage behind upon the army's first movement, as those officers who served in the previous war in America, will have learned that they must accept living in soldiers' tents, and that all their baggage consisted of a knapsack. As soon as there is an opportunity to allow the baggage which was left at Ticonderoga, to be brought here without hindering the transport for the magazines, General Burgoyne will grant that pleasure for all the officers so they may obtain all possible commodities. Lord Pidderson is named aide-de-camp for General Burgoyne. Governor Skene is designated as commissary to administer the oath of loyalty to those inhabitants seeking protection, and to administer all other tasks requiring his services as ordered, in the countryside.

Mr. Ochsley is designated as wagon master for the army. Captain Garther is to return to England. Anyone wishing to send letters must submit them by eleven o'clock noon, on the fourteenth.

One officer, and 20 men are to be sent to the camp of Major General von Riedesel in order to accept the horses meant for the use of the army. NB - The English are to provide this detachment. If there are sick individuals in the regiment, who can be returned to health in the hospital at Ticonderoga sooner than in the camp, then each brigade is to submit a list at once.

- - - - - - -

Hesse-Hanau Order Book

Orders from Major General von Riedesel
Although there is hope that fresh meat can be delivered to the regiments in a few days, each regiment is to draw eight days' salted-meat for the present, so that there will never be a shortage of provisions, in case the fresh meat should ever be missing.

- - - - - - -

Orders in Camp at Castleton, 15 July 1777
Passwords - St. Alexander and Weymouth
Watch - Lieutenant von Bischhausen; 3 non-commissioned officers, 1 drummer, and 39 privates

- - - - - - -

Orders in Camp at Castleton, 16 July 1777
Passwords - Wilhelm and Castle
Watch - Ensign von Weyhers; 3 non-commissioned officers, 1 drummer, and 39 privates
The officers may attempt to obtain horses, for which purpose each regimental chief is to be allowed to send 1 officer and a small detail out into the local region to buy horses for cash, but this must be done with great care.

- - - - - - -

Orders in Camp at Castleton, 17 July 1777
Passwords - St. Louisa and Lincoln
Watch - Lieutenant Seiffert; [3 non-commissioned officers], 1 drummer, and 30 privates
Work detail - Lieutenant Siebert; 1 non-commissioned

Hesse-Hanau Order Book

officer, and 12 privates

Orders in Camp at Castleton, 18 July 1777
Passwords - St. George and Dorset
Watch - Lieutenant von Geyling; 3 non-commissioned officers, 1 drummer, and 39 privates

Each regiment is to submit the names of its sutlers and others who are attached to the regiment to Adjutant General Kingston. All individuals who wish to sell items for the use of the army are to report to the adjutant general, also, so that their character can be checked, and those who are trading with the soldiers without permission, or who sell cognac to the Indians can be most severely punished. The disturbance between the German and the English troops on the 16th was caused by the sale of cognac, and some English soldiers forgot themselves to the extent that they violated one of the strictest articles concerning conduct, and attacked the guard. When, in the future, either an English or a German soldier conducts himself so that the good relations between the two nations, which until now have been so praiseworthy, and which between good troops must always be maintained, should be damaged, those individuals causing such to happen, are to be severely punished. As the inspector for the hospital finds it necessary that two wives, from each regiment of the army, must be provided to care for the sick and wounded, the

Hesse-Hanau Order Book

regimental chiefs are to give the necessary orders.

- - - - - - -

Orders in the Camp at Castleton, 19 July 1777
From Major General von Riedesel

Passwords - St. Barbara and Blandford
Staff officers of the day - Major von Menge
Watch - Lieutenant von Buttlar; 3 non-commissioned officers, 1 drummer, and 39 privates
Picket - Lieutenant Bischhausen; 2 non-commissioned officers, 1 drummer, and 30 privates

Dr. Nox, presently assigned to the hospital, claims that sick and wounded have arrived at the hospital without having proper uniform items, etc. Therefore, it is recommended to the regiments that those men, who have something missing, should have those items sent to the hospital at Carillon, and a list of those items accompany them in the future, according to the orders of last year. At the same time, the hospital requests that two women per regiment be ordered to tend the sick according to the general order of 18 February. The regiments are not to raise any difficulties in complying therewith, as they are to be well paid. When the regiments receive oxen or cows, the weight is to be reported at once by the regimental quartermaster to the respective commissaries, so that it can be known, first, if, and for how long, the regiment is supplied with meat, and so that accounts can be properly maintained with the English commissariat.

Hesse-Hanau Order Book

A general rule is that every detachment, before it is relieved, is to send a lance corporal each time to the brigade from which the new detachment is to come, to show the new detachment the place where it is to go.

Orders in Camp at Castleton, 20 July 1777
Passwords - St. Timothy and Marlborough
Watch - Lieutenant von Lindau; 3 non-commissioned officers, 1 drummer, and 39 privates

----

Orders in Camp at Castleton, 21 July 1777
Passwords - St. Cecelia and Sarum
Watch - Lieutenant Count von Puckler; 3 non-commissioned officers, 1 drummer, and 39 privates
Picket - Lieutenant von Buttlar; 2 non-commissioned officers, 1 drummer, and 30 privates

It has become a practice that individual non-commissioned officers, and even privates, leave the regiments and pass the outposts, on the pretext of buying horses for the officers. This is completely contrary to the intent of the recently issued order, and although the general wishes, with the greatest pleasure that the officers might obtain horses, it is not possible that individuals, or small groups, be allowed to move away from the regiment. If the providers want to send for horses, they are to apply to the regimental chiefs, and one or two officers can undertake the business, which must be conducted by turns, of buying horses.

Hesse-Hanau Order Book

This must then be reported by the commanders of regiments, which are camped here, to Brigadier Specht, and from Lieutenant Colonel Breymann's Corps, to Lieutenant Colonel Breymann, and four to six men must be assigned for their security. The reporting must be done so that it is known what details have left the camp. Lieutenant Colonel Breymann has also received the order not to allow anyone, not accompanied by an officer, to pass the outpost.

Letters for the Hesse-Hanau Regiment can be picked up at Skenesborough by a non-commissioned officer with a bateau. As it is possible in a few days, that many crossings will be made on the bridge leading to the Hesse-Hanau Regiment, the general highly recommends that it be put in the best condition, and relies upon Captain Pausch to fix it so that the battalion can march across without any difficulties.

- - - - - - -

Orders for the Commanders who must then Notify their Officers

According to the report which Major General von Riedesel has received concerning the extent which the English regiments have reduced their officers' baggage, it has been determined that all the officers sleep in non-commissioned officer or musketeer tents, and take nothing with them but their bedding and a pair of canteens, and have sent all other officer and company equipment back to Ticonderoga. As soon as

Hesse-Hanau Order Book

the regiments have entered camp at Skenesborough, ready to march to Fort Anne, no more bateaux will be brought passed the rapids than are necessary to transport the tents, ammunition, and the reduced baggage and provisions, which at the most is to be only two bateaux per company. The bateaux are to bring the allowed items to Fort Anne, where all the items are to be unloaded again, and from there all the cargo is apparently to be carried on land. The bateaux, going as far as Fort Anne, are then to be sent back to Skenesborough, where all the other bateaux are to wait for their return, and then all go back to Ticonderoga. All those bateaux, with as few boatmen as possible, are to be tied one behind the other, so that the front ones can pull the others.

There is reason to hope that General Burgoyne will be able to deliver two wagons with Canadian horses to each company for carrying ammunition, soldiers' tents, and as much officer baggage as possible, on land. If the officers use their own pack horses, and if the three wagons per regiment with oxen, which were delivered from here, are retained, and together with what they can load on the Canadian wagons, without overloading them, they should be able to determine those items which they can take for their own use, or what must be left behind, without making it necessary for Major General von Riedesel to hear further complaints and remonstrations. When the order to march is given, if Major von Riedesel learns the time before hand, then the tents are to be struck the day before, and loaded on the battalion's three wagons, and the officers' baggage taken to the bateaux on travois so as to be loaded therein, so that on the following day the regiment will have nothing to do but enter the bateaux, and continue their march to Skenesborough. The regimental quartermasters, quartermaster sergeants, and their guards are to move ahead with the tents so as to arrive at the new camp sites early enough to be able to lay them out. The empty wagons with the oxen, the surplus cattle, and the unencumbered officers' pack horses are to go early enough the next day to reach Skenesborough, but must not allow themselves to be seen by the English camp, but rather remain in the area where the Breymann Corps had last camped. After the regiments have entered camp, they can allow the mentioned wagons and pack horses to follow after dark. As a precaution, the companies must not forget to take their two pack saddles with them, so that if something on the Canadians' wagons breaks, the load can be put on the horses and carried in that manner. Above all, it is necessary that every regiment do everything possible in every situation, because accidents do happen which no general in the world can correct or give assistance. In order to lighten the baggage more, the large blankets should not be taken along, but sent to

Hesse-Hanau Order Book

Ticonderoga.

Orders in Camp at Castleton, 23 July 1777
Passwords - St. Priquet and Shipenham
Watch - Lieutenant Siebert; 3 non-commissioned officers, 1 drummer, and 39 privates

----

Orders in Camp at Castleton, 24 July 1777
Passwords - St. Justin and Troma
Watch - Lieutenant von Trott; 3 non-commissioned officers, 1 drummer, and 39 privates
Picket - Lieutenant von Lindau; 2 non-commissioned officers, 1 drummer, and 24 privates

Hesse-Hanau Order Book

The Hesse-Hanau Regiment, as soon as it has finished cooking this afternoon, is to embark in its bateaux, with the Artillery, which has camped with it, and move to Skenesborough However, as it is too far to enable the regiment to enter camp this evening, it is to land in the area where the German bateaux have recently stood, and remain bivouacked at that place overnight. The regiment must not approach too near the bridge with the bateaux, so that the bateaux for the entire left wing can remain in order of battle. The regiment is to enquire immediately upon its arrival as to who has the responsibility of taking the bateaux past the rapids, which are necessary to take the musketeers' tents, provisions, and ammunition from Skenesborough to Fort Anne, and will ensure that the bateaux are past the rapids before the other regiments arrive. Captain Gerlach, who has gone to Skenesborough today, is to do everything to provide the regiment with intelligence in this situation, and direct the regiments as to their camps tomorrow morning.

The captured rebels are to be taken to Ticonderoga tomorrow morning, by an escort of 1 officer and 20 men. As soon as the army marches, a detachment of 50 English, 50 Germans, and 50 Provincials is to be left at Skenesborough for a few days, and so as to weaken the battalions as little as possible, this detachment is to consist of convalescents. This

Hesse-Hanau Order Book

information is provided, because it is assumed that some of the sick who are in the hospital and unable to march with the army, may be so far recovered as to be able to perform this duty. The brigadiers are to inform the quartermaster general how many bateaux are needed to deliver the men to the hospital, and Major General von Riedesel is to determine the appropriate number for the sick from the left wing, and send them to East Creek.

Tomorrow morning as many wagons as can be made ready are to be prepared to go with the army, with two horses each, and the necessary drivers. Brigadier Powell is to assign the necessary escort. This escort, as soon as the horses and wagons have reached the neighborhood, near Fort Anne, are to serve there as a guard force until the army arrives, and are to take their knapsacks, blankets, and three days' provisions with them. The drivers are to take grass and a ration of oats for one day with them. The oats must be withheld however, until the horses have had to work hard. Lieutenant Etherington is designated provost for the army, and is to keep a guard force of 1 non-commissioned officer and 10 English soldiers, and an equal number of Germans with him at all times. This guard is to be relieved every fourteen days. As soon as the army enters a new camp, an appropriate house is to be sought out for the provost, behind the army. Except for the patrol that the troops make daily,

Hesse-Hanau Order Book

and occasionally at night, in order to maintain discipline in camp, the provost is responsible for strictly enforcing the orders of the eighteenth of this month. He is also to inspect the huts and tents behind the camp, and as soon as he encounters anyone selling cognac to the soldiers, women, Indians, or officers' servants, without permission of the adjutant general, and without a certificate signed by their officer, they are to be arrested immediately, their possessions taken from them, and their residence set on fire.

This order is to be made known to all the individuals who accompany the army and camp outside the line. As soon as the provost guard is established, all captives are to be delivered to them, and turned over to the watch designated for that task. The German Dragoons are to provide 1 non-commissioned officer and 10 men for the provost guard, until the arrival of the left wing. One subaltern and 25 men of the picket are to be posted by the staff officer of the day, where the picket of the Fraser Brigade had previously been posted. Each regiment is to furnish a bateau to Quartermaster General Valentine.

- - - - - - -

Orders in Camp at Skenesborough, 25 July 1777
Passwords - St. Rosalie and Conterbourg
Staff officer of the day - Major von Passern
Watch -

Hesse-Hanau Order Book

Tomorrow the regiments have a day of rest and are to receive further orders concerning the march on the day after tomorrow. All the bateaux with the rest of the officers' baggage, company items, and similar things are to be sent back to Carillon from here, day after tomorrow. Only as many men are to be provided by each company, under the command of an officer, as are absolutely necessary to take them away, and the bateaux can be tied one behind the other, so that it will only be necessary to have oarsmen in the leading bateaux, and the others can follow without men. This will spare many crews. It is the responsibility of the battalion commanders to use their best judgment in assigning men. As these bateaux are to be delivered through Lake George, and designated men are to be used for that, except for the crews that take the bateaux to Carillon, one, two, or three bateaux, according to how many are truly needed, are to bring them back, and for the guarding of the equipment of the brigade, 1 officer from the Specht Regiment, 1 officer from Lieutenant Colonel Breymann's Corps, and 10 men per regiment, who can be men who are exhausted, are to remain there. The crews who return in the bateaux are to turn them in to local commander, Major Erwin, and then follow the army from here to Fort Anne. With these departing bateaux, all the sick are to be sent, also. The regiments are not to retain anything except the small, and in the recent orders

Hesse-Hanau Order Book

specified baggage, plus the musketeers' tents, ammunition, and two pack saddles per company, The regiments will be in the best position after today to know what they can carry with them on land. All those items are to be placed in the newly acquired bateaux on the other side of the rapids, and the battalions are then to march on land, and the baggage on the water, in two sections. Each bateau is to be occupied by 5 men, and each battalion is to provide 1 officer to accompany them. Of the four regiments that are in the line here, 2 officers and 50 men are to be furnished the evening before our departure, who are to remain here under the command of Major Erwin at Skenesborough. This detachment may include those who are exhausted, and men suffering from diarrhea. With the bateaux returning to Carillon, the regiments are to send those officers going to Canada to pick up recruits, and they are to bring back all the otherwise necessary items, and all the equipment belonging to them, also the watch coats, delivered pack saddles, scythes, medicine chests, etc., which the regiments, except the detachment under Lieutenant Colonel Ehrenkrook, left behind. When the officers arrive at Carillon, they are to report to Commander Ludewig, who has promised to take them across to St. John. Therefore, the Grenadier Battalion is to send 1 officer so as to better supervise the transportation of equipment. If the regiments have so nearly finished using their bateaux, that they can be sent away tomorrow, that is all the better, and the regiments do not need to wait for one another. As the Hesse-Hanau Regiment has no individuals bringing their equipment from Canada, it will be best to talk to Lieutenant Colonel Ehrenkrook, so that he sends a detachment of his Hessian command to escort the baggage to St. John, from which place the equipment can be brought in the large ship and needs no further escort.

For the picket, 2 officers from the Specht Regiment and 1 non-commissioned officer and 10 men from each regiment.

The regiments which have obtained entrenching tools from the Hesse-Hanau Artillery, are to return them to Captain Pausch and get their receipts back. Captain Pausch received the order to transport the tools, and if the regiments find it necessary later, they can obtain the tools again with a receipt.

Orders in Camp at Skenesborough, 26 July 1777
Passwords - St. Mathew and Winbourne
Watch - Ensign von Weyhers; 3 non-commissioned officers, 1 drummer, and 39 privates
Work detail - Lieutenant von Geyling; 1 non-commissioned officer, 1 drummer, and 6 privates

The bateaux being sent from here to Carillon may depart as soon as they wish without waiting for one another, and the officers going to Three Rivers may

Hesse-Hanau Order Book

also depart with this opportunity.

- - - - - - -

Orders in Camp at Skenesborough, 27 July 1777
Passwords - St. Geoffrey and Shelborne
Staff officer of the day - Lieutenant Colonel Lentz
Watch - Lieutenant von Geyling; 3 non-commissioned officers, 1 drummer, and 39 privates
Reserve picket - Ensign von Geyling; 1 non-commissioned officer, 1 drummer, and 12 privates
Detail to Carillon - Lieutenant Seiffert; 1 non-commissioned officer, and 12 privates

When the bateaux arrive, they will be delivered to the regiments by Captain Gerlach, from the left wing to the right, beginning with the corps of Lieutenant Colonel Breymann receiving the same. The Hesse-Hanau Artillery follows this corps, and the Hesse-Hanau Regiment follows last. The Breymann Corps is to pack everything in the bateaux this evening, except tents, and the tents are to be struck tomorrow morning at exactly three o'clock. As soon as the tents have been loaded into the bateaux each is to depart for Fort St. Anne with 5 men. One captain from the corps is ordered on this detail, 1 officer regiment [This seems to indicate an omission in the copy of the German text.] These bateaux will not return to the corps, until at Fort St. Anne. Therefore, the battalions are to take two days' cooked meat with them. Lieutenant Colonel Breymann remains with tomorrow's guard on the same

Hesse-Hanau Order Book

road between here and Fort St. Anne, where Caprain Gerlach is to be, so as to indicate the location of the camp.

The Hessian Artillery follows the corps of Lieutenant Colonel Breymann tomorrow. All pack horses and wagons follow this road to Fort St. Anne, empty. If bateaux still arrive early enough tomorrow, the Rhetz and Speth Regiments are to continue their march in the same manner, followed by the Riedesel and Hesse-Hanau Regiments. They may march by regiments as far as Fort St. Anne, without having to be together in brigade formation, and each regiment is to bivouac near Conten's House, so as to reach Fort St. Anne in two days. At the same time, they are to note orders concerning the Breymann Corps, and the regiments, which have not received their bateaux tomorrow, are to remain standing until the day after tomorrow. Brigadier Specht is to move out with the first regiment, and Brigadier von Gall is to remain here until the last troops have marched. Tomorrow morning the detail of 50 men remaining here is to be sent to Major Erwin. For information, General von Riedesel departs day after tomorrow, and will make the trip to St. Anne in one day.

- - - - - - -

Hesse-Hanau Order Book

Orders in Camp at Skenesborough, 28 July 1777
Passwords - St. Bernard and Biddeford
Watch - Ensign von Geyling; 3 non-commissioned officers, 1 drummer, and 39 privates
Work detail, to remain behind - Lieutenant von Trott; 1 non-commissioned officer and 12 privates

- - - - - - - -

Orders in Camp at Fort St. Anne, 29 July 1777
Passwords - St. Edward and Exmouth
Staff officer of the day - Major von Menge
Orders concerning the Pickets to follow
Watch - Lieutenant von Buttlar; 3 non-commissioned officers, 1 drummer, and 39 privates

As soon as the wagons arrive, four wagons are to be turned in by the corps of Lieutenant Colonel Breymann, one by the Hesse-Hanau Regiment, and six by the von Specht Brigade. These are to transport the English tents, and then are to return. As soon as the English regiments have marched, the German regiments are to enter their camp, and Captain Gerlach is to give directions. As soon as the bateaux arrive, they are to be unloaded, and each regiment is to pick up its own baggage. When the bateaux have been unloaded, and all the people have finished cooking, the bateaux are to be sent back, but with only 3 men in each. One officer, and 1 non-commissioned officer may be assigned to that detail by each regiment, and 1 captain is to be assigned to command from the Rhetz

Hesse-Hanau Order Book

Regiment, who is to have command over all those troops. The bateaux are to be delivered to Skenesborough, to the Department Quartermaster General Harving, and receipts obtained. The troops are then to return on land. Each regiment is to assign 1 non-commissioned officer to the wagons. Each regiment is to receive from the Hesse-Hanau Artillery, two bateaux, each of which is to be manned and transported by 3 individuals. At the blockhouse, a detachment of 1 officer and 30 men.

Orders from Headquarters

Tomorrow, Fraser's Advance Corps is to march and camp on the other side of Fort Edward. The Indians, Canadians, and armed Provincial troops are to cover the front and flanks of the Advanced Corps. The headquarters is to be located in the red house near Fort Edward, and is to be covered by the Dragoon Regiment, which is to camp on the plain. The right wing is to camp on the far side of the height, the other side of the plain. As the transportation of provisions and equipment of the Advanced Corps, and the right wing have been held up due to the shortage of wagons, it is necessary that the left wing remain at Fort Anne until the tents and equipment have reached the regiments. General von Riedesel is to provide sufficient detachments to bring the bateaux from Fort St. Anne to Skenesborough. As soon as the

Hesse-Hanau Order Book

detachments have brought the bateaux down, they are to rejoin their regiments. The Provincials and Canadians, who are armed, are to march this afternoon, with an appropriate number of their own officers, to Fort St. Anne, in order to help with the duty with the bateaux. Secondly, thereafter, to take the bateaux across the portage to Skenesborough, and from there to Carillon, where they are to receive weapons, and then, proceed across Lake George to join their own corps. The several regimental and battalion chiefs must insure, therefore, that the wagons for transporting the baggage are not too heavily loaded. The weakness of the wagons and their maintenance require the strictest adherence to this order, and the service will be less endangered if the regiments make several trips to pick up their baggage, rather than leave it behind, due to broken wagons and ruined horses en route. These orders are especially applicable to all officers and commissaries involved in the transportation of provisions. The brigadiers are therefore responsible, that where there is fruit or grass near their camps, an extra guard be posted to ensure its use for the army's animals. In case that it should be ordered, that a detachment of regular troops, or the Canadians, is to join the Indians, it is to be under the command of Major Kemble, except in the situation when the commander, who commands the regular troops, has seniority over the major. Major Kemble is

Hesse-Hanau Order Book

to receive his orders from Brigadier Fraser, pending further orders.

- - - - - - -

Orders in Camp near Fort St. Anne, 30 July 1777
Passwords - St. Gervas and Newcastle
Watch - Lieutenant von Lindau; 3 non-commissioned officers, 1 drummer, and 39 privates
Work detail - Lieutenant Siebert; 1 non-commissioned officer, and 4 privates
Staff officer of the day - Major von Ehrenkrook

    As General Burgoyne reminded General von Riedesel again this evening, that all wagons were to be turned in to the wagon master general, General Riedesel is compelled to take them from the regiments, and the regiments are to send all issued wagons to Captain Gerlach, who will indicate the place where they are to be turned in, so they can be turned in to the wagonmaster general.

    When in the future, our regiments march from here, everything that the officers can not carry on their horses, such as the tents, ammunition, and provisions, which the regiment needs for three days, is to be left in the camp. One officer per regiment, and 20 men are to be left therewith. The order has also been given to the wagonmaster general by General Burgoyne, that in the future, when equipment is being transported, he is to remain behind so as to determine how the English differ from us. If the officers can not transport all

Hesse-Hanau Order Book

their belongings at one time, they must send their horses back to make a second trip.

For the reserve picket, each regiment is to provide 10 privates, 2 non-commissioned officers, and 1 officer. The von Riedesel Regiment is to provide the captain for the reserve picket. Those pickets are to move out ahead of their regiment, be alert, and remain dressed during the night, and always ready, in their tent, to move out at the first alarm.

Orders from Headquarters
in Camp near Fort Edward, 31 July 1777

Passwords - St. Basil and Loyne
Watch - Lieutenant von Geyling; 3 non-commissioned officers, 1 drummer, and 39 privates
Picket - Lieutenant von Buttlar, in reserve

When the left wing, under the command of Major General von Riedesel moves out of its camp, Brigadier von Gall, with the Hesse-Hanau Regiment, is to remain in place, under Major General von Riedesel, until the provisions for the army for ten days, have arrived at Fort Anne, and the empty bateaux have been sent back.

Orders in Camp at Fort St. Anne, 1 August 1777
Passwords - St. Thomas and Paempff
Staff officer of the day - Major von Passern
Watch - Ensign von Geyling; 3 non-commissioned

Hesse-Hanau Order Book

officers, 1 drummer, and 39 privates

Picket - Lieutenant von Bischhhausen; 1 non-commissioned officer, and 30 privates

Blockhouse watch - 1 non-commissioned officer, and 7 privates

    At five o'clock tomorrow morning, general march is to be beaten at the Breymann Corps and left wing. At general march, the quartermaster sergeants and guards are to assemble at the Jaeger Company, after which they are to march immediately to the new camp near Fort Edward. The regiments are to strike their tents with the general march, pack them with the ammunition on the wagons to be delivered this evening, and when assembly is beaten at six o'clock, at which time the weapons are to be taken in hand, march out from the right with the Breymann Corps, and also the Specht Regiment Corps, and be ahead of the Riedesel Regiment.

    The pack horses can go beside the column, but not between the regiments. However, the wagons are all to follow behind the column in the same order as the regiments. Should the wagons which General Burgoyne promises, not arrive this evening, or before the march, the tents and ammunition must be left here under the guard of 1 officer and 20 men, until the wagons arrive, so as to bring these items to the regiments. Provisions are to be received today, for three days. The detail at the blockhouse is to be relieved this evening by 1 non-commissioned officer and 8 men from the Hesse-Hanau Regiment. Brigadier von Gall is assigned command of the detachment here at Fort St. Anne, and retains the Hesse-Hanau Regiment under his orders. He is to remain here until meat for ten days has actually arrived, and the bateaux returned. Then the brigadier is to break camp, and close with the army.

- - - - - - -

Orders in Camp at Fort St. Anne, 2 August 1777
Passwords - Sabina and Berwick
Staff officer of the day - Lieutenant Colonel Speth
Watch - Lieutenant von Eschwege; 3 non-commissioned officers, 1 drummer, and 39 privates
Picket - Ensign von Weyhers; 2 non-commissioned officers, and 25 privates

The regiments must remain ready to march, and as soon as the wagons arrive, and the order to march is given, be ready to break camp. The detail at the blockhouse is to be relieved by the Hesse-Hanau Regiment again, and Brigadier von Gall is responsible for everything pertaining to the detail, according to instructions disseminated to them yesterday, because the other three regiments must always be in a condition to move out..

- - - - - - -

Hesse-Hanau Order Book

Orders in Camp at Fort St. Anne, 3 August 1777
Passwords - St. Xavier and Glomorgen
Watch - Lieutenant von Buttlar; 3 non-commissioned officers, 1 drummer, and 39 privates
Picket - Lieutenant von Eschwege; 2 non-commissioned officers, 1 drummer, and 25 privates

- - - - - - - -

Orders in Camp at Fort Edward, 5 August 1777
Passwords - St. James and Bristol
Watch - Lieutenant Count von Puckler; 3 non-commissioned officers, 1 drummer, and 39 privates
Picket - Lieutenant Siebert; 2 non-commissioned officers, 1 drummer, and 25 privates

As it appears that the order concerning the transportation of officers' baggage has not been fully understood, it is herewith made known that neither on orders of the King nor the orders of General Carleton, are any changes in the transportation to be made. Those officers who do not fully understand this order, must as opportunity presents, acquire their own horses, but not forget that the order not to buy horses from the Indians, is always to be obeyed. An officer with 20 men, and the appropriate non-commissioned officers from the line, is to take all prisoners to Fort George. Those regiments which have sutlers, must not keep them behind their camp, and must forbid them, most sharply, to sell cognac to the English as well as the Indians, because situations occur that English

Hesse-Hanau Order Book

soldiers get drunk, commit excesses, and then say they bought the cognac behind the German regiments. All sutlers are herewith notified not to risk selling cognac to the Indians nor the English, be it any amount, as not only will the cognac be taken from him, but he will no longer be permitted to serve as a sutler.

- - - - - - - -

Orders in Camp at Fort Edward, 6 August 1777
Passwords - St. Joseph and Boston
Watch - Lieutenant von Bischhausen; 3 non-commissioned officers, 1 drummer, and 39 privates
Pickets - Ensign von Weyhers; 2 non-commissioned officers, 1 drummer, and 25 privates

It is assumed that the deserters from the 53rd Regiment were scalped by the Indians. His Excellency, Lieutenant General Burgoyne, is so completely convinced of the good character of the soldiers of his army, as to fear that should the desertions from the army increase, then despite every precaution to prevent desertions, it is to be strictly ordered that one hour after leaving the company, a list is to be sent to headquarters by the personnel present with the company, so that a detachment of Indians, who have orders to scalp deserters can be sent after the deserters immediately. If wagons are to be used for transportation by the regiments, or for the sick, they must thereafter be returned to the wagonmaster general by those who use them.

Hesse-Hanau Order Book

Orders in Camp at Fort Edward, 7 August 1777
Passwords - St. Lucretia and Bourton
Picket - Lieutenant Count von Puckler; 2 non-commissioned officers, and 35 privates
Work detail - Lieutenant von Geyling; 2 non-commissioned officers, and 144 privates
Watch - Ensign von Weyhers; 3 non-commissioned officers, 1 drummer, and 39 privates

All wagons, oxen, and horses which belong to the King and are now in the various regiments, are to be delivered to the wagon master general at once, in order to be used for the transport of provisions for the army. Lieutenant Bailey of the 20th Regiment is designated as the assistant to the quartermaster general.

Orders in Camp at Fort Edward, 7 August 1777
From Major General von Riedesel

As, since moving into camp here, General von Riedesel has learned that all the bateaux are to be brought behind the portage at Carillon, in order to carry provisions to Fort George, which will mean a long delay until the baggage can be brought here, or it is to be feared, that the baggage will be unloaded from the bateaux, and the bateaux with provisions come here, now in order to have the baggage much closer, as soon as enough vehicles are available to carry it here, General Riedesel has requested General Burgoyne to

Hesse-Hanau Order Book

send a detachment to Fort George and from there to go to Carillon, and obtain as many bateaux on this side of the portage as are necessary to carry all the equipment at that place to Carillon, and to bring the baggage to Fort George. As His Excellency, General Burgoyne, has agreed with this arrangement, all the regiments are to send a detachment, as they think necessary, under the command of an officer, and the necessary non-commissioned officers, and supplied with provisions for two days, to Fort George tomorrow morning at five o'clock in order to pick up as many bateaux in Carillon as five men can manage, as well as pick up the baggage which we sent back from Skenesborough to Carillon, in order to have it taken to Fort George. One captain is to command this entire detail. Those regiments which already have officers with the baggage at Carillon, are to send 1 non-commissioned officer with the detail from here, and the 10 men per regiment, who are among the necessary crew, are to bring the bateaux with the baggage here, in so far as they are healthy. The captain who has the command is to receive a letter from General von Riedesel to the commandant at Fort George, who is Lieutenant Colonel Anstruther, so that he will issue as many bateaux at Fort George, as are necessary to bring 24 or 25 men in each bateaux to Carillon. This appears to be one bateau per regiment, and in this manner he is to travel to Carillon, where he is to deliver a second

Hesse-Hanau Order Book

letter to Brigadier Hamilton, from Riedesel, whereby he is to receive as many bateaux on this side of the portage as each regiment has necessary to bring back the baggage, which it has at Carillon. He is to load the baggage, protect it from moisture, assign 5 men to each bateau, which each regiment has loaded, and depart from Fort George. The captain remains finally, until everything has left. Whereas the bateaux, in which the baggage is, arrives at Fort George, the captain is to determine if houses, or possibly barns, are available in which the baggage can lie very dry, and securely defended by the garrison from the fort. In this case, he is to allow it to be unloaded, and stored separately by regiments. If that situation is not possible, the things must remain lying in the bateaux, and protected as well as possible by blankets, and whatever is available. When the captain has taken care of everything , he is to return to the camp here with the entire crew, except for 1 non-commissioned officer and 10 men per regiment. One officer from the Breymann Corps and 1 officer from Specht Brigade remain behind to secure the equipment at Fort George. Those regiments which have sick needing hospital care, can use this opportunity to send them along to the hospital at Carillon. As the Hesse-Hanau Regiment is to be given a much easier route, from St. Anne to Skenesborough, by Major Erwin, than all the English bateaux had to use in traveling to Carillon,

Hesse-Hanau Order Book

and from there onward to Fort George, General von Riedesel allows Brigadier General von Gall, if he wishes to permit it, to allow his command to bring the baggage from Carillon to Fort George by the water route.

- - - - - - -

Orders from Headquarters, 1 August 1777

The already long established order concerning soldiers leaving the camp, is being very poorly observed. Troops have been seen three miles from camp, others have nearly considered deserters and rebels, by the Indians, and been shot at. The officers will recall that the orders in the camp at Crown Point, that as soon as four shots are fired, the entire army is to move out, is still valid during the entire campaign, and just now, we are only three miles from the enemy. Also, they are never to go so far from the enemy, that in case of an alarm, they can not be the first to take up arms. The companies are to take roll call twice a day, and once at night. If it is necessary to obtain water, it is a standing suggestion to the regiments, to which the order does not apply, that obtaining water is always authorized, and must always be supplied by sending an appropriate detail, when the water is too far from the camp.

- - - - - - -

Hesse-Hanau Order Book

Orders in Camp at Fort Edward, 8 August 1777
Passwords - St. Anne and Biggleswade
Picket - Lieutenant von Buttlar; 2 non-commissioned officers, 1 drummer, and 25 privates
Watch - Lieutenant von Geyling; 3 non-commissioned officers, 1 drummer, and 39 privates

- - - - - - - -

Orders in Camp at Fort Edward, 9 August 1777
Passwords - St. David and Convey
Watch - Ensign von Geyling; 3 non-commissioned officers, 1 drummer, and 39 privates
Picket - Lieutenant Siebert; 2 non-commissioned officers, 1 drummer, and 25 privates

Brigadier Powell is to relieve Brigadier Hamilton at Carillon. The 53rd Regiment is to march tomorrow to relieve the 62nd Regiment. The provision wagons which return, are to transport the regimental baggage. Four companies are to embark at Fort George, and the four other companies are to remain there until the bateaux of the 62nd Regiment return. The company of Captain Money is to march as soon as the 62nd Regiment has arrived at Fort George, so as to join the advance corps of the army. The company of Captain

Hesse-Hanau Order Book

Boucherville is to march to Fort George to relieve the company of Captain Money. At eleven o'clock tomorrow morning, religious services are to be held before the front of the line, and in the headquarters.

- - - - - - -

Orders in Camp at Fort Edward, 10 August 1777
Passwords - St. Peter and Truro
Picket - Ensign von Weyhers; 2 non-commissioned officers, 1 drummer, and 26 privates
Watch - Lieutenant Eschwege; 3 non-commissioned officers, 1 drummer, and 39 privates

The soldier Anton Fasselabend, who has been sentenced to death by a court-martial, is to be executed at eleven o'clock tomorrow morning before the front of the Riedesel Regiment. Tomorrow morning, at the English camp, a court-martial is to sit for two English soldiers, with the names William Skeen and Johann Doring. No detail or single soldier is to be detached from the regiment, without having a signed certificate from the regimental commander indicating for how long provisions have been issued. Without such a certificate, no commissary provisions are to be issued to the troops.

- - - - - - -

Hesse-Hanau Order Book

Orders in Camp at Fort Edward, 11 August 1777
Passwords - St. Mathew and Penzana
Picket - Lieutenant von Geyling; 2 non-commissioned officers, 1 drummer, and 25 privates
Watch - Lieutenant Siebert; 3 non-commissioned officers, 1 drummer, and 39 privates

Brigadier von Gall orders that daily, one officer, two non-commissioned officers, one drummer, and thirty privates are to be in the moving-out picket. Therefrom, the officer is to send out, at three o'clock tomorrow morning, one non-commissioned officer and six privates on patrol, half way to Fort Edward. They must return by nine o'clock, when the officer and the picket are withdrawn. At four o'clock in the afternoon, the same patrol, with a non-commissioned officer and six men leave the camp, make the same patrol as they made in the morning, and must return again by nine o'clock in the evening. The picket is to provide one [non-commissioned] officer and ten privates every evening, the non-commissioned officer and six privates for the fire watch, and four men, one of whom is a lance corporal at the water, where the trees stand opposite, to establish a post this side of the water. A non-commissioned officer and the six men

Hesse-Hanau Order Book

on the fire watch are to make their patrol during the early morning, at three-thirty, to Skenesborough, six miles distance, to the two first houses, and again in the evening at four o'clock.

- - - - - - - -

Orders in Camp at Fort Edward, 12 August 1777
Passwords - St. Luke and Dartmouth
Watch - Lieutenant von Buttlar; 3 non-commissioned officers, 1 drummer, and 39 privates
Picket - Lieutenant von Lindau; 2 non-commissioned officers, 1 drummer, and 25 privates

- - - - - - -

Orders in Camp at Fort Edward, 13 August 1777
Passwords - St. John and Ipswich
Picket - Ensign von Geyling; 2 non-commissioned officers, 1 drummer, and 25 privates
Watch - Lieutenant von Lindau; 3 non-commissioned officers, 1 drummer, and 39 privates

This afternoon, the army provisions, to and including the 16th are to be received. At five o'clock this afternoon, as many bateaux are to be issued as are needed to transport the field equipment for the regiments, and the regimental quartermasters are to accept them. As, however, it is wished that the troops

Hesse-Hanau Order Book

practice making rafts, the regimental chiefs are to insure that they are instructed in this practice. The model was made that rafts eighteen feet long and nine feet wide are the best for passing the narrow and flat stretches of water this side of Fort Miller. Tomorrow the army marches in columns from the right. At daybreak general march is to be beaten, and at the same time the regimental quartermasters, with the quartermaster sergeants and guards depart. When it so happens that the regiments must camp at places where other troops have previously camped, the regimental quartermasters must insure that the terrain is properly cleaned, before the regiment enters camp. An hour after general march, assembly is to be beaten, and the regiments are then to march out. As many people as are necessary must be ordered to load and row the bateaux and rafts. All pack horses and vehicles which belong to the officers must march behind the column. The provost is to follow behind the baggage. The court-martial of which Lieutenant Colonel Hill is president, is dissolved. Baron Salans, of the 9th Regiment, is to do duty with Captain Fraser's Corps, pending further orders. Mr. Munro is designated as captain for the bateaux, and is to serve in the detachment of the quartermaster general. The two kegs of Madeira wine, 3 kegs of rum, a sack of coffee, a sack of barley, two tubs of butter, and two rolls of tobacco, which were laid on a provisions cart in such a secretive manner, were given to the commissary for safeguarding, and it is to be further ordered as to how they are to be distributed.

Orders of Major General von Riedesel

The rear guard is to consist of one officer, two non-commissioned officers, and 30 privates. They are to halt at the right wing of the English line, and remain there until the army and equipment following behind it, and the wagons and pack horses, have marched out. Then, it is to follow the army, but is not to enter the camp before all the vehicles and pack horses have entered. [The repetition of a portion of the above, which appears in the German text, has not been made in this translation.] At the same time, this rear guard must not tolerate any stragglers behind the army. As the two regiments, von Riedesel and Specht, are rather far from the place where the bateaux can enter, the provision has been made that six wagons can deliver the baggage of those regiments, to the place which is

Hesse-Hanau Order Book

as close as the bateaux can come. Brigadier Specht is to have an officer reconnoiter how far up the river the bateaux can come, and as soon as the wagons arrive, the things are to be loaded in the wagons, and taken to the place where the bateaux are, so that they can be put in the bateaux, and when it comes the turn for the tents, which must be the last items, the tents are to be struck, and the troops are to remain in bivouac this night. The six wagons are to be used until nothing more of the brigadier's, or any regimental items remain above, and then the wagons are to be sent to the von Rhetz Regiment, which must send a detail here to receive them. If not enough bateaux have been distributed to the regiments, as are necessary to bring all the regimental items, the bateaux are to go again and pick up the remaining items. The regiments must then leave a proportionate guard by the items left lying here, which is to enter camp with the final transport. The von Rhetz Regiment is to march at daybreak, leaving an appropriate guard with the tents and baggage, and the regiment is to enter camp here, at Fort Edward, at about the place where the general guard and baggage detail of the von Riedesel Regiment previously stood. For help in transporting

Hesse-Hanau Order Book

regimental equipment, the von Rhetz Regiment is to receive six wagons from Brigadier Specht, to carry the items, and if they can not carry everything in one trip, they must make two trips. When the final baggage of the von Rhetz Regiment is brought in, the detail left behind is to rejoin the regiment, although the officer of the detail, and a portion of the men must remain in camp, until the two companies of the Hesse-Hanau Regiment have arrived, which are to take over the von Rhetz Regiment's posts.

Orders in Camp at Fort Edward, 14 August 1777
Passwords - Valentine and Watton
Watch - Lieutenant Count von Puckler; 3 non-commissioned officers, 1 drummer, and 39 privates

----

Orders in Camp at Fort Edward, 15 August 1777
Passwords - St. Theodosius and Trusy
Watch - Ensign von Weyhers; 3 non-commissioned officers, 1 drummer, and 39 privates

Tomorrow morning, after the changing of the guard, the quartermaster sergeants and guards are to go with Ensign and Adjutant Heerwagen to lay out the new camps, and at two o'clock this afternoon, the

Hesse-Hanau Order Book

camp is to be changed.

Orders in the Camp of the General Quarters
At Duar, 16 August 1777

Passwords - Lawrence and Pezbourgh [Pittsburg?]

Watch - Ensign von Geyling; 3 non-commissioned officers, 1 drummer, and 39 privates

The sentence of the court-martial concerning the two soldiers of the 47th Regiment, who committed highway robbery, is that each is to receive 1,000 lashes. Provisions are to be received tomorrow.

Hesse-Hanau Order Book

Orders in Camp at Fort Duar, 17 August 1777
Passwords - Ferdinand and Madrid
Watch - Lieutenant von Trott; 3 non-commissioned officers, 1 drummer, and 39 privates

An effort has been made from the left wing of this expedition to obtain such a supply of cattle and provisions so that the line would be in a condition to continue the march. As this effort has failed because of the fortunes of war, therefore the troops must halt for a few days, to allow the movement of foodstuffs. The various regiments are to use this opportunity to collect their sick and convalescents. The 47th Regiment is to march to [Fort] Edward tomorrow, where it is to receive orders from General Phillips. The regiment is to assume responsibility for the prisoners taken by Lieutenant Colonel Breymann, and such others as are here. The flour taken from the enemy must be delivered to the commissariat.

The vehicles and wagons taken from the enemy are to be delivered to the Breymann Corps and the 47th Regiment tomorrow, and then turned in to the wagon master general. [The repetition of a portion of the above, which appears in the German text on pages 235 and 236, has not been made in this translation.] As the bridge over the Hudson river has been taken away, building materials must be assembled in order to build another, better bridge. If no orders have been issued, foraging is to be carried out every morning at

Hesse-Hanau Order Book

six o'clock, and all the servants are to assemble together at the 47th Regiment. There is always to be one officer, 2 non-commissioned officers, and eighteen men with them, as a covering party: the officer from the Hesse-Hanau Regiment, one non-commissioned officer from the Rhetz Regiment, and the other from the 47th Regiment; six men from the Rhetz Regiment, seven from the Hesse-Hanau Regiment, and five from the 47th Regiment. This detail is not only to protect the foragers, but is to prevent excesses and marauding, for which the officer is responsible. The Artillery is to send its foragers with the detail. No individual person, without an accompanying non-commissioned officer, or at a post designated by the battalion commander, is to go beyond the outposts, otherwise, they are to be placed in arrest and punished as such by the regiments. The retreat shot at evening is to be fired by a 12-pound cannon, before the 47th Regiment. Orders are to be announced every morning at eleven o'clock, which the brigade-majors and adjutants are to pick up from Deputy Adjutant General Poellnitz, and at this time, all questions and reports from the regiments, are to be made to General von Riedesel. As Brigadier General von Gall, under the orders of General von Riedesel, as he commands the line here, all reports are to be made to him should General von Riedesel be absent, and he will also then, give out the orders.

Hesse-Hanau Order Book

Orders of General von Riedesel
[Following the Battle of Bennington, 16 August 1777]

The corps of Lieutenant Colonel Breymann is to send its wounded with the wagons which brought the flour to Doctor Hess at the hospital, where they are to be taken into the houses and every measure taken for their care. Both regiments are to send their surgeons also, in order to provide the best care for officers as well as privates. General von Riedesel extends his highest praise to both battalions for their bravery, and declares that it was not their fault that they could not completely defeat the enemy, but that the time lapse between the two attacks, by the corps of Baum and Breymann, was the cause that both corps could not unite. Honor is always present for troops which conduct themselves well, and the general herewith thanks Lieutenant Colonel Breymann as much for his demonstrated fortitude, as for his good dispositions, which allowed him to withdraw from the battle. The same applies to Major von Barner for the bravery, which he demonstrated during this opportunity. And, as the general does not wish to neglect everyone who distinguished themselves, but the senior officers, he is sending a report to His Highness and will himself, at all times, acknowledge the merit that the officers displayed during this opportunity. Although this expedition was not as successful as was anticipated, there is no reason to be downcast, but we must wait

Hesse-Hanau Order Book

for another opportunity to again recapture that which was lost. When the coming day has past, and possibly other troops have been found who have returned, Lieutenant Colonel Breymann is to submit a casualty list of both battalions.

Orders in Camp at Duar, 18 August 1777
Passwords - Carleton and Quebec
Watch - Lieutenant von Eschwege; 3 non-commissioned officers, 1 drummer, and 39 privates
Captain for Inspection - Captain von Schachten

As some officers have made a habit of using wagons and oxen meant for royal use, for the transportation of their personal baggage, preventing the transportation of provisions, and breaking the wagons, and ruining the horses, it is strictly ordered that no wagons or horses, meant for royal service, are to be used under any pretext unless the wagon master, or other supervisor of the horses, is informed. Those supervisors are not to allow a provisions wagon to be taken for any other use except the transportation of provisions, nor bateaux without a specific order from General Burgoyne, the quartermaster general, or his assistant. Nor should any officer who commands a post, interfere the least bit with the provisions vehicles, except for those needed for transporting provisions.

Hesse-Hanau Order Book

Orders of Brigadier von Gall

The brigadier orders that in the companies and by the regiments strict attention is to be given and maintained that no soldier is to go about with bare feet, without shoes and socks, because the regimental surgeon believes this to be mainly responsible for the soldiers suddenly becoming sick and suffering great pain. Second - all sending-out of soldiers, for whatever reason, is expressly forbidden. In case a private should be dispatched, it must be reported to the staff by the company. Third - The officers and company chiefs are to give strict observance that when a regiment marches out that a tent block is never rolled up in the tent, because experience shows that some tents have been rolled and have been torn by so doing. Each and every company should and must insure that the privates' tents are well maintained and are in a usable condition. Tomorrow morning [the command] is to march. At six o'clock, general march is to be beaten and at seven o'clock, assembly. Therefore, Lieutenant von Buttlar, two non-commissioned officers from the Leib Regiment [sic - Company ?], and the Colonel's Company, and one drummer, and twenty privates per company, are ordered on a combat patrol. Three [two illegible words], which are to remain behind in camp here, and this detail is to be relieved by one lance corporal and three men of the blockhouse guard, at four o'clock

Hesse-Hanau Order Book

tomorrow morning.

- - - - - - -

Orders in Camp at Duar, 19 August 1777
Passwords - Patrick and Cork
Watch - Lieutenant Siebert; 3 non-commissioned officers, 1 drummer, and 39 privates

- - - - - - -

Orders of 20 August 1777
In Camp at John's House
Staff officer of the day - Lieutenant Colonel Lentz
Watch - Lieutenant von Lindau; 3 non-commissioned officers, 1 drummer, and 39 privates
Foraging detail - Lieutenant von Eschwege; 1 non-commissioned officer, 1 drummer, and 6 privates
Picket - Ensign von Weyhers; 2 non-commissioned officers, 1 drummer, and 25 privates

Duty remains the same as yesterday, with the appropriate field and fire watches. Each regiment is to have one officer, 2 non-commissioned officers, and 25 privates in the picket, which is to move out at the proper time during the evening. The pickets are to march out from each regiment's *place d'armes* after being inspected, and having drilled, and are to go to their designated posts, where they are to be briefed by the officer who commanded the picket on the preceding night. The picket is to return to the camp at five-thirty in the morning. At three-thirty in the morning, the picket is to send a patrol, consisting of

Hesse-Hanau Order Book

one non-commissioned officer and four men to St. Anne, and another to Fort Edward. If they meet patrols from those places, when underway, they are to exchange about everything new. After each has exchanged the name of the commanding non-commissioned officer, or lance corporal, each patrol is to return to its camp and report to the officer who commanded the picket, who is then to make a further report. Rhetz Regiment and Hesse-Hanau Regiment are to draw lots to see which one patrols to Fort Edward, and which to St. Anne. If this corps is so well situated, that trenches and such defensive preparations are unnecessary, then not only the orders of General Burgoyne to be observed, but also the requirements by General von Riedesel, that the troops are to be kept working on the defenses by making defensive positions before the guards, and connecting them with the line. Deputy Quartermaster General Gerlach is to instruct the workers, and each regiment is to work on that section which is before its camp, supplying one officer, 3 non-commissioned officers, and fifty men. They are to begin work at five o'clock in the morning, and work until eleven o'clock, and work during the afternoon from three until retreat. The entrenching tools are to be received at the artillery park by each regiment, in the morning, and returned again in the evening. When each regiment has completed its assigned work, this work detail is

Hesse-Hanau Order Book

finished. As part of this work, it is also required that the regiments make a communications path with a width of one foot, for the pickets which are in woods, from one sentry to the next, and the woods must also be cleared from the path from the officer's post to the sentries, so that a person can also ride along the footpath. As the regiments are quite near to one another, the latrine for the 47th Regiment is to be made on its left flank, for Rhetz Regiment, ahead of its right wing, and for the Hesse-Hanau Regiment, before its front, and to maintain sanitation, they must be changed frequently.

Orders in Camp at John's House
21 August 1777

Passwords - Mathilda and Consentin
Staff officer of the day - Major von Lucke
Watch - Lieutenant Bischhausen; 3 non-commissioned officers, 1 drummer, and 39 privates
Work detail - Ensign Weyhers; 3 non-commissioned officers, and 48 men
Picket - Captain von Schachten, Lieutenant Count von Puckler; 2 non-commissioned officers, 1 drummer, and 25 privates

Captain of the picket from Hesse-Hanau, the officer for the foraging detail to be from the Rhetz Regiment, non-commissioned officers to be from the 47th Regiment and the Hesse-Hanau Regiments,

Hesse-Hanau Order Book

seven privates from the Hesse-Hanau Regiment, six from Rhetz Regiment, and five from the 47th Regiment. The pickets are to remain at the same place, occupying posts the same as yesterday, where the staff officer of the day established them. The regiments are strictly forbidden from shooting in the vicinity of the camp site. The foraging detail is to go out just like this morning. The two non-commissioned officers for patrolling are to be provided by the 47th and Rhetz Regiments. The two regiments must decide which patrols to Fort Edward and which one to Fort Anne. Of the three regiments which are here, fifty-three men are to be transferred to the English Artillery, eighteen from the Rhetz Regiment, twenty from the Hesse-Hanau Regiment, and fourteen privates from the 47th Regiment. These men are to be detached every day, but do not need to transfer to the English Artillery, except in case of an attack.

- - - - - - - -

Orders from Headquarters at Duar

As four German recruits from various English regiments have twice been absent from company formation, and it is assumed that they have deserted, Indians and Provincial troops have been sent out to find them, and it is hoped that they will either be brought back, or scalped. His Excellence is so completely convinced of the loyalty of this army, as to fear that the desertions will only increase if the

Hesse-Hanau Order Book

soldiers are drunk or seduced to desertions by the enemy. There is reason to believe that such individuals have been sent into our camp by the enemy, and sought to get the men to desert by promises, and with a fluency in the German language. In order to insure that those sent-in individuals receive their just punishment, a reward of one hundred Thaler is to be awarded to individuals who can expose them, having seen that one of that type of person spoke with the soldier. In order to prevent such conversations, sentries are to be attentive that no person who is not a soldier, or an officer's servant, is allowed in camp. The provost, all patrols, and guards, must inquire, in case they see strangers in the camp, what they are doing there. It is herewith made known that in case a sentry, patrol, Provincial or Indian captures a deserter, a twenty Thaler reward is to be paid. Should the deserter run away however, and then be shot dead, the Indians are to bring in his scalp.

Hesse-Hanau Order Book

Orders in Camp at John's House, 22 August 1777
Passwords - St. Agnes and Sorel
Staff officer of the day - Major Erwin
Watch - Lieutenant von Bischhausen; 3 non-commissioned officers, 1 drummer, and 39 privates
Picket - Lieutenant von Geyling; 2 non-commissioned officers, 1 drummer, and 25 privates
Work detail - Lieutenant von Lindau; 3 non-commissioned officers, and 48 privates

Captain of the picket from the 47th Regiment; officer with the foragers from the 47th Regiment, one non-commissioned officer each from the Rhetz and Hesse-Hanau Regiments. The patrol to Fort Anne from the Hesse-Hanau Regiment, and to Edward from the 47th Regiment. The work detail to remain with the Artillery, tomorrow morning is to be one non-commissioned officer and seven men from the Hesse-Hanau Regiment. There is to be no drill this evening.

- - - - - - - -

Orders in Camp at John's House, 23 August 1777
Passwords - St. John and Arc
Staff officer of the day - Major von Passern
Watch - Ensign von Weyhers; 3 non-commissioned officers, 1 drummer, and 39 privates
Picket - Ensign von Geyling; 2 non-commissioned officers, 1 drummer, and 25 privates
Work detail - Lieutenant von Trott; 3 non-commissioned officers, and 48 privates

Hesse-Hanau Order Book

Captain of the picket to be from the Rhetz Regiment; officer for the foraging detail from the Hesse-Hanau Regiment. Hesse-Hanau Regiment to send a patrol to Fort Edward, and the Rhetz Regiment to St. Anne. There is to be drill this evening, and church is to be held after guard mount.

- - - - - - -

Orders in Camp at John's House, 24 August 1777
Passwords - Sicily and Theley
Staff officer of the day - Lieutenant Colonel Sutherland
Watch - Lieutenant von Geyling; 3 non-commissioned officers, 1 drummer, and 39 privates
Picket - Captain von Schachten; 2 non-commissioned officers, 1 drummer, and 25 privates

Captain of the picket to be from the Hesse-Hanau Regiment; the officer for the foraging detail from the Rhetz Regiment. One non-commissioned officer from the Hesse-Hanau Regiment, and one from the 47th Regiment. The 47th Regiment to send a patrol to Fort Anne, and the von Rhetz Regiment to Fort Edward. Vinegar is to be issued today, to the regiments, by proportions. Tomorrow the regiments are to receive four days' rations.

- - - - - - -

Orders in Camp at John's House, 25 August 1777
Passwords - St. Theresa and Paderborn
Staff officer of the day - Lieutenant Colonel Lentz

Hesse-Hanau Order Book

Watch - Lieutenant von Trott; 3 non-commissioned officers, 1 drummer, and 39 privates
Picket - Lieutenant von Eschwege; 2 non-commissioned officers, 1 drummer, and 25 privates
Work detail - Lieutenant von Bischhausen; 3 non-commissioned officers, and 48 privates

Captain of the picket to be from the 47th Regiment; officer for the foraging detail from the 47th Regiment, one non-commissioned officer each from the Hesse-Hanau and Rhetz Regiment. The 47th Regiment to patrol to Fort Edward, and the Hesse-Hanau Regiment to Fort Anne. Rum is to be received this evening, and no sutler is to sell cognac to an Englishman nor to the Brunswickers, pending further orders. The path to the outposts is to be cleared. No sutler is to buy uniform items from the English. The brigadier orders that no soldier is to leave the camp, whether with or without a non-commissioned officer. At the same time, a detachment of one captain, two officers, six non-commissioned officers, and eighty men is to be provided, which is to assemble here at John's House, where the English Artillery is located. The 47th Regiment is to provide one captain, two non-commissioned officers, and twenty-two men; the von Rhetz Regiment one officer, two non-commissioned officers, and twenty-eight men; and the Hesse-Hanau Regiment one officer, two non-commissioned officers, and thirty men. This detachment is not to carry

Hesse-Hanau Order Book

knapsacks, but is to carry one day's provisions. The officer for the detail is to be Lieutenant von Lindau.

- - - - - - -

Orders in Camp at John's House, 26 August 1777
Passwords - Marie and Jerusalem
Watch - Lieutenant von Geyling; 3 non-commissioned officers, 1 drummer, and 39 privates
Picket - Lieutenant Siebert; 2 non-commissioned officers, 1 drummer, and 25 privates
Work detail - Lieutenant von Eschwege; 3 non-commissioned officers, and 48 privates

Captain for the picket is to be from the von Rhetz Regiment; the officer for the foraging detail from the Rhetz Regiment. One non-commissioned officer each, from the Hesse-Hanau and 47th Regiments. Rhetz Regiment to patrol to Fort Anne; Hesse-Hanau Regiment to Edward. As it has been proven that a non-commissioned officer of the Rhetz Regiment sold material for a shirt to a soldier of the 47th Regiment, and it is against orders for a soldier to sell uniform items, he has been sentenced to be put in an uncomfortable position for 24 hours, and this is to be made known, so that no one will sell anything to the English without prior approval.

- - - - - - -

Hesse-Hanau Order Book

Orders in Camp at John's House, 27 August 1777
Passwords - St. Magdalene and Babylon
Staff officer of the day - Major Erwin
Watch - Lieutenant Eschwege; 3 non-commission4d officers, 1 drummer, and 39 privates
Picket - Captain von Geren; 2 non-commissioned officers, 1 drummer, and 25 privates

Captain for the picket is to be from the Hesse-Hanau Regiment; the officer for the foraging detail from the Hesse-Hanau Regiment; non-commissioned officers from the Rhetz and English 47th Regiments. Rhetz Regiment is to patrol to Edward; 47th Regiment to Fort Anne. Work on the regimental defenses in camp to continue until the line laid out by Captain Gerlach is completed. The patrol which has gone to Fort Anne previously, is to go no more than half way to the other side of the dam, where the houses stand, determine if anything new has occurred, and then return to camp. They will no longer make contact with another patrol, because the Hesse-Hanau detachment, which was previously there, has departed. Although the order has been given several times previously, that the vegetables are not to be taken from any house where there are inhabitants, and even less so from where a guard detachment is, now each non-commissioned officer with a foraging party is notified that he must be responsible for insuring that this order is carried out. Furthermore, such details sent out to get vegetables are to consist of not more than eight or ten men. However, complaints to the contrary, frequently reported by the inhabitants of the houses, are that forty or fifty men, or larger, are sent out from the camp, who frequently seize the inhabitants' complete supply of vegetables. As it is against all regulations to send out detachments without the prior knowledge of the general who commands a corps, and taking vegetables from an inhabitant who still occupies his house is against General Burgoyne's orders, in the future, not a single detachment is to leave the camp without the general having first been notified as to how many men the regiment intends to send, and no such detachment is to be ordered out until it is known which houses are empty and where vegetables are available. The individual who commands such a detachment must be specifically instructed not to begin taking vegetables without being first convinced that no one occupies the house. Therefore, all detachments sent out, without having informed the general beforehand, are to be considered as marauders, and the outer posts, as well as the patrols, which are so ordered, must bring them in under arrest. As a foraging detail is ordered to protect the houses each day, at the place where all the officers keep their horses, they are to use them for foraging with this escort. It appears however, that some officers do not allow the use of their horses for

Hesse-Hanau Order Book

foraging detail, but keep them only for themselves. Furthermore, it is to be made known that single foragers are to be arrested as marauders, and are to be sent to the regiments. As one non-commissioned officer of the Rhetz Regiment, who was properly instructed by his commander, took more vegetables than ordered to take, from houses in which there were people, he is, for disobedience of orders, to lie in an uncomfortable position for forty-eight hours. Likewise, a detachment of the Hesse-Hanau Regiment foraged, not only where there was an inhabitant, but even where there was a guard. Therefore, Brigadier von Gall is to have an investigation of this matter conducted, and is to punish the individual who disobeyed orders, and compensate the owner.

- - - - - - -

Hesse-Hanau Order Book

Orders in Camp at Headquarters at Duar

Several punishable offenses, which have been committed by a driver and other persons attached to the army, require a field court-martial of the type similar to the courts used in garrison. Therefore, one is to be established, consisting of a captain and four subalterns from the line, to conduct trials of the mentioned persons according to the content of acts of Parliament, against the disrespectful insubordination and desertion. Captain Money, deputy quartermaster general, is designated as commissary in matters relating to the royal horses, and is empowered to acquire a definite number of horses for the King's service, by means of a proper contract. It has become apparent that some of the King's horses have been taken for individual use, and it is known that such were lost in the woods just before a pending march. Therefore, all regimental commanders are to conduct an exact investigation concerning those individuals who might have made themselves guilty of such an exceptionally crime. It is difficult to imagine that an officer could participate in an undertaking so disadvantageous to the King, which could result in his downfall, without being cashiered. On the other hand, it is even more necessary to make known to all sutlers, officers' servants, Provincials, and everyone who follows the army, or is dependent thereon, regardless of whom that might be, who is inclined to put a royal

Hesse-Hanau Order Book

horse to his own use, without the department of the quartermaster general considering it necessary, that he shall face a court-martial for theft. All officers of the department of the quartermaster general are likewise forbidden, without the express order of General Burgoyne, or without specific and unavoidable circumstances which affect the army, to give permission for a royal horse to be used on a particular service. At the same time, any agent, commissary, driver, wagon master, etc., who perhaps thinks he can lose, or loses royal horses, wagons, harnesses, etc., or who allows those mentioned things to be changed from the service they were intended for, is herewith informed that he will be most severely punished. As long as a brigadier commands at Ticonderoga, he is to command both English brigades with the army. At noon tomorrow, a horse auction is to be held at the tent near the headquarters, for those officers who have a desire to buy a horse, and can be there at the designated time.

- - - - - - - -

Orders in Camp at John's House, 28 August 1777
Passwords - George and Windsor
Staff officer of the day - Major von Passern
Watch - Lieutenant Siebert; 3 non-commissioned officers, 1 drummer, and 39 privates
Picket - Lieutenant Count von Puckler; 2 non-commissioned officers, 1 drummer, and 25 privates

Hesse-Hanau Order Book

Work detail - Ensign von Geyling

Captain for the picket is to be from the 47th Regiment; the captain for the foraging detail from the 47th Regiment. Non-commissioned officer to patrol for the 47th Regiment to Edward; for Hesse-Hanau to St. Anne. Shooting in the vicinity of the camp is again forbidden, because several shots were heard near the camp yesterday. Also, a cannoneer of the Royal Artillery was caught and brought in by a patrol, because he was shooting pigeons before the Rhetz Regiment. He was released by General von Riedesel however, as it was his first offense.

All guards in the camp, when they hear shooting close by, whether at day or night, are to send patrols at once to the place where the shots were fired, and the individual who did the shooting is to be placed in arrest, and brought to General Riedesel's general guard.

Orders in Camp at John's House, 29 August 1777
Passwords - St. Joseph and Portugal
Staff officer of the day - Lieutenant Colonel Sutherland
Watch - Lieutenant von Buttlar; 3 non-commissioned officers, 1 drummer, and 39 privates
Picket - Lieutenant Bischhausen; 2 non-commissioned officers, 1 drummer, and 25 privates
Foraging detail - Ensign von Geyling

Hesse-Hanau Order Book

Captain for the picket is to be from the Rhetz Regiment; the officer for the foraging detail from the Hesse-Hanau Regiment. Non-commissioned officer of the Rhetz Regiment to patrol to Fort Anne; of Hesse-Hanau to Fort Edward.

Orders from Headquarters at Duar House

The greatest economy in issuing and receiving provisions, now and in the future, is to be a regular duty and an object of the greatest importance. The fate of the entire campaign can depend on that, and the necessary conservation of the previous supply of slaughtered cattle requires the closest attention. Up to now and even yet, nothing can be slaughtered except for the sick, and for these first, only the sick, and for all others, fresh meat can be delivered, only in completely exceptionally necessary situation. The regimental commanders are therefore to submit, on their honor, a report of the necessary portions needed for their sick, to the commisariat the day before the entire army is to be supplied with provisions again; and in the future, the fresh provisions are to be received according to their submitted reports, when a sufficient number of slaughter cattle have been collected. All possible attention will be used in order to obtain the best results, and for officers to use to ease the situation, and notice will be given when fresh meat can be supplied, instead of salted provisions.

Hesse-Hanau Order Book

Orders in Camp at John's House, 30 August 1777
Passwords - Carl and Castle
Staff officer of the day - Lieutenant Colonel Lentz
Watch - Lieutenant von Lindau; 3 non-commissioned officers, 1 drummer, and 39 privates
Picket - Ensign von Weyhers; 2 non-commissioned officers, 1 drummer, and 25 privates

Captain of the picket to be from the Hesse-Hanau Regiment; the officer for the foraging detail from the Rhetz Regiment; non-commissioned officer from the Hesse-Hanau Regiment. The English to patrol to Fort Anne; Rhetz Regiment to Edward.

The posts in the camp are to challenge anyone passing them during the night. It is not necessary however, as it is in the camp, to demand the password, if patrols or details pass with weapons. The posts however, which are outside the camp, however, must require the password, after giving the challenge.

- - - - - - -

Orders from the Headquarters at Duar House

Undoubtedly, there has been considerable confusion during the sale of horses between the soldiers and the inhabitants, and horses, which often were stolen by the inhabitants were bought by officers who did not know that, at a cheap price. To prevent this in the future, and so that the officers are not cheated in this matter, it is herewith ordered that no officer or other person is to buy more horses on his own, and all inhabitants who bring horses to sell, when it is determined that they are their own property, are to be informed that they may sell them before the great tent at headquarters at twelve o'clock noon. Each soldier or inhabitant who is discovered to have stolen horses, or by another pretext seeks to deceive, is to be severely punished therefore. It is hoped, that no officer will buy horses anywhere else except at the publicly authorized place. All cattle that are brought into camp, are also to be brought to this commission, and then delivered to the commissariat. The regiments will see that when they buy cattle for themselves, the army thereby suffers a serious loss. The quartermaster general department is to receive its orders from Major General Phillips, and submit its report to him. Mr. Robertson has been designated as commissary general of the various Provincial corps assigned to the army. Lieutenant Wilkinson has been designated an assistant with the Engineer Corps.

- - - - - - - -

Orders in Camp at John's House, 31 August 1777
Passwords - St. Mark and Venice
Staff officer of the day - Major von Lucke
Watch - Lieutenant Count von Puckler; 3 non-commissioned officers, 1 drummer, and 39 privates
Picket - Lieutenant von Trott; 2 non-commissioned officers, 1 drummer, and 25 privates
    Captain for the picket is to be from the 47th

Hesse-Hanau Order Book

Regiment; the officer for the foraging detail from the 47th Regiment. For patrolling to Fort Anne, a non-commissioned officer from the Hesse-Hanau Regiment, and to Fort Edward, from the Rhetz Regiment. At exactly five o'clock tomorrow morning, a detachment consisting of one officer, two non-commissioned officers, and 25 men is to assemble here at the John's House, This detachment is to take three days' provisions along, and Deputy Quartermaster General Harrington is to give instructions. From each regiment, two axes are to be taken along, and the men are to carry their knapsacks. The 47th Regiment is to provide one officer, and six men for this detachment, the Rhetz Regiment one non-commissioned officer, and nine men, and the Hesse-Hanau Regiment, one non-commissioned officer, and ten men, for a total of one officer, two non-commissioned officers, and twenty-five men.

Orders from Headquarters at Duar

Tomorrow morning, at the advance corps of Brigadier Fraser, a general court-martial is to sit, consisting of officers of this corps. It is too try the soldier Walter Harris, of the Light Infantry Company, of the 53rd Regiment, for inciting Wilhelm Bell, soldier of the Light Infantry Company, of the 24th Regiment, and Joseph Brooks, soldier of the Light Infantry Company, of the 53rd Regiment, to desert to

Hesse-Hanau Order Book

the rebels, and for having shown his own intention of deserting.

The End

Rosters Of The Hesse-Hanau Hereditary Prince Infantry Regiment Pausch Artillery Company The Chasseur Corps and Hesse-Cassel Recruits

Rosters

Roster of the Hesse-Hanau Hereditary Prince Infantry Regiment

Staff - [Mustered Nijmegen, 22 March 1776]
QM - 2nd Lt. Charles Augusta Sartorius
Auditor - Paul Guillaume Schefer
Chaplain - Erneste Theobald
Aide - Jacques Heerwagen
Armorer - Philippe Hein
Surgeon Major - Jeremie Heidelbach
Drum Major - Leonhard Klie
Provost - Adam Urbach
Provost's Valet - Jean Schmidt
Musicians - Adam Muller; Andre Emmert;
   Christophle Justorf; George Justorf;
   Jean Andra; and Jean Rabe

Company Colonel Gall - [Mustered Nijmegen, 22 March 1776]
Colonel - Guillaume Rudolphi Gall and his batman
   Captain - Charles Auguste Scheel (Absent on QM matters), and his batman
2nd Lt. - Frederic Geyling, and his batman
Ensign - Henry Siebert, and his batman
1st Sgt - Jean George Eiffert
Sgt - Christophle Dehnhard
Sgt Nicolas Beist
QM Sgt - Henry Krug

Rosters

Captain-at-arms - Caspar Eckel
Surgeon - Jean George Gruge
Color Bearer - George Baumert
Corporal - Jean Schmidt
Corporal - Adam Kolepp
Drummers - Michael Reichmann; Jean Philippe Wissenbach; Caspar Starck

Anspesades

Henry Bommersheim
George Stamm
Henry Deckmann
Nicolas Lotz

Nicolas Kressel
Sebastian Metzler
Chretien Muller
Conrad Gruner

Soldiers

Conrad Forter
Adam Zipf
Jean Klue
Guillaume Becker
Daniel Charles Boos
Michael Alter
Conrad Klees
Caspar Kitz
Christophle Donges
Augustin Velten
Jean Manckel
Henry Schumm
Jean Traut
Jean Schmitt, Med.
Philippe Crass

Maurice Lehr
Godefroid Westphal
Jean Mercker
Philippe Seibert
Jean Schmidt, Sr.
Philippe Charles Tack
Francois Scmid
Martin Muller
Guillaume Treulieb
Conrad Heyl
Conrad Behr
Jean Kester
Philippe Traut
George Conrad
Johanne Bruhmann

Rosters

Conrad Zeul
Conrad Bender
Etienne Kunes
Adam Amend
Michael Stock
Pierre Schonburger
George Frederic Diehl
Pierre Breitwiesser
Philippe Menck
Caspar Hess
Nicolas Werner
Jean Wachtershauser
Jean Homann
Conrad Hinckel
George Beist
Jean Fehl
Jean Kaus
Henry Diehl
George Freyensener
Jacques Gering
Frederic Frischkorn
Jean Lindebauer
Wendel Kammerer
Ulric Zeth
Pierre Fix
Pierre Engel
Jean Seelich
Johannes Kammerer

Conrad Spahn
Michael Bartold
Henry Beck
George Beck
Johannes Kammerer
Laurent Kessler
Jean Liller
Henry Hufner
Chretien Schefer
Melchior Schmitt
George Heyl
Auguste Bender
Caspar Klober
Conrad Henzel
Conrad Lowenstein
Conrad Werheim
Jean Bartman
Henry Aumann
Adam Henzler
Christophle Traut
Henry Kunkel
Pierre Stroh
Jean Muller
Martin Schefer
Guillaume Arnold
Jean Will
Nicolas Cress
Nicolas Door

Rosters

Company Lieutenant Colonel Lentz, Mustered at Nijmegen, 22 March 1776

Lt. Col. Jean Christophle Lentz, and his batman
Captain Frederic Geismar, and his batman
2nd Lt. Charles Lindau, and his batman
Ensign Frederic Louis Kampfer, and his batman
1st Sgt Hernry Staasy
Sgt. Melchior Kolepp
Sgt. Caspar Claus
QM Sgt. Louis Becker
Captain-at-arms Adam Kirchhof
Corporals Andrea Koch; Jean Sauer;
Color Bearer George Frederic Schellenberg
Drummers Jean Weber; Louis Rauch; and Martin Heck

Anspesades

Nicolas Jahn	Nicolas Zehner
Guilllaume Muller	Conrad Bach
Isaac Bauscher	Caspar Linck
Henry Voltz	Charles Knoblaoch

Soldiers

Valentin Bolst	Charles Weibling
Charles Schott	Henry Kunkel
Henry Krieg	Jean Schenck
Panorave Hassner	Jean Rub
Nicolas Schmidt	Caspar Henning
Conrad Roth	Conrad Muller
Henry Uhrledig	Henry Westphal

Rosters

Nicolas Klie	Henry Behr
Nicolas Beist	Pierre Zehner
Philippe Bender	Henry Resch
Nicolas Uffermann, Sr.	Nicolas Resch
Philippe Muller	Henry Schilling, Sr.
Conrad Bremer	Daniel Klier
Michail Huffner	Nicolas Kolb
Jean Beck	Pierre Schwab
Philippe Petri	Caspar Epp
Henry Alt	Michael Adami
Henry Lehberg	Leonhard Kratz
Pierre Geyer	Jean Zinckhan
Jean Merbott	Frederic Koch
Wendel Leib	Conrad Voltz
Conrad Manche	Nicolas Hammann
Jean Madern	Jean Blumler
Thome Petri	Pierre Schroeder
Nicolas Uffermann, Jr.	Henry Faber
Jean Lotz	George Gobel
Jean Weigand	Conrad Bauer
Henry Stickel	Jean Rau
George Vogel Berger	Laurent Kramer
Walter Best	Pierre Mahlo
Pierre Hartmann	Christophle Still
Philippe Baumann	Henry Schilling, Jr.
Valentin Fix	Pierre Weissenstein
Henry Pulver	Pierre Hetterich
Pierre Weigand	Adam Rub

Rosters

Jean See
Michael Kunckel
Laurent Borckmann
Adam Scchwab
Nicolas Alter
Jean Schwind
Hartmann Weil
Christophle Gurker

Charles Zorbach
Conrad Schreiner
Nicolas Keiser
Nicolas Horn
Jacques Frantz
Philippe Reges
Engelbert Kappes

Rosters

Company of Major Martens, Mustered at
Nijmegen, 22 March 1776

Major Henry Martens (as captain), and his batman
Captain Frederic Louis Schoell (as 1st Lt.), and his batman
2nd Lt. Louis Canorinus, and his batman
Ensign Louis Hohorst, and his batman
1st Sgt. Auguste Kitz
QM Sgt. Nicolas Stoppel
Sgts. - Henry Manikel, and Adam Metzler
Captain-at-arms Henry Keisser
Color Bearer Henry Fuhr
Corporals - Jean Orth, and George Beiker
Drummers - Chretien Leonhard; George Schreiber; and Jean Neunobel

Anspesades

Henry Motter	Jean Enrick
Henry Freiter	Jean Behr
Jean Schefer, Jr.	Conrad Beiker
Nicolas Ungar, Med.	Philippe Trau

Soldiers

Sigmond Bender	Philippe Bensing
Caspar Schmitt	Jean Senzel
Conrad Ruppel	Pierre Gruner
J0ean Gumbel	Andre Ebert
Pierre Hammann	Guillaume Breidenbach
Philippe Honnig	Daniel Waller, Jr.
Andre Ungar, Sr.	Valentin Bauscher

Rosters

Adam Zipsy	Esare Klinkershus
Jean Obrish	Adam Vetton
Henry Scherer	Henry Krafft
Caspar Gobel	Philippe Heyl
Henry Schwab	Jean Schuler
Marten Voltz	Andre Ungar, Jr.
Louis Roth	Caspar Borner
Caspar Rul	Frederic Farber
Guillaume Bertz	Balhasar Muller
Jean Lehr	Jean Roth
Martin Hurh	Jean Seiler
Conrad Traband	George Rullmann
Jean Braumann	Guillaume Merschel
Philippe Henrich	Henry Schwarzhaupt
Henry Mertz	Conrad Schmitt
Jean Muller, Jr.	Christophle Krein
Conrad Simon	Laurent Baussum
Jean Gutermuth	Henry Henzel
Jean Broll	Caspar Muller
George Hachenberger	Philippe Krebs
George Siegel	Philippe Locher
Jean Hoffmann	Frederic Bernges
Jean Traband	Jean Ohl
Laurent Werner	George Dettler
Henry Brust	Henry Crest
Jean Bauscher	Paul Schlaush
Henry Reitz	Philippe Roth
Louis Bugler	Henry Bender

Rosters

George Stein
Christophle May
Balthasar Diehl
Balthasar Schefer
Laurent Werheim
Jean Jolepp
Jean Lotz
Jean Weyd

George Schmitt
Henry Linck
Theodor Dechert
Guilllaume Obrich
Thome Schad
Auguste Weimar
Sebastian Kratz

Rosters

Company Captain Germann, Mustered at Nijmegen, 22 March 1776

Captain Frederic Germann, and his batman
1st Lt. Maurice Buttlar, and his batman
2nd Lt. Chretiern Eschwege, and his batman
Ensign Ernest Weyhers, and his batman
1st Sgt. Samuel Vaupel
QM Sgt. Henry Lentz
Sgts. - Philippe Schefer; Henry Orth
Surgeon Guillaume Gottschalck
Captain-at-arms Frederic Bockel
Color Bearer Jacques Haumann
Corporals - Pierre Weber; George Vempel
Drummers - Guillaume Giese; Jacques Gewalt; and George Kitz

Anspesades

Hieronime Schweinsberger	Philippe Heinzinger
Henry Kohller	Henry Beuker
Jean Schoner	Jean Koch
Jean Zimmermann	Christophle Wiskerman

Soldiers

Philippe Walt	Jacques Pfaff
Philippe Bruckmann	Henry Fischer
Conrad Orth	Pierre Ewalt
Daniel Ruffer	Conrad Krieg
Frederic Weingartner	Conrad Traut
Jean Kohler	Philippe Lange
Louis Hoene	Frederic Stein

Rosters

Paul Breidenbach	Conrad Finzel
George Mahr	Philippe Ruhl
Philippe Mahr	Jean Lind
Conrad Morter	Jean Weil Sickenberger
Philippe Klinckerfus	Jean Henzel
Jean Hallatschka	Henry Eidelenz
Jean Schauberger	George Kolepp
Guillaume Lotz	Caspar Kempf
Philippe Hinckel	Daniel Bechtold
Jean Lack	Philippe Bockel
Conrad Bickes	Caspar Maul
Joachim Rauch	Urban Hiessner
Jean Weizel	Andre Bieling
Jean Glas	Conrad Reis
Melchior Parner	Jean Datzner
Jean Adam Bolender	Andre Krafft
Caspar Weltor	Caspar Kolepp
Jacques Tack	Hartmann Groth
George Charles Unger	Frederic Christ
Jean Seltzer	Jean Lapp
Michael Herber	Jean Bellinger
Guillaume Engelhard	Pierre Stein
George Schadel	Conrad Sommerlade
Nicolas Schmitt	Conrad Ewald
Christophle Diehl	Caspar Bechtel
Jacques Eiffert	George Ziegl;er
Caspar Backer	Philippe Lemung
Conrad Krebs	Adam Jost

Rosters

George Conrad Fuhr
Melchior Schmitt
Jacques Schmitt
Charles Lentz
Jean Rosenberger
Pierre Bode
Fredceric Keiser
Etienne Linck

Christophle Henrich
Conrad Schefer
Nicolas Pohl
Conrad Schlinglust
Pierre Fengel
Jean Filsinger
Jacques Schaffer

Rosters

Hanau Infantry Recruits, Mustered at
Nijmegen, 15 March 1777
Ensign Guillaume Geyling, and his batman
QM Sgt. Charles Frederic Zipf
Color Bearers - Fraancois Pape; Charles Christople Metzger; and Chretien Freericv Werner
Fifer Conrad Ziewe
Drummer George Hoffmann

Soldiers

Gottlieb Muller	Conrad Schimming
Chretien Kuntzly	Michael Remy
Guilllaume Grimm	Jean Herrmann
Xavier Gruber	George Aufleider
Jean Gruber	Thadeus Hemmerle
George Spengler	Pierre Hoffmann
George Rappert	Chretien Muller ***
Louis Theodor Burckhard	Chretien Keppenhahn
Conrad Stein	George Muhl
Guillaume Frederic Linss	Leonhard Heyl
Paul Anschultz	Christople Wideram
Adolph Zehner	Conrad Fires
Engelhard Ludwig	Jost Kohler
Andreas Diehl	Philippe Dietz
Michael Brodbeck	George Bechtold
Jean Trabandl	Jacques Pfeiffer
Jean Muller, Sr.	Jean Werling
Jean Linss	Jean Mayer
Nicolas Bohm	George Funck

Rosters

Henry Heidenreich	Adam Kirchner
Jean Muller, Jr.***	Pierre Kenner
Tobia Jacobi	Jean Fischer
Ehrenfrid Knoch	Martin Zinckhan
George Korn	Thoma Schneider
Gottlieb Krancke	Jean Iffland
Adam Mergenthal	Gerhard Schmidt
Martin Meuer	Conrad Bayer
Henry Mayer	Frederic Mayer
Jean Haussner	Charles Frederic Sohl
Jean Fuss	Adam Uhl
Balthasar Knauss	Valentin Christenz
Henry Iffland	Maurice Becker***
Philippe Holl	Conrad Spielmann

*** Deserted in Holland on 24 March 1777

Rosters

Hanau Infantry Recruits, Mustered at Hanau, 12 November 1777

Auditor Conrad Wachs
QM Sgt. Henry Henzel
Corporal Caspar Zeh
Surgeons - Chretien Klemm; Guillaume Schitter; and Auguste Robat
Drummers - Conrad Seebach; Samuel Otto; and Conrad Drill

Soldiers

Jean Bewalle
Jacques Fleischmann
Reinhard Merckel
Antoine Marowfsky
Jean Crest
Theophile Schauer
Eckhard Happel
Henry Feuerbach
Louis Berard
Theodor Kling, Jr.
Henry Nubel
Leonhard Krieg
Christoph Ballas
Henry Holger
Etienne Gambel
Jean Lindner
Conrad Dummler
Michael Hirsch
Louis Heisterreich
Henry David
George Deschmar
Guillaumes Veith
Paul Hermann
Frederic Mullner
Jacques Kling, Sr.
Frederic Hessler, Jr.
Jacques Datz
Christoph Hessler, Sr.
George Topfer
George Siebert
Hermann Bange
Balthasar Ermentraut
Joseph Menzer
Kraft Hofmann
Michel Geschke
Jacques Wemzel

Rosters

Anselme Spanier	George Bender
Guillaume Diefenbach	Christoph Dummler
Valentin Christanz	Jean Sulger
Balthasar Klentsch	Chretien Schwalm
Jean Bornkessel	Christoph Kuhn
Nicolas Lange	Jean Barth
Chretien Humrich	Henry Keller
Guillaume Muss	Jean Para
Frederic Georgi	George Braunkart
Jean Gscheidle	George Loter
Conrad Emmerich	George Gischer
Antoine Knapp	Adam Brior
Frederic Hieronymus	Andre Weber
Conrad Jacobi	Leopold Rohre
Henry Rasch	Henry Felger
Joachim Muller	George Rottner
Caspar Weber	Jean Korn
Christoph Franisko	Adam Leick
George Kraus	Valentin Stock
Nicolas Rodiger	Jacques Haag
Jean Beil	Joachim Betzel
Louis Reichenbach	Adam Bauer
Jean Vicario	Christoph Ganss
Etienne Rosch	Caspar Schad
Joseph Butz	Philipp Mehrling
Nicolas Kreckel	Michel Asmus
Adam Weimar	George Nauheimer
Benjamin Capitsky	Jean Zinck

Rosters

Jacques Werner
Daniel Cramer
Christoph Schmoll
Francois Fetzer
Jean Kertzner
Francois Hofmann
Henry Schmid
Louis Heicke
Frederic Kretzler
Caspar Schuch
Philipp Werner
Theophile Berens
Martin Diehl
Jean Rullmann
Henry Gotz
Henry Feul
Michel Kessler
Martin Bross

Joachim Maisch
Henry Cramer
Gottlieb Stier
Antoine Baldauf
Godefroy Hofmann
Philipp Gerhard
Jean Porbach
Jean Porth
Jean Wilhelm
Michel Hiller
Nicolas Schnetter
Henry Stoll
Frederic Hopfenrath
Henry Schneider
Caspar Heck
Leonhard Bauer
Jean Gunckel

(23651, f 32; f 33; f 34; f 107, 22 Mar 76; f 91, 15 Mar 77; f 117, 24 Mar 77; f 222, 12 Nov 77)

Rosters

Hesse-Hanau Artillery Company of Captain Pausch, Mustered at Nijmegen, 24 May 1776

Captain Georg Pausch (or Peusch or Paeusch), and his batman
1st Lt. Guillaume Dufais, and his batman
2nd Lt. George Dittmar Spangenberg, and his batman
2nd Lt. Michael Bach, and his batman
Surgeon Herman Melchior Eberths
Drummers - Ulrich Schreiber; Jean Keysser; and Jacques Billiu

Bombardiers

Jean Moerschell	Louis Saltzmann
Conrad Wall	Jean Muller
Charles Louis Hausmann	Jacques Leiss
Jean Frederic Wochler	Jean Hoff
Jean Louis Enosse	Jacques Engelhard
George Henry Dickhaut	

Cannoneers

George Tempell	Henry Muller
Gottlob Louis Gallafres	Guillaume List
Phillipe Schneider	Asmus Goede
Philippe Fintzell	Jean Doerrbecker
Pierre Bauer	Conrad Hamann
Jean George Lora	Conrad Schmiett
Conrad Horst	Andre Lotz
Jean Paul Kustner	Frederic Lempect
Wenzell Biehl	Balthasar Loos

Rosters

Conrad Bangerd	Michel Uffelmann
George Seltzer	Jean Orbach
Henry Paul Stroh	Pierre Eichmann
Henry Uffer	Jacques Born
David Zorbach	Pierre Diehl
Joachim Leibold	Guillaume Lochmann
Henry Nantz	Mathias Bender
Thomas Fils	Jean Pflug
Nicolas Bender	George Klempell
Caspar Ermetraut	Pierre Sentzell
Pierre Scheffer	George Heyd
George Zorbach	Paul Hartmann
Pierre Kappes	Jean Muller, Sr.
Bernhard Braun	Jean Guillaume Boch
Michel Paul	Pierre Waller
Hartmann Hess	Jean Schroder
Henry Koerber	Michel Willmann
Valentin Raab	Jean David Pfulfer
Jacques Keittell	Henry Zohn
Jean George Schwab	Thomas Weil
Louis Elsesser	Jean George Reck
Jean Lotz	Jean Petzinger
Adam Hansellmann	Thiery Reuter
Chretien Koch	Balthasar Hoffmann
Christophle Haenischfeeger	Jacques Leonard
Jean Muller, Jr.	Jeremie Bischoff
Pierre Metzler	Jean George Walter
Conrad Hahn	Henry Orbach

Rosters

Jean Forbaon	Frederic Scheefer
Pierre Wegmann	Pierre Funck
Jean George Becker	Nicolas Sentzell
Nicolas Wectzell	Jean Rossmer
Frederic Rutscher	Balthasar Lochmann
Jean Kohber	Caspar Roerber
Philippe Haut	Augustus Erdmann
Pierre Ernstdorff	Jean Adam Krebs

Wagonmaster Jean George Zicklamm
Master Marshal Henry Broct
Marshal of the Company Nicolas Muller
Master Wheelwright Jean Lossberger
Company Wheelwright Caspar Spahn
Saddle Maker Bernhard Eichellmann
Master Valet Daniel Keysser

Valet d'Artillerie

Jean Haarenfeenger	Pierre Quelmann
Jean Gottlieb Hatler	Hubert Fuchs
Michel Schmidt	Michel Heckmann
Jean Thomas Roth	Joseph Felsenheim
Jean George Siebert	Jean Pierre Focht
Mathias Kuhn	Jean Kihron

Rosters

Artillery Recruits, Mustered at Nijmegen, 15 March 1777

Bombardier Charles Frederic Hestermann
Surgeon Eberhard Unger

Cannoneers

Jean Dorr	Bernhard Sschenger
Andree Hoffmann	Andree Muller
George Zischler	George Bandel
Jean Spahn	Pierre Rapp
George Haenlein	Jacque Ecker
Sebastienne Kreuzer	Adam Kappes
Michael Simon	Chrretien Weber
Valentin Heyl	Conrad Orbel
George Hab	Mathia Haupt
Jean Leschhern	Francois Michael Menzer
Jean Frischkorn	Chretien Finck
Gregor Schaeffer	Leonhardt Schmidt
Jean Handel	

Artillery Recruits, Mustered at Hanau, 12 November 1777

Cannoneer

Daniel Bauer	Jean Remshard
Christoph Sauerwein	George Pahr
Henry Happel	Jean Fredrich
Daniel Hennig	Conrad Knorr

Rosters

Jacques Huber	Joseph Elzer
Philipp Klein	Leonhard Meyer
Conrad Kuhn	Philipp Grubenstein
Elias Bleich	Rudolph Fleckstein
Nicolas Volmert	Conrad Unschuck
Jean Olgen	Jean Mertz
Martin Stroh	Jean Traband
Bernhard Fischer	Frederic Hildner
Frederic Desselberger	Conrad Sauer
George Schmid	Caspar Fischer
Jean Jahn	Adam Carl

(23651, f 44, 24 May 76; f 91, 15 Mar 77; f 222, 12 Nov 77)

The Artilllery Company rosters were previously published in *Georg Pausch's Journal and Reports of the Campaign in America,* Bruce E. Burgoyne's translation, published by Heritage Books, Inc. (Bowie, Md., 1996)

Rosters

Hesse-Hanau Chasseur Corps

Staff, Mustered at Nijmegen, 11 April 1777

Adjutant Wilhelm von den Velden
Auditor Reinhard Kaup
Surgeon Major Xavier Bender
Provost Neumeister
Armorers - Justus Bergstraesser and Johann Richter
Regimental QM Ernst Staudinger
Valet de Charriot - Lorentz Wagemann, Christian Weinlein; Michel Dieterich; Leonhard Ortner; and Michel Wurtz

Staff, Mustered at Quebec, 4 August 1783

Provost George Neumeister
Armorers - Jean Richter and Justus Bergstraesser
Valet de Charriot - Leonhard Ortner and Caspar Mack

Company Lieutenant Colonel Creuzbourg
Mustered at Nijmegen, 11 April 1777

Lt. Col. Creuzbourg (as Captain), and his batman
1st Lt. Siegmont Storck, and his batman
2nd Lt. Friederich Jung, and his batman
Sgt. Major Christian Horn
Sgt. Carl Filzhoffer
QM Sgt. Simon Creuzbourg
Captain-at-arms Martin Simon

Rosters

Surgeon Nicolas Mezler
Corporals - Eckart Menzell; Conrad Loltig; Reichenhard Horst; Ludwig Krafft; Daniel Sternbring, and Caspar Hoehn (in America)
Corps de Chaisse - Andreas Henssel; Adam Pfeiffer; and Friederich Clauss

Chasseurs

Michael Trumper	Jacob Muller
Christian Kuckumus	Paul Fuchs
Herrnrich Thoene	Herrnrich Christanz
Conrad Henning	Johann Weissenstein
Friederich Nolte	Conrad Nenzell
Johann Bockell	Conrad Rolffs
Herrnrich Keibb	Rudolph Rach
Wilhelm Schwarz	Christian Wiessener
Adam Kruling	Johann Pfeiffer
Christian Fischer	Balthasar Maier
Michael Mangell	Friederich Hirschberger
Christian Schlatterer	Johann Hoffmann
Friederich Strebel	Gottlieb Spatz
Anthon Griessinger	Wilhelm Schneider
Anthon Karbbe	Heinrich Hammel
Anthon Massorea	Peter Bermes
Friederich Streich	Balthasar Hoffmann
Anthon Grundler	Matheus Rumpf
Johann Dornmer	Gottfried Boetger
Christian Eppinger	Christian Aumhauer
Georg Stern	Christian Holzerner

Rosters

Anthon Emmerich
Frantz Reischel
Thomas Schaeffer
Georg Nieding
Conrad Glatterer
Johann Wittmann
Heinrich Lauer
Wilhelm Muller
Johann Kulung
Adam Bangert
Johann Wenderich
Christian Hildebrand
Matheus Obrich
Johann Berg
Friederich Moos
Christoph Berg
Christian Low
Jacob Sentner
Caspar Spahn
Michel Gluck
Friederich Dorffer
Johann Danz
Heinrich Jordan
Michel Weidner
Heinrich Schmidt
Gottfried Kressler

Gottfried Marreck
Frederich Grauling
Julius Peter
Johann Korn
Johann Rauch
Conrad Dufft
Bernhard Donges
Johann Fischer
Johann Kuhn
Johann Schmitt
Lorentz Teller
Jacob Schaeffer
Christoph Baier
Philipp Wagner
Conrad Reichenbach
Christian Bode
Conrad Fluhrer
Johann Roppert
Friederich Bayer
Johann Weber
Urban Muller
Conrad Roppert
Christian Tramm
Caspar Degen
Andreas Kuntze

Rosters

Company Colonel Creuzbourg,
Mustered at Quebec, 4 August 1783

QM Sgt. Frederic Graeter
Corporals - Frederic Peters; Adam Raubenheimer;
Conrad Rolfs; and Antoine Grundler

Chasseurs

Julius Peter
George Fischer
Sammuel Hermann
Frederic Dorffer
Chretien Low
Guillaume Muller
Henri Hammell
Jean Kuwatsch
Henri Jordan
Guillaume Hildebrand
Gebhard Nieding
Conrad Reichenbach
Conrad Muller
Jean Hoffmann
Jean Filzhofer
Christophle Epppinger
Erhard Egner
Conrad Dufft
Conrad Fluhner
Chretien Wiesner
Jean Dantz

Chretien Fischer
Jean Korn
Caspar Degen
Pierre Schattack
Gottlieb Spatz
Henri (no other name)
Adam Bangert
George Helmuth
Guillaume Kunsitler
Jean Jaeckell
Jacques Kulong
George Trumper
Joseph Grysingher
Jacques Hoffmann
George Schusmmer
Conrad Klatterer
Rudolphe Rach
Pierre Reill
Godefroid Marreck
Pierre Boland
August Neuburger

Rosters

Godefroid Boetger	Andre Henssell
Jean Muller	Chretien Zurcker
Jacques Schaefer	Philippe Wagner
Frederic Hensse	Conrad Roppert
Bernhard Doenges	Chretien Wenderich
Charles Weissenstein	Frederic Gratsch
Chretien Bobe	Jean Stubenhauer
Henri Schroth	Henri Hein
Andre Lauer	Conrad Bodenbinder
George Baier	Jean Bauer
Henri Grauling	Guillaume Schneider
Conrad Henzell	Christoph Baier
Jean Roppert	Pierre Muller

Rosters

Company Captain Francken, Mustered at Nijmegen, 11 April 1777

Captain Hermann Albrecht Francken, and batman, Wilhelm Metzler
1st Lt. Adolphe Neuberg Leth, and his batman, Cornelius Ringeler
2nd Lt. Johan August Kraft, and his batman, Johannes Nicks
Sgt. Major Ernst Wilhelme
Sgt. Carl Wuth
QM Sgt. Johan Ludow Dosch
Captain-at-arms August Einfeld
Corporals - Kukemus (in America); Wilhelm Krauss; Johan Friedrich Roos; Carl Wittmann; Jacob Corel; and Anthon Most
Surgeon Gotthilf Borgius
Corps de Chaisse - Johan Herman Winckler; Conrad Gertmann; and Peter Heilman

Chasseurs

Christoph Dahn	Emanuel Costenbader
Stephan Gottschalck	Joseph Bentz
Martin Eidam	Georg Menges
Johan Leonhard Pillmann	Conrad Fischer
Johan Georg Krass	Friedrich Gehring
Georg Bruchhoff	Carl Antoine
Johannes Hofmann	Henrich Rapp
Johan Winter	Phillip Stickel

Rosters

Valentinn Stahl	Jacob Rossmann
Johannes Heller	Johannes Wust
Nicolas Krebs	August Schuster
Friedrich Utz	Franz Siebenhaar
Joseph Schlaug	Georg Geiger
Johannes Lotz	Johannes Ruppel
Georg Bach	Phillip Starck
Georg Hofmann	Carl Kulb
Johaannes Munter	Johannes Muller
Peter Rath	Johan Martin
Johan Peter Wiesenecker	Christoph Werner
Heinrich Umstatter	Joseph Eickel
Ludwig Trober	Wilhelm Hufnagel
Joseph Trostler	Johannes Findel
Conrad Lauch	Peter Jockel
Martin Amman	Ludwig Nohr
Wilhelm Fuhrmann	Wilhelm Roth
Mathias Heyl	Johann Wagener
Ludwig Wagener	Jost Friederick
Johann Eickel	Heinrich Zimmerman
Adam Stephan	Lorenz Maefai
Heinrich Stein	Georg Major
Johann Neizel	Antoine Roos
Leonhard Kitzsteiner	Michael Lederer
Johannes Fetter	Christian Port
Wilhelm Schmitt	Adam Schlereth
Balthasar Braun	Georg Theilheimer
Erhard Koch	Jacob Hufschmith

Rosters

Marcus Pflug
Caspar Schnabel
Phillip Hauser
Johannes Ifland
Georg Stilling
Phillip Diderich
Johannes Seydil
Caspar Hock
Johan Herman Kessler
Georg Geiselmeyer
Friederich Muller
Johannes Atlon
Mathias Meyer

Anthon Roth
Simon Gyldner
Paul Geisler
Peter Ebersbach
Andreas Kobbel
Georg Knabenschug
Caspar Mack
Johannes Erck
Martin Bentz
Jacob Schmith
Michael Steinberger
David Frey

Company Major Francken, Mustered at Quebec, 4 August 1783

Sgt. Conrad Amman
QM Sgt. Frederic Pforius
Corporals - Dominic Baumbronn and Martin Eydam

Chasseurs

Daniel Crammer
Antoine Regenbogen
Jean Zorn
George Theilheimer
Pierre Heillmann
Frederic Munnich
Henri Pelz

Conrad Gerthmann
Jacques Rossmann
Adam Schlerett
Chretien Porth
Jean Armbrecht
August Glaubenskind
Godefroid Bauer

Rosters

Francois Veith	Frederic Wagner
Jean Martin	Jean Boehmreuther
Joseph Ergell	Jean Klebonitz
Pierre Jockell	Jean Kunkler
George Bach	Joseph Trostler
Jean Latz	Philippe Kunger
Henri Heinnemann	Mathieu Heill
Henri Rapp	Andre Moller
Nicolas Krebs	Liborie Hertz
Jean Wagner	Jacques Schmith
Chretien Stemmetz	August Schuster
George Stilling	Jean Schneider
Henri Stein	Francois Siebenhaar
George Knabenschuhe	Guillaume Poehrer
Laurent Ehrensperger	David Frey
Joseph Bentz	Michel Steger
Guillaume Schmith	Stephan Gottschall
Wolfgang Siry	Theodor Moyer
Guillaume Wolff	Leonhad Nol
Jean Frantz	Jean Adlon
Michel Dietrich	Jean Fetter
Michel Liederer	Charles Thienell
Jean Leibenfeder	Mathieu Meyer
Anthoine Barthell	Simon Gildner
Simon Beaudair	George Gerger
Lucas Barban	George Berner

Rosters

Company Captain Wittgenstein, Mustered at
Nijmegen, 11 April 1777

Captain Wittgenstein, and his batman, Jean Eberhard
   Mattheus
1st Lt. Meijern, and his batman (no name)
2nd Lt. Hochstetter, and his batman, Jean Martin
   Richter
Sgt. Major Frederic Dehrn
Sgt. Chretien Stauberand
QM Sgt. Daniel Krug (in America)
Captain-at-arms Jean Adam Bormann
Corporals - Henri Auguste Weinrich; George Keyser;
   Jean Caspar Klozbuger; Joseph Bosen; Jean Pierre
   Ziegenhayn; and Jean George Meijn
Surgeon - Jean Conrad Ullrich
Corps de Chaisse - Adam Klein; Jean Funck; and Elias
   Schneider

Chasseurs

Jacob Landoehr	Frederic Singer
Carl Frederic Salomo Friderici	Andre Bernheimer
Joseph Fuchs	Jean George Weiss
Guillaume Kunstler	Michael Steinbach
Christophle Semmingen	Jean Leonhard Holzberger
Jean Henri Kreisther	Jacques Kurz
Valentin Scheid	Adam Simon

Rosters

Chretien Schroeder
Jean Frederic Deries
George Beitniz
Pierre Francisce Alsdorf
Jean Gottlob Richter
Jean Chretien Jackisch
Jean Henri Fischer
Anton Chretien Schaefer
Jean Riedel
Jean Fasnacht
Chretien Guillaume
    Nungesser
Jean Bernard Deisinger
Gottefrid Stein
Wendel Umm
Jean Paul Heerdt
Andre Schmid
George Collignon
Adam Hofmann
Charles Gras
Jean Hartmann
Francisce Holzer
Henri Wolf
Pierre Albert
Nicolas Krafft
Jean George Umpfenbach
Jacque Henckel
Michael Meinone

Daniel Fiesele
Jean Ofermann
Caspar Busch
Gottefrid Roose
Jean Henri Larch
Frederic Knab
George Paul Muller
Henri Turck
Jean Henri Fatschel
Frederic Georgi

George Wagner
Chretien Dieterich
Dietrich Heyl
Jean Philipp Schmid
Jean Hermann
Andre Heinlein
Jean Gottefrid Seibt
Jean Geist
Jean Becker
Jean Daniel Thomas
Jean George Finsterer
Frederic Kunckel
Valentin Steinmacher
Jean Bender
Daniel Zellmann
Caspar Wolf
Pierre Hessler

Rosters

Jacque Kummerle
Jean Henri Gluth
Louis Grimm
Jean Dreher
Jean Philipp Wilckens
Benjamin Schmorr
Pierre Pfeiffer
Nicolas Koll
Joseph Erwin Alsdorf
Philipp Heijn
Christophle Klug
Jean Koch
Frederic Weiss
Benjamin Gotz
Gottefrid Ammon

Conrad Rhein
Christophle Burckhard
Jacque Dieterich
Guillaume Roges
Louis Steger
Daniel Meijen
Pierre Schneider
Jean Roth
Jean George Vehler
Joseph Batz
Nicolas Emmerich
Jean Frederic Rhein
Theophil Hazdorf
Henri Schreiber

Company Captain Wittgenstein, Mustered at Quebec, 4 August 1783

Sgt. Antoine Most
QM Sgt. Henri Lerch
Corporals - Caspar Busch; Frederic Storr; George Meijn; and Pierre Ziegenhain

Chasseurs

Valentin Scheid
George Finsterer
Guillaume Schilling
Jean Bender

Adam Klein
Paul Herth
Francois Holzer
Philippe Hein

Rosters

Jacques Henkell
Jacques Bauer
Michel Meinone
Frederic Kunckell
Paul Muller
Jean Passnacht (Fassnacht?)
Laurent Wagemann
Pierre Hessler
Jean Schaum
Henri Fischer
Godlieb Mauck
Caspar Claus
Guillaume Singer
Christophle Seinimgen
Henri Fatschell
Guillaume Nongesser
George Prosy
Andre Heinlein
Valentin Schmith
Christophle Kuhlmann
Chretien Hoehn
Christophle Burckard
Charles Krass
Henri Eissenkolben
Conrad Albert
Andre Schmith
Conrad Rhein
Francois Huck

Jean Dreher
Benjamin Schmorr
Benjamin Goetz
Frederic Michaetis
Godefroid Kellerstein
Bernhard Emmerich
Philippe Schmith
Henri Schreiber
Joseph Batz
Jean Becker
Dietrich Heill
Jean Ifflandt
Leonhard Diller
Martin Stamin
Frederic Knab
Godefroid Ammon
Frederic Rhein
Guillaume Reges
Bernhard Ritter
Daniel Thomas
Martin Thiser
Nicolas Kohle
Francois Guthsmith
Henri Claus
Martin Stamm
Godefroid Roose
Henri Holzhaussen
Adam Hoffmann

Rosters

Leonhard Holzberger
Jacques Kummerle
Francois Alsdorff
Christophle Graetschmann
Daniel Zellmann
Jean Hermann

Jean Ditzell
Erwin Alsdorff
Georg Beithnitz
Elias Schneider
Bernhard Deissinger

Rosters

Company Captain Kornrumpf, Mustered at Nijmegen, 15 March 1777

Captain Caspar Henry Kornrumpf, and his batman
1st Lt. Philip Jacque Hildebrand, and his bat man
2nd Lt. George Scheurer, and his batman
1st Sgt. Frederich Schaffer
Sgt. Jean Finck
QM Sgt. Jean Beyer
Captain-at-arms Caspar Grill
Corporals - Jacques Meyer; Conrad Hartz; Louis Schwimmer; Guillaume Beck; Jacques Meyer; Jacque Fuhr (in America); and Joseph Pirie (held at Mainz)
Surgeon Sebastienne Burgi

Chasseurs

Frederich Krug	Chretien Schmidt
David Diehon	Jean Heerich
Pierre Spielmann	Henry Spangerberg
George Fuhr	George Wille
Christophle Durbeck	Jean Voelp
Jean Ebert	Valentin Assehau
Henry Lindebauer	Henry Krebs
Henry Hensch	Charle Finck
Adam Funck	Fredrich Wimmer
Christopphle Krosser	Chretien Eckell
Henry Schopner	Mathias Prod

Rosters

Jacque Schmidt (held at Mainz)	George Krum
Adam Spahn	Pierre Reymont
Henry Stahrenfenger	Lambert Baehr
Antoine Geckell	Henry Moller
Conrad Schnabel	Pierre Brand
Henry Kaip	Jean Werner
Gottleib Bedlich	Samuel Wittsack
Guillaume Hartmann	Jean Gerbhard
Louis Heine	Babtiste Streitel
Michael Engel	George Deissing
Pierre Rupert (held at Mainz)	Henry Mebius
Guillaume Kratz	Jean Stroth
Jean Greff	Feorge Wallisser
Daniel Bauch	Hartman Voigt
Conrad Silberling	Nicolas Weigand
Michael Schaffer	Ernst Sturm
Joseph Reinhardt	Melchior Kirsch
Albert Kling	George Weibell
Philippe Bauscher	Melchior Mack
Samuel Stentzell	Conrad Schultz
Oswald Weigand	Jean Diehl
Conrad Feith	Caspar Kurtz
Jost Stein	Frederich Bretreich
Jacque Bruekfieb	Frederich Bruekfieb
Nicolas Wagner	Henry Hilchen
Henry Bohm	Jean Kalkhoff
Paul Schuckard	Louis Zipf

Rosters

Chretien Lemaire	George Vehs
Henry Riede	Ernst Gerhard
Antoine Jordan	Nicolas Matheus
George Schaffer	Caspar Reitz
Leonhard Weinem	Martin Dettman
Jean Kopp	Alexandre Freiburger
Guillaume Martin	Jospeh Kessler
Philip Schluchterlein	Michael Schneider
Lorent Ilten	Nicolas Gullery
George Paster	George Pannemuller
Conrad Schaffer	Henry Heygefeldt
Balthasar Seibert	Jean Diehl
Henry Fahrein	

Company Captain Castendyck, Mustered at Quebec, 4 August 1783

Surgeon Sebastien Burgy
Corporal Jacques Werner

Chasseurs

Jacques Meyer	Nicolas Gullerie
Jean Diehl	Jean Graeff
Laurent Jiten	Conrad Feith
Peter Raymondt	Henri Schenck
Nicolas Weigand	George Deissinger
Philippe Deuhler	Chretien Seelander
Henri Keuss	Henri Schoepner
Philippe Starck	Anthoine Goeckell

Rosters

Paul Schuckard
Mathieu Proth
Hartmann Voigt
Sammuel Withsack
Jacques Sereny
Christophle Kroeser
Conrad Schaefer
George Paster
Jean Kopp
Jean Wagner
Michel Meixner
Henri Boehm
Henri Detrie
Guillaume Harthmann
George Fessner
Nicolas Wagner
Casimir Kreissler
Erneste Gerhard
Balthasar Seibert
Albert Kling
Jean Preller
Frederic Hoffmann

Melchior Kayser
Oswald Weigand
George Krumm
Andre Borckell
Melchior Kirsch
Chretien Lemaire
Frederic Weibell
Conrad Schultz
Guillaume Kratz
Henri Mebius
Nicolas Schaefer
George Gross
Conrad Schnabell
Joseph Rheinhard
George Sussner
Chretien Henning
Sammuel Stenzell
Henri Launhard
Frederic Weininer
Jean Calckhof
Leonhard Weinem
Jean Stirner

Rosters

Chasseur Recruits, Mustered at
Hanau, 12 November 1777

Lt. Fredric Schacht, and his batman

Chasseurs

Fredric Pforrius	Jean Ifland
Jean Stahl	Valentin Nichtern
Gottlieb Gottesheim	Chretien Schmid
Auguste Neuberger	Chretien Klein
Pierre Schawack	Fredric Wagner
Jacques Werner	Leonhard Diller
Henry Heyn	George Riehl
Bernard Noach	Pierre Weber
Theodore Meyer	Guillaume Schilling
Samuel Hemann	Jean Demke
Henry Holzhausen	Guillaume Wolff
Dominique Pambrun	Theophile Kellerstein
Jean Schmid	Francois Veith
Conrad Ammann	Charles Thenell
Jean Knauth	Theophile Much
Antoine Regenbogen	Charles Grundherr
Jean Lulay	George Prosi
Caspar Clauss	George Pub
Jean Stirner	Fredric Leubenreder
Louis Klein	Jean Franz
Francois Schaller	Melchior Keyser
Henry Schenck	Francois Ehrlich
Henry Pelz	Bernard Ritter

Rosters

Fredric Hyder
Henry Dettry
Leonhard Nohe
Fredric Richter

Jacques Sereny
Jean Seidel
Henry Eisenkolben
Simon Beauclair

Company Captain Hildebrandt, Mustered at
Quebec, 4 August 1783

Surgeon George Stubinger
QM Sgt. Henri Charles Wittmann
Corporals - Louis Zeillmann and Chretien Schwalm

Chasseurs

David Bohle
George Suss
Friedrich Lentze
Conrad Weber
Francois Hoffmann
Rudolphe Goedicke
George Pickell
Martin Dittlie
Daniel Collivo
Chretien Bauer
Jean Schubert
Albrecht Baier
Martin Blech
Henri Breitenbach
Conrad Wiesell
Gotthard Schaefer

Dietrich Koelscher
George Binder
Jacques Liedell
Frederic Lelm
Frederic Blummell
Balthasar Kock
Jacob Bischoff
Jean Stauber
Frederic Hoffmann
Gottlob Beickert
Barthell Grunsteidell
Jean Muller
Jean Becker
Jean Emmerich
Jean Stadermann
Michel Lichtenwalter

Rosters

Gottlieb Schentzell Theodor Goebell
Pierre Ullrich Daniel Wollendorf
Conrad Wegener George Koehler

(23651, f 89, 15 Mar 77; f 162; f 163; f 165; f 1678,
11 Apr 77; f 222, 12 Nov 77; 21812, f 120m 4 Aug 83)

Rosters

Recruits for Units of Hesse-Cassel

Infantry Recruits, Mustered at Nijmegen, 28 March 1777

2nd Lt. Carl August Corngrebel, and his batman
Ensign George Louis Motz, and his batman
Ensign Louis Grau, and his batman
Ensign Johan J. Werner, and his batman
Ensign F. A. Becker, and his batman
Ensign Carl W. Trott, and his batman
Auditor Carl Dietrich Meisterlin
Surgeons Joseph Malchebrey and Ziriax Claus
Drummers - Martin Schneider; Herman Meyer; Jacob Fahrenbach; Philip Appel; Peter Geis; Philip Schaefer; Carl August Hacke; Friedrich Noding; Friedrich Moller

Soldiers

Anthon Ehgard	Conrad Kapler
Johan Schaefer (held at Coblenz)	Johan Henrich Voment
Jacob Lahrum (held at Coblenz)	Mathias Schmid
Johan Henrich Riefel	Johan Henrich Rau

Rosters

Johan Meissell	Ernst Marck
Johan Justus Gundlach	Jacob Luschka
Johan George Blesman	Johan Rothe
Wilhelm Bohlander	Johan Friedrich Mebus
Johan George Stang	Henrich Specht
Johan Wilhelm Ludewig	Philip Jacob Kuntzinger
Michael Eberhard	Carl Joseph Zimmerman
Johan Conrad Rauschenberg	Christian Etzer
George Wilhelm Schneider	Friedrich Kloes
Joseph Bernhard Knapfigt	Jacob Stumph
Henrich Ochs	Hartman Fochs
Samuel Ruebeling	Hans Claus Voelcker
Christian Friedrich Richtsteur	Rudolph Eberth
Johannes Petri	Christian Meysner
Johannes Nauman	Hartman Waldschmid
Conrad Thieredott	Johannes Faerber
Thileman Jacob Joseph Compiz	Casper Morsch
Johann Theis Schuster	Christian Langen Schwart
Henrich Meyer	David Storck
Jacob Pfanno	Johannes Steinhauer
Frantz Niederhuber	Johannes Heinickel
Friedrich Schneider (held at	Johan Michael Flamant

Rosters

Coblenz)
Johan Henrich Groos
Johan Jacob Andreas
Friedrich Riemenschneider

Paul Werths
Johan Valentin Herman
Johan Gottlob Meyer
Friedrich Nauman
Wiegand Klimmenhagen
Johan Jacob Wambach
Johan Adam Rutz
Conrad Lotz
Philip Music
Philip Gerhard Hild
   (held at Coblenz)
Gottfried Lauberth

Johan Jacob Nopper

Johan Philip Franck
Johan Gabriel Walzer
Johannes Christ
Frantz Anton Steinhauer

Johan Adam Klop
Ephraim Traeger
Henrich Andreas
   Dewsner
Arnold Gerhard
Henrich Luckard
Johannes Ortwein
Johannes Gerlach
Ludewig Becker
Gerlack Zaun
Ludewig Schmid
Conrad Moller
Jacob Brav

Johan Adam Schuberth
Johannes Plantzky (held
   at Coblenz)
Joseph Kramant (held
   at Coblenz)
Alexander Joseph Wild
Christian Braun
Johan Georg Somer
Jacob Schindling

Rosters

Johan Jacob Eisele
Johan Mertens (held at Coblenz)
Johan Henrich Schmid
Johan Michael Kilborn
Johannes Krausse
Christoph Roman
Carl Henrich Fiedler
Gottlob Friedrich Diphold
Johan Martin Sondeman
Johannes Steinhoff
Johannes Fuckell
Johan Dietrich Schaeffer
Michael Kornman
Jacob Lahr
Johan Balthasar Konig
Henrich Jacob Friedge
Johannes Kuegeler
Johan Caspar Gildau
Arnold Jonus (held at Coblenz)
Johannes Menzel
Johan Gotfried Lowe
Christian Anton Ratnau
George Goebell

Caspar Methe
Johannes Blum
Henrich Rude
Joseph Schmid
Andreas Mehlmann
Justus Schrader
Herman Finger
Franciscus Mahler
Johan Wilhelm Knopf
Johan Adam Becker
Johan Jost Rubert
Daniel Jacob Luber
Caspar Ender
Peter Landman
Christian Mayntz
Joseph Heydelman
Johannes Seyn
Johannes Kropf
Daniel Jaeger
Bernhard Wachtell
Henrich Eschinger
Johan Paul Thomas
Christian Wirsing

Rosters

Johan Georg Stam
Johannes Schmid
Johan Christian Datge
Johan Friedrich Peplate
Andreas Pfeiffer
Johan Ulrich Sigmund
Philip Neis
Christian Bilner
Henrich Kress
Matheus Wiegand
Johan Conrad Weisman
Henrich Sandig
Johan Adam
Balthasar Wiegand
Wilhelm Siebelitz
Johan Conrad Schroder
George Raphka
Conrad Weber
Henrich Kollerman (deserted at Coblenz)
Johan Peter Weismaurer
Friedrich Avell
Michael Kellerman
Frantz Joseph Vogd

Johannes Grunder
Johannes Rippert
George Kauffman
Jacob Reis
Johan Jacob Schilt
Johannes Schaeffer
Lambertus Gliem
Friedrich Geusser
Johannes Friedrick
Wilhelm Koch
Melchior Hoeflich
Caspar Heuser
Johan Conrad Dehn
Conrad Kruel
Anton Meyer
Stephan Vogd
Frantz Krim
Carl Anton Heim

Johannes Kollerman
Stephan Daegler
Wilhelm Muller
Johan Georg Wiedman
Johannes Gaehling

Rosters

Johannes Schambach
Nicolas Schwinghamer
  (held at Coblenz)
Johan Georg Helli
Jacob Straus
Joseph Thiel
Johan Christian Lasky
Bartholomaus Kramer
Joseph Schall
Jacob Kropfinger
George Boland
Johan Adam Griech
Johan Henrich Michael
Johan Henrich Alter
Martin Kraemer
Martin Schellhaas
Johan Friedrich Schmid
Johan Henrich Strebe
Philip Weydeman
Christian Friedrich Rensch
Johan Andreas Koeneman
Christoph Gruen
Wendel Brauer
Johan Jost Ransheimer

Johannes Volcker

Johannes Heihl
Joseph Kieffer
Joseph Ulm
Philip Jacob Satler
George Bock
Jacob Janson
Jacob Fischer
Peter Pfeiffer
Franciscus Gottlob
Michael Lehe
Asmuth Haller
Daniel Deyenhard
Lorentz Schellhaas
Nicolaus Foerster
Johannes Jueneman
Henrich Sestman
Peter Schwartzbich
Johan Henrich Koch
Philip Vogeler
Jacob Hoffmann
Johannes Klein
Martin Loh

Rosters

Pierre Erhard
Johannes Feurstein
Johan George Briesman
Henrich Haselbach
Johan George Herche
Johan Wilhelm Sprizersbach
Philip Brueck
Joseph Schaefer (held at
 Coblenz)
Christian Wirsing

Peter Buelon
Matheus Feder (died enroute
 to port)
Johan George Scherring
Joseph Koch
Johan Martin Strueter
Volckman Benjamin Luci
Anton Eisenschneider
Johan Peter Ruthard
Clemens Kramer
Joseph Degend
Johannes Schobert
Balthasar Wuest (held at

Daniel Ludwig Busch
Johannes Bonhard
Johan Adam Reitz
Johan Philip Herche
Wendel Michell
Johan Matheus Michel
Martin Leutenbach

Gottlieb Martin
Johan Conrad
 Gerstung
Conrad Jaeger

Henrich Theer
Bernhard Roth
Johan Wilhelm Haas
Johan Ricus
Johan Martin Lies
Daniel Hellinger
Johannes Reichhard
Michael Bornheimer
Lorentz Gubernator
George Stophell

Rosters

Coblenz)
Wilhelm Christoph Schaper
Wilhelm Schaefer
Johannes Roemeli
Henrich Fiezy
Carl Henrich Werner
Peter Loefler
Johan Friedrich Wilhelm
   Tanneberg
Anton Hemmerling
Johan Adam Dor
Wilhelm Matheus Zumbe
Adam Hachborn
Caspar Leinroth
Johannes Jungk
Johannes Dietrich
Henrich Kayser (held at
   Coblenz)
Friedrich Daniel Kumersheim
Anton Gerzell
Philip Peter Geitz
Johan Gottlieb Metzler
Jacob Anton Michael
Andreas Kuersch

Frantz Mechler
Johan Henrich Prosuhn
Johann Gottlieb Dell
Johan Friedrich Jaeger
Johan Dietrich Rothe
Henrich Becker
Andreas Scheermesser

Johan Peter Glaser
Jacob Kirschner
Caspar Leusler
Jacob Hartman
Johannes Ort
Henrich Kirschner
Christoph Winter
Johan George Hutzel

Valentin Ackerman
Henrich Moller
Johannes Kraus
Caspar Bochler
Johan Florey
Johan Henrich Beutell
Caspar Grunele

Rosters

Wilhelm Thieleman
Johan Friedrich Ritter
Peter Schaefer
Johan Reinhard
Conrad Kresser
Caspar Schaus (held at Coblenz)
Adam Johan Jacob Sohn

Philip Eberhard
George Waltzmuller
Jacob Mueller
Georg Peter Niebergal

Friedrich Hartman
Anton Beck
Friedrich Gottlieb
Augustin Licht
Johannes Paul
Henrich Posde
George Becker
Martin Erb
Caspar Schuster
Johan Conrad Metze

Ludewig Hirschhauser
Johannes Schaefer
Wilhelm Printz
Anton Krebs
Johan Hoffrath

Henrich Balthes
Joachim Gerhard Martins
Adolph Eberhard
Philip Walther
Johan Georg Dierich
Samuel Christian Leopold
Johannes Schmid
Martin Georgius
Wilhelm Vogd
Joseph Kalmey
Peter Christoph Debus
Andreas Flomeyer
Henrich Klein
Johan Conrad Muller
Johannes Grisan
Henrich Muller

Rosters

Johannes Saurland
Frantz Engelbreit (held at Coblenz)
Henrich Becker
Johannes Schranck
Carl Wilhelm Schultz
Johan Ulrich Feith
George Drick
Frantz Scheimar
Leonhard Claudi (held at Coblenz)
Henrich Fruhrath (held at Coblenz)
Christian Otto
Herman Eckel
Conrad Martin
Johannes Hoeck
Peter Kraus (held at Coblenz)
Conrad von der Weyd
Johan Adam Eislaub

Johannes Flach

Henrich Korner
Johannes Debey
Celenius Hochley
Nicolaus Haberstich
Johan Caspar Brueck
Philip Martin Thoma
Philip Jacob Geis

Johannes Braun

Anton Bohl
Conrad Kiehlman
Johannes Steinweg
Johan George Kober
Benedictus Schuman
Georg Wilhelm Kramer
Jacob Schiltheis

Rosters

Physically Unfit - Not sent to America

Johannes Pfeffer
Johan Andreas Funck
Henrich Borck
Johannes Micus

Bernhard Grunder
Ludewig Erdman
Conrad Thiel
Daniel Schneider

Barthel Paul
Christian Engel Balhorn

Frantz Baratt
Johannes Kangiesser
Henrich Spriesterbach
Nicolaus Bolcke
Caspar Roemer
Friedrich Dehn
Jacob Froehner
Johan Nicolaus Hocke
Jacob Werner

Johan Caspar Ortwein
Johannes Lapp
Peter Buchin
Georg Friedrich Reibold
Johannes Hartung
Elias Goebich
Hartman Kaufman
Johan Henrich Hebenhard
Peter Sintz
Johan Jacob Wetzler
George Horn
Johannes Dickhaut
Jacob Johannes
Wilhelm Brill
Matheus Maser
Johannes Bauer
Bartholomaus Faber
George Henrich Lange
Johannes Conradi

Rosters

Henrich Kraft   Rudolph Bellinger
George Schmitz   Peter Auel
Michael Hoeck   Christian Reuter
Philip Miesel   Johan Elias Spalt
Johannes Stoband   David Riescht

Rosters

Chasseur Recruits, Mustered at Nijmegen, 28 March 1777

1st Lt. Frederic Adam Jules Wangenheim, and his batman

Sgts. - Johannes Sussebach and Johann Peter Oehm

Corporals - Carl August Giebner; Peter Wilhelm Schoenauer; Burckhard Conrad Cordemann; and Johann Christoph Muller

Sugeon Burckhart Keil

Chasseurs

Herrmann Deichmeyer
Caspar Brandau
Johan Gottfried Leopold
Johann Ledersack
Reinhard Happel
Johann Wilhelm Ullius
Johann George Knaust
Philipp Roppeter
Johann Krug
Johann Diedrich Hecht
Johann Conrad Muller, Jr.
Friedrich Theodor Abt
Johann Sebastian Schuchen
Johann Ernst Oesterling
Johan George Schramm
Christian Gottlieb Boehme
Johann Gottfried Santer

Philipp Landsiedel
Jacob Klein
Johann Hohlbein
Johann Kolbe
Carl Niester
Dietrich Meyer
Andreas Biermann
Johann David Arndt
Ernst Goebert
Anton Haarbusch
Johann Georg Apell
Wilhelm Keil
Martin Liberam
David Wandrock
Gottfried Hauer
Conrad Roeder
Johann Schwarz

Rosters

David Muhlenhenck
Michael Ruppert
Conrad Deege
Heinrich Wilhelm Schmid
Daniel Wilhelm Krausse
Johann Conrad Muller, Sr.
Johann Philipp Klintwort
Johann Heinrich Schoenewoltz
Johann Conrad Hildebrand

Conrad Schreiber
Diedrich Wilhelm
Christian Breye
Peter Schneider
David Port
Gottfried Muller
Georg Kugeler
Justus Fingerling

(23651, f 139; f 145, 28 Mar 77)

Index

Index

----, Henri 254
ABT, Friedrich Theodor 284
ACKERMAN, Valentin 279
ACKERMANN, K 13
ADAM, Johan 276
ADAMI, Michael 233
ADLON, Jean 259
ALBERT, Conrad 263 Pierre 261
ALSDORF, Joseph Erwin 262 Pierre Francisce 261
ALSDORFF, Erwin 264 Francois 264
ALT, Henry 233
ALTER, Johan Henrich 277 Michael 230 Nicolas 234
AMEND, Adam 231
AMMAN, Conrad 258 Martin 257
AMMANN, Conrad 269
AMMON, Godefroid 263 Gottefrid 262
ANDRA, Jean 229
ANDREAS, Johan Jacob 274
ANSCHULTZ, Paul 241
ANSTRUTHER, John 146 Lt Col 191
ANTOINE, Carl 256
APELL, Johann Georg 284
APPEL, Philip 272
ARMBRECHT, Jean 258
ARNDT, Johann David 284
ARNOLD, Benedict 29 Gen 29 Guillaume 231
ASMUS, Michel 244
ASSEHAU, Valentin 265
ATLON, Johannes 258
AUEL, Peter 283
AUFLEIDER, George 241
AUMANN, Henry 231
AUMHAUER, Christian 252
AVELL, Friedrich 276
BACH, Conrad 232 Georg 257 George 259 Lt 147 Michael 143 246
BACKER, Caspar 239
BAEHR, Lambert 266
BAIER, Albrecht 270 Christoph 253 255 George 255
BAILEY, Lt 190
BALDAUF, Antoine 245
BALHORN, Christian Engel 282
BALLAS, Christoph 243
BALTHES, Henrich 280

BANDEL, George 249
BANGE, Hermann 243
BANGERD, Conrad 247
BANGERT, Adam 253-254
BARATT, Frantz 282
BARBAN, Lucas 259
BARNER, 162 Maj 95
BARR, William 40
BARTH, Jean 244
BARTHELL, Anthoine 259
BARTMAN, Jean 231
BARTOLD, Michael 231
BATZ, Joseph 262-263
BAUCH, Daniel 266
BAUER, Adam 244 Chretien 270 Conrad 233 Daniel 249 Godefroid 258 Jacques 263 Jean 255 Johannes 282 Leonhard 245 Pierre 246
BAUM, 205 Friedrich 9
BAUMANN, Philippe 233
BAUMBRONN, Dominic 258
BAUMERT, George 230
BAUSCHER, Isaac 232 Jean 236 Philippe 266 Valentin 235
BAUSSUM, Laurent 236
BAYER, Conrad 242 Friederich 253
BEAUCLAIR, Simon 270
BEAUDAIR, Simon 259
BECHTEL, Caspar 239
BECHTOLD, Daniel 239 George 241 Lt 149
BECK, Anton 280 George 231 Guillaume 265 Henry 231 Jean 233
BECKER, F A 272 George 280 Guillaume 230 Henrich 279 281 Jean 261 263 270 Jean George 248 Johan Adam 275 Louis 232 Ludewig 274 Ludwig 108 Maurice 242
BEDLICH, Gottleib 266
BEHR, Conrad 230 Henry 233 Jean 235
BEICKERT, Gottlob 270
BEIKER, Conrad 235 George 235
BEIL, Jean 244
BEIST, George 231 Nicolas 229 233
BEITHNITZ, Georg 264
BEITNIZ, George 261
BELL, Capt 5 Wilhelm 226
BELLINGER, Jean 239 Rudolph 283

Index

BENDER, Auguste 231 Conrad 231 George 244 Henry 236 Jean 261-262 Mathias 247 Nicolas 247 Philippe 233 Sigmond 235 Xavier 251
BENSING, Philippe 235
BENTZ, Joseph 256 259 Martin 258
BERARD, Louis 243
BERENS, Theophile 245
BERG, Christoph 253 Johann 253
BERGER, George Vogel 233
BERGSTRAESSER, Justus 251 251
BERMES, Peter 252
BERNER, George 259
BERNGES, Frederic 236
BERNHEIMER, Andre 260
BERTZ, Guillaume 236
BEST, Walter 233
BETZEL, Joachim 244
BEUKER, Henry 238
BEUTELL, Johan Henrich 279
BEWALLE, Jean 243
BEYER, Jean 265
BICKES, Conrad 239
BIEHL, Wenzell 246
BIELING, Andre 239
BIERMANN, Andreas 284
BILLIU, Jacques 246
BILNER, Christian 276
BINDER, George 270
BISCHHAUSEN, Lt 79 82 85 93 114 132 153 157 167 210 222
BISCHOFF, Jacob 270 Jeremie 247
BLECH, Martin 270
BLEICH, Elias 250
BLESMAN, Johan George 273
BLUM, Johannes 275
BLUMLER, Jean 233
BLUMMELL, Frederic 270
BOBE, Chretien 255
BOCH, Jean Guillaume 247
BOCHLER, Caspar 279
BOCK, George 277
BOCKEL, Frederic 238 Philippe 239
BOCKELL, Johann 252
BODE, Christian 253 Pierre 240
BODENBINDER, Conrad 255
BOEHM, Henri 268
BOEHME, Christian Gottlieb 284
BOEHMREUTHER, Jean 259
BOETGER, Godefroid 255 Gottfried 252
BOHL, Anton 281
BOHLANDER, Wilhelm 273
BOHLE, David 270
BOHM, Henry 266 Nicolas 241

BOLAND, George 277 Pierre 254
BOLCKE, Nicolaus 282
BOLENDER, Jean Adam 239
BOLST, Valentin 232
BOMMERSHEIM, Henry 230
BONHARD, Johannes 278
BOOS, Daniel Charles 230
BORCK, Henrich 282
BORCKELL, Andre 268
BORCKMANN, Laurent 234
BORGIUS, Gotthilf 256
BORMANN, Jean Adam 260
BORN, Jacques 247
BORNER, Caspar 236
BORNHEIMER, Michael 278
BORNKESSEL, Jean 244
BOSEN, Joseph 260
BOUCHERVILLE, Capt 194-195
BRAND, Pierre 266
BRANDAU, Caspar 284
BRANDES, Ensign 87 Ernst Christian Heinrich 61
BRAUER, Wendel 277
BRAUMANN, Jean 236
BRAUN, Balthasar 257 Bernhard 247 Christian 274 Johannes 281
BRAUNKART, George 244
BRAV, Jacob 274
BREIDENBACH, Guillaume 235 Paul 239
BREITENBACH, Henri 270
BREITWIESSER, Pierre 231
BREMER, Conrad 233
BRETREICH, Frederick 266
BREYE, Christian 285
BREYMANN, Heinrich 115 Lt 159 Lt Col 74 76 118 124 127 129-130 133 143 151 162 169 176 179-181 203 205-206
BREYMENN, Lt Col 129
BRIESMAN, Johan George 278
BRILL, Wilhelm 282
BRIOR, Adam 244
BROCHT, Henry 248
BRODBECK, Michael 241
BROLL, Jean 236
BROOKS, Joseph 226
BROSS, Martin 245
BRUCHHOFF, Georg 256
BRUCKMANN, Philippe 238
BRUECK, Johan Caspar 281 Philip 278
BRUEKFIEB, Frederick 266 Jacque 266
BRUHMANN, Johanne 230
BRUST, Henry 236
BUCHIN, Peter 282
BUELON, Peter 278

Index

BUGLER, Louis 236
BURCKARD, Christophle 263
BURCKHARD, Christophle 262 Louis Theodor 241
BURGI, Sebastienne 265
BURGOYNE, 155 Gen 9 63 75-76 95 116-119 123 126 131 138 141 144-145 148 150 156 162 164 170 184 186 190-191 206 209 218 221 John 9 63 95 Lt Gen 189
BURGY, Sebastien 267
BUSCH, Caspar 261-262 Daniel Ludwig 278
BUTTLAR, Lt 113 Maurice 238
BUTZ, Joseph 244
CALCKHOF, Jean 268
CANORINUS, Louis 235
CAPITSKY, Benjamin 244
CARL, Adam 250
CARLETON, Gen 27-30 34-36 39 43 47 49-50 52 71 188 Gov 31 Guy 25 33 109
CASTENDYCK, Capt 267
CHRIST, Frederic 239 Johannes 274
CHRISTANZ, Herrnrich 252 Valentin 244
CHRISTENZ, Valentin 242
CLARKE, Adj 127 Commisaary Gen 135 Commissary 140
CLAUDI, Leonhard 281
CLAUS, Caspar 232 263 Henri 263 Ziriax 272
CLAUSS, Caspar 269 Friederich 252
CLERC, 137 141
CLERKE, Commissary Gen 142
CLEVE, Friedrich Christian 38
COLLIGNON, George 261
COLLIVO, Daniel 270
COMPIZ, Thileman Jacob Joseph 273
CONRAD, George 230
CONRADI, Johannes 282
CONTEN, 180
CORBIN, Capt 43 71 111 Mr 110
CORDEMANN, Burckhard Conrad 284
COREL, Jacob 256
CORNGREBEL, Carl Auguste 272
COSTENBADER, Emanuel 256
CRAMAHE, Lt Gov 49
CRAMER, Daniel 245 Henry 245
CRAMMER, Daniel 258
CRASS, Philippe 230
CRESS, Nicolas 231
CREST, Henry 236 Jean 243
CREUZBOURG, Col 254 Lt Col 251 Simon 251
DAEGLER, Stpehan 276

DAHN, Christoph 256
DANTZ, Jean 254
DANZ, Johann 253
DATGE, Johan Christian 276
DATZ, Jacques 243
DATZNER, Jean 239
DAVID, Henry 243
DEBEY, Johannes 281
DEBUS, Peter Christoph 280
DECHERT, Theodor 237
DECKMANN, Henry 230
DEEGE, Conrad 285
DEGEN, Caspar 253-254
DEGEND, Joseph 278
DEHM, Johan Conrad 276
DEHN, Friedrich 282
DEHNHARD, Christophle 229
DEHRN, Frederic 260
DEICHMEYER, Herrmann 284
DEISINGER, Jean Bernard 261
DEISSING, George 266
DEISSINGER, Bernhard 264 George 267
DELL, Johann Gottlieb 279
DEMCKE, Capt-at-arms 87
DEMKE, Jean 269
DENECKE, Friedrich Ludwig 61
DERIES, Jean Frederic 261
DESCHMAR, George 243
DESSELBERGER, Frederic 250
DETRIE, Henri 268
DETTLER, George 236
DETTMAN, Martin 267
DETTRY, Henry 270
DEUHLER, Philippe 267
DEWSNER, Henrich Andreas 274
DEYENHARD, Daniel 277
DICKHAUT, George Henry 246 Johannes 282
DIDERICH, Phillip 258
DIEFENBACH, Guillaume 244
DIEHL, Andreas 241 Balthasar 237 Christophle 239 George Frederic 231 Henry 231 Jean 266-267 267 Martin 245 Pierre 247
DIEHON, David 265
DIERICH, Johan Georg 280
DIETERICH, Chretien 261 Jacque 262 Michel 251
DIETRICH, Johannes 279 Michel 259
DIETZ, Philippe 241
DILLER, Leonhard 263 269
DIPHOLD, Gottlob Friedrich 275
DITTLIE, Martin 270
DITZELL, Jean 264

Index

DOENGES, Bernhard 255
DOERRBECKER, Jean 246
DONGES, Bernhard 253 Christophle 230
DOOR, Nicolas 231
DOR, Johan Adam 279
DORFFER, Frederic 254 Friederich 253
DORING, Johann 195
DORNMER, Johann 252
DORR, Jean 249
DOSCH, Johan Ludow 256
DOUGLAS, Commander 29
DREHER, Jean 262
DRICK, George 281
DRILL, Conrad 243
DUFAIS, Guillaume 246
DUFFT, Conrad 253-254
DUMFORT, Lt 137
DUMMLER, Christoph 244 Conrad 243
DUNN, Mr 46
DURBECK, Christophle 265
EBERHARD, Adolph 280 Michael 273 Philip 280
EBERSBACH, Peter 258
EBERT, Andre 235 Jean 265
EBERTH, Rudolph 273
EBERTHS, Herman Melchior 246
ECHWEGE, Lt 161
ECKEL, Caspar 230 Herman 281
ECKELL, Chretien 265
ECKER, Jacque 249
EGNER, Erhard 254
EHGARD, Anthon 272
EHRENKROOK, 148 Carl Friedrich 154 Lt Col 177-178
EHRENSPERGER, Laurent 259
EHRLICH, Francois 269
EICHELLMANN, Bernhard 248
EICHMANN, Pierre 247
EICKEL, Johann 257 Joseph 257
EIDAM, Martin 256
EIDELENZ, Henry 239
EIFFERT, Jacques 239 Jean George 229
EIKTS, Lt 149
EINFELD, August 256
EISELE, Johan Jacob 275
EISENKOLBEN, Henry 270
EISENSCHNEIDER, Anton 278
EISLAUB, Johan Adam 281
EISSENKOLBEN, Henri 363
ELSESSER, Louis 247
ELZER, Joseph 250
EMMERICH, Anthon 253 Bernhard 263 Conrad 244 Jean 270 Nicolas 262
EMMERT, Andre 229

ENDER, Caspar 275
ENGEL, Michael 266 Pierre 231
ENGELBREIT, Frantz 281
ENGELHARD, Guillaume 239 Jacques 246
ENGLAND, King Of 4 31
ENOSSE, Jean Louis 246
ENRICK, Jean 235
EPP, Caspar 233
EPPINGER, Christian 252
EPPPINGER, Christophle 254
ERB, Martin 280
ERCK, Johannes 258
ERDMAN, Ludewig 282
ERDMANN, Augustus 248
ERGELL, Joseph 259
ERHARD, Pierre 278
ERMENTRAUT, Balthasar 243
ERMETRAUT, Caspar 247
ERNSTDORFF, Pierre 248
ERWIN, Maj 149 176-177 180 192 213
ESCHINGER, Henrich 275
ESCHWEGE, Chretiern 238 Lt 195 217
ETHERINGTON, Lt 174
ETZER, Christian 273
EWALD, Conrad 239 Peter 108
EWALT, Pierre 238
EYDAM, Martin 258
FABER, Bartholomaus 282 Henry 233
FAERBER, Johannes 273
FAHREIN, Henry 267
FAHRENBACH, Jacob 272
FARBER, Frederic 236
FASNACHT, Jean 261
FASSELABEND, Anton 195
FASSNACHT, Jean 263
FATSCHEL, Jean Henri 261
FATSCHELL, Henri 263
FAUCITT, William 34
FEDER, Matheus 278
FEHL, Jean 231
FEITH, Conrad 266-267 Johan Ulrich 281
FELGER, Henry 244
FELSENHEIM, Joseph 248
FENGEL, Pierre 240
FESSNER, George 268
FETTER, Jean 259 Johannes 257
FETZER, Francois 245
FEUERBACH, Henry 243
FEUL, Henry 245
FEURSTEIN, Johannes 278
FIELDER, Carl Henrich 275
FIESELE, Daniel 261
FIEZY, Henrich 279
FILS, Thomas 247

Index

FILSINGER, Jean 240
FILZHOFER, Jean 254
FILZHOFFER, Carl 251
FINCK, Charle 265 Chretien 249 Jean 265
FINDEL, Johannes 257
FINGER, Herman 275
FINGERLING, Justus 285
FINSTERER, George 262 Jean George 261
FINTZELL, Philippe 246
FINZEL, Conrad 239
FIRES, Conrad 241
FISCHER, Bernhard 250 Caspar 250 Chretien 254 Christian 252 Conrad 256 George 254 Henri 263 Henry 238 Jacob 277 Jean 242 Jean Henri 261 Johann 253
FIX, Pierre 231 Valentin 233
FLACH, Johannes 281
FLAMANT, Johan Michael 273
FLECKSTEIN, Rudolph 250
FLEISCHMANN, Jacques 243
FLOMEYER, Andreas 280
FLOREY, Johan 279
FLUHNER, Conrad 254
FLUHRER, Conrad 253
FOCHS, Hartman 273
FOCHT, Jean Pierre 248
FOERSTER, Nicolaus 277
FORBAON, Jean 248
FORSTER, 148
FORTER, Conrad 230
FOSTER, Maj 141
FOY, Capt 34 44 E 60 Edward 34
FRANCK, Johan Philip 274
FRANCKEN, Capt 256 Hermann Albrecht 256 Maj 258
FRANISKO, Christoph 244
FRANTZ, Jacques 234 Jean 259
FRANZ, Jean 269
FRASER, 101 153 182 Alexander 74 115 Brig 158-159 184 226 Capt 198 Gen 115 127 151 Simon 74 100
FREDRICH, Jean 249
FREHER, Jean 263
FREIBURGER, Alexandre 267
FREITER, Henry 235
FREY, David 258-259
FREYENSENER, George 231
FRIDERICI, Carl Frederic Salomo 260
FRIEDERICK, Jost 257
FRIEDGE, Henrich Jacob 275
FRIEDRICK, Johannes 276
FRISCHKORN, Frederic 231 Jean 249
FROEHNER, Jacob 282

FRUHRATH, Henrich 281
FUCHS, Hubert 248 Joseph 260 Paul 252
FUCKELL, Johannes 275
FUHR, George 265 George Conrad 240 Henry 235 Jacque 265
FUHRMANN, Wilhelm 257
FUNCK, Adam 265 George 241 Jean 260 Johan Andreas 282 Pierre 248
FUSS, Jean 242
GAEHLING, Johannes 276
GALL, Brig 82 98 Guillaume Rudolphi 229
GALLAFRES, Gottlob Louis 246
GAMBEL, Etienne 243
GANSS, Christoph 244
GARTHER, Capt 164
GECKELL, Antoine 266
GEHRING, Friedrich 256
GEIGER, Georg 257
GEIS, Peter 272 Philip Jacob 281
GEISELMEYER, Georg 258
GEISLER, Paul 258
GEISMAR, Frederic 232 Friedrich 73
GEIST, Jean 261
GEITZ, Philip Peter 279
GEORGE, King Of England 54
GEORGI, Frederic 244 261
GEORGIUS, Martin 280
GERBHARD, Jean 266
GERGER, George 259
GERHARD, Arnold 274 Erneste 268 Ernst 267 Philipp 245
GERING, Jacques 231
GERLACH, Capt 118 127-128 135 173 179-181 184 217 Deputy Quartermaster Gen 209 Heinrich 76 Johannes 274
GERMANN, Capt 238 Frederic 238
GERSTUNG, Johan Conrad 278
GERTHMANN, Conrad 258
GERTMANN, Conrad 256
GERZELL, Anton 279
GESCHKE, Michel 243
GEUSSER, Friedrich 276
GEWALT, Jacques 238
GEYER, Pierre 233
GEYLING, Frederic 229 Guillaume 241
GIEBER, Carl August 284
GIESE, Guillaume 258
GILDAU, Johan Caspar 275
GILDNER, Simon 259
GISCHER, George 244
GLAS, Jean 239
GLASER, Johan Peter 279
GLATTERER, Conrad 253
GLAUBENSKIND, August 258

Index

GLIEM, Lambertus 276
GLUCK, Michel 253
GLUTH, Jean Henri 262
GOBEL, Caspar 236 George 233
GOEBELL, George 275 Theodor 271
GOEBERT, Ernst 284
GOEBICH, Elias 282
GOECKELL, Anthoine 267
GOEDE, Asmus 246
GOEDECKE, Johann Conrad 33
GOEDICKE, Rudolphe 270
GOETZ, Benjamin 263
GOTTESHEIM, Gottlieb 269
GOTTLIEB, Friedrich 280
GOTTLOB, Franciscus 277
GOTTSCHALCK, Guillaume 238 Stephan 256
GOTTSCHALL, Stephan 259
GOTZ, Benjamin 262 Henry 245
GRAEFF, Jean 267
GRAETER, Frederic 254
GRAETSCHMANN, Christophle 264
GRAS, Charles 261
GRATSCH, Frederic 255
GRAU, Louis 272
GRAULING, Frederich 253 Henri 255
GREFF, Jean 266
GRIECH, Johan Adam 277
GRIESSINGER, Anthon 252
GRILL, Caspar 265
GRIMM, Guillaume 241 Louis 262
GRISAN, Johannes 280
GROOS, Johan Henrich 274
GROSS, George 268
GROTH, Hartmann 239
GRUBENSTEIN, Philipp 250
GRUBER, Jean 241 Xavier 241
GRUEN, Christoph 277
GRUGE, Jean George 230
GRUNDER, Bernhard 282 Johannes 276
GRUNDHERR, Charles 269
GRUNDLER, Anthon 252 Antoine 254
GRUNELE, Caspar 279
GRUNER, Conrad 230 Pierre 235
GRUNSTEIDELL, Barthell 270
GRYSINGHER, Joseph 254
GSCHEIDLE, Jean 244
GUBERNATOR, Lorentz 278
GUIGY, 66 98
GULLERIE, Nicolas 267
GULLERY, Nicolas 267
GUMBEL, Joean 235
GUNCKEL, Jean 245
GUNDLACH, Johan Justus 273
GURKER, Christophle 234
GUTERMUTH, Jean 236
GUTHSMITH, Francois 263
GYLDNER, Simon 258
HAAG, Jacques 244
HAARBUSCH, Anton 284
HAARENFEENGER, Jean 248
HAAS, Johan Wilhelm 278
HAB, George 249
HABERSTICH, Nicolaus 281
HACHBORN, Adam 279
HACHENBERGER, George 236
HACKE, Carl August 272
HAENISCHFEEGER, Christophle 247
HAENLEIN, George 249
HAHN, Conrad 247
HALASCHKA, Pvt 84-85
HALLATSCHKA, Jean 239
HALLER, Asmuth 277
HAMANN, Conrad 246
HAMILTON, 149 Brig 133 155 160 192 194 Gen 132 138 155 Gustavus 74 132 James 137
HAMMANN, Nicolas 233 Pierre 235
HAMMEL, Heinrich 252
HAMMELL, Henri 254
HANDEL, Jean 249
HANSELLMANN, Adam 247
HAPPEL, Eckhard 243 Henry 249 Reinhard 284
HARRINGTON, Deputy Quartermaster Gen 226
HARRIS, Walt 226
HARTHMANN, Guillaume 268
HARTMAN, Friedrich 280 Jacob 279
HARTMANN, Guillaume 266 Jean 261 Paul 247 Pierre 233
HARTUNG, Johannes 282
HARTZ, Conrad 265
HARVING, Quartermaster Gen 182
HASELBACH, Henrich 278
HASSNER, Panorave 232
HATLER, Jean Gottlieb 248
HAUER, Gottfried 284
HAUMANN, Jacques 238
HAUPT, Mathia 249
HAUSER, Phillip 258
HAUSMANN, Charles Louis 246
HAUSSNER, Jean 242
HAUT, Philippe 248
HAZDORF, Theophil 262
HEBENHARD, Johan Henrich 282
HECHT, Johann Diedrich 284
HECK, Caspar 245 Martin 232

Index

HECKMANN, Michel 248
HEERDT, Jean Paul 261
HEERICH, Jean 265
HEERWAGEN, Adj 201 Ensign 201 Jacques 229
HEERWAGON, Ensign 80 106 Jacob 79
HEICKE, Louis 245
HEIDELBACH, Jeremie 229
HEIDENREICH, Henry 242
HEIHL, Johannes 277
HEIJN, Philipp 262
HEILL, Dietrich 263 Mathieu 259
HEILLMANN, Pierre 258
HEILMAN, Peter 256
HEIM, Carl Anton 276
HEIN, Henri 255 Philippe 229 262
HEINE, Louis 266
HEINICKEL, Johannes 273
HEINLEIN, Andre 261 263
HEINNEMANN, Henri 259
HEINZINGER, Philippe 238
HEISTERREICH, Louis 243
HELLER, Johannes 257
HELLI, Johan Georg 277
HELLINGER, Daniel 278
HELMUTH, George 254
HEMANN, Samuel 269
HEMMERLE, Thadeus 241
HEMMERLING, Anton 279
HENCKEL, Jacque 261
HENKELL, Jacques 263
HENNIG, Daniel 249
HENNING, Caspar 232 Chretien 268 Conrad 252
HENRICH, Christophle 240 Philippe 236
HENSCH, Henry 265
HENSSE, Frederic 255
HENSSEL, Andreas 252
HENSSELL, Andre 255
HENZEL, Conrad 231 Henry 236 243 Jean 239
HENZELL, Conrad 255
HENZLER, Adam 231
HERBER, Michael 239
HERCHE, Johan George 278 Johan Philip 278
HERMAN, Johan Valentin 274
HERMANN, Jean 261 264 Paul 243 Sammuel 254
HERRMANN, Jean 241
HERTH, Paul 262
HERTZ, Liborie 259
HESS, Caspar 231 Dr 205 Hartmann 247
HESSE-CASSEL, Hereditary Prince Of 62

HESSLER, Christoph Sr 243 Frederic Jr 243 Pierre 261 263
HESTERMANN, Charles Frederic 249
HETTERICH, Pierre 233
HEUSER, Caspar 276
HEYD, George 247
HEYDELMAN, Joseph 275
HEYGEFELDT, Henry 267
HEYL, Conrad 230 Dietrich 261 George 231 Leonhard 241 Mathias 257 Philippe 236 Valentin 249
HEYN, Henry 269
HIERONYMUS, Frederic 244
HIESSNER, Urban 239
HILCHEN, Henry 266
HILD, Philip Gerhard 274
HILDEBRAND, Christian 253 Guillaume 254 Jacque 265 Johann Conrad 285
HILDEBRANDT, Capt 270
HILDNER, Frederic 250
HILL, Lt Col 137 150 159 198
HILLE, Capt-at-arms 87 Maj 141
HILLER, Michel 245
HINCKEL, Conrad 231 Philippe 239
HIRSCH, Michael 243
HIRSCHBERGER, Friederich 252
HIRSCHHAUSER, Ludewig 280
HOCHLEY, Celenius 281
HOCHSTETTER, Lt 260
HOCK, Caspar 258
HOCKE, Johan Nicolaus 282
HOECK, Johannes 281 Michael 283
HOEFLICH, Melchior 276
HOEHN, Caspar 252 Chretien 263
HOENE, Louis 238
HOFF, Jean 246
HOFFMAN, Jacob 277 Jean 236
HOFFMANN, Adam 263 Andree 249 Balthasar 247 252 Francois 270 Frederic 268 270 George 241 Jacques 254 Jean 254 Johann 252 Pierre 241
HOFFRATH, Johan 280
HOFMANN, Adam 261 Francois 245 Georg 257 Godefroy 245 Johannes 256 Kraft 243
HOHLBEIN, Johann 284
HOHORST, Louis 235
HOLGER, Henry 243
HOLL, Philippe 242
HOLZBERGER, Jean Leonhard 260 Leonhard 264
HOLZER, Franciscse 261 Francois 262
HOLZERNER, Christian 252
HOLZHAUSEN, Henry 269

293

Index

HOLZHAUSSEN, Henri 263
HOMANN, Jean 231
HONNIG, Philippe 235
HOPFENRATH, Frederic 245
HORN, Christian 251 George 282 Nicolas 234
HORST, Conrad 246 Reichenhard 252
HOURT, Mr 142
HUBER, Jacques 250
HUCK, Francois 263
HUFFNER, Michail 233
HUFNAGEL, Wilhelm 257
HUFNER, Henry 231
HUFSCHMITH, Jacob 257
HUMRICH, Chretien 244
HURH, Martin 236
HUTZEL, Johan George 279
HYDER, Fredric 270
IFFLAND, Henry 242 Jean 242
IFFLANDT, Jean 263
IFLAND, Jean 269 Johannes 258
ILTEN, Lorent 267
INGAR, Nicolas 235
JACKISCH, Jean Chretien 261
JACOBI, Conrad 244 Tobia 242
JAECKELL, Jean 254
JAEGER, Conrad 278 Daniel 275 Hermann 138 Johan Friedrich 279
JAHN, Jean 250 Nicolas 232
JANSON, Jacob 277
JITEN, Laurent 267
JOCKEL, Peter 257
JOCKELL, Pierre 259
JOHANNES, Jacob 282
JOLEPP, Jean 237
JONUS, Arnold 275
JORDAN, Antoine 267 Heinrich 253 Henri 254
JOST, Adam 239
JUENEMAN, Johannes 277
JUNG, Friederich 251
JUNGK, Johannes 279
JUSTORF, Christophle 229 George 229
KAIP, Henry 266
KALBFLEISCH, Grenadier 92
KALKHOFF, Jean 266
KALMEY, Joseph 280
KAMMERER, Johannes 231 231 Wendel 231
KAMPFER, Frederic Louis 232
KANGIESSER, Johannes 282
KAPLER, Conrad 272
KAPPES, Adam 249 Engelbert 234 Piere 247

KARBBE, Anthon 252
KAUFFMAN, George 276
KAUFMAN, Hartman 282
KAUP, Reinhard 251
KAUS, Jean 231
KAYSAR, Henrich 279
KAYSER, Melchior 268
KEIBB, Herrnrich 252
KEIL, Burckhart 284 Wilhelm 284
KEISER, Fredceric 240 Nicolas 234
KEISSER, Henry 235
KEITTELL, Jacques 247
KELLER, Henry 244
KELLERMAN, Michael 276
KELLERSTEIN, Godefroid 263 Theophile 269
KEMBLE, Maj 183
KEMPF, Caspas 239
KEMPFER, Ensign 86 Friedrich Ludwig 79
KEMPNER, Ensign 106
KENNER, Pierre 242
KEPPENHAHN, Chretien 241
KERTZNER, Jean 245
KESSLER, Johan Herman 258 Jospeh 267 Laurent 231 Michel 245
KESTER, Jean 230
KEUSS, Henri 267
KEYSER, George 260 Melchior 269
KEYSSER, Daniel 248 Jean 246
KICKMAN, Maj 138
KIEFFER, Joseph 277
KIEHLMAN, Conrad 281
KIHRON, Jean 248
KILBORN, Johan Michael 275
KINGSTON, Adj Gen 166 Adj Gen Maj 151
KIRCHHOF, Adam 232
KIRCHNER, Adam 242
KIRSCH, Melchior 266 268
KIRSCHNER, Henrich 279 Jacob 279
KITZ, Auguste 235 Caspar 230 George 238
KITZSTEINER, Leonhard 257
KLATTERER, Conrad 254
KLEBONITZ, Jean 259
KLEES, Conrad 230
KLEIN, Adam 260 262 Chretien 269 Henrich 280 Jacob 284 Johannes 277 Louis 269 Philipp 250
KLEMM, Chretien 243
KLEMPELL, George 247
KLENTSCH, Balthasar 244
KLIE, Drummer 141 143 Leonhard 107 229 Nicolas 233 Quartermaster 108
KLIER, Daniel 233

Index

KLIMMENHAGEN, Wiegand 274
KLINCKERFUS, Philippe 239
KLING, Albert 266 268 Jacques Sr 243 Theodor Jr 243
KLINKERSHUS, Esare 236
KLINTWORT, Johann Philipp 285
KLOBER, Caspar 231
KLOES, Friedrich 273
KLOP, Johan Adam 274
KLOZBUGER, Jean Caspar 260
KLUE, Jean 230
KLUG, Christophle 262
KNAB, Frederic 261 263
KNABENSCHUG, Georg 258
KNABENSCHUHE, George 259
KNAPFIGT, Joseph Bernhard 273
KNAPP, Antoine 244
KNAUSS, Balthasar 242
KNAUST, Johann George 284
KNAUTH, Jean 269
KNOBLAOCH, Charles 232
KNOCH, Ehrenfrid 242
KNOPF, Johan Wilhelm 275
KNORR, Conrad 249
KOBBEL, Andreas 258
KOBER, Johan George 281
KOCH, Andrea 232 Andreas 94 Chretien 247 Corp 94 Erhard 257 Frederic 233 Jean 238 262 Johan Henrich 277 Joseph 278 Wilhelm 276
KOCK, Balthasar 270
KOEHLER, George 271
KOELSCHER, Dietrich 270
KOENEMAN, Johan Andreas 277
KOERBER, Henry 247
KOHBER, Jean 248
KOHLE, Nicolas 263
KOHLER, Jean 238 Jost 241
KOHLLER, Henry 238
KOLB, Corp 108 Nicolas 233
KOLBE, Johann 284
KOLEPP, Adam 230 Caspar 239 George 239 Melchior 232
KOLL, Nicolas 262
KOLLERMAN, Henrich 276 Johannes 276
KONIG, Johan Balthasar 275
KOPP, Jean 267-268
KORN, 244 George 242 Jean 254 Johann 253
KORNER, Henrich 281
KORNMAN, Michael 275
KORNRUMPF, Capt 265 Caspar Henry 265
KRAEMER, Martin 277

KRAFFT, Andre 239 Henry 236 Ludwig 252 Nicholas 261
KRAFT, Henrich 283 Johan August 256
KRAMANT, Joseph 274
KRAMER, Bartholomaus 277 Clemens 278 Georg Wilhelm 281 Laurent 233
KRANCKE, Gottlieb 242
KRASS, Charles 263 Johan Georg 256
KRATZ, Guillaume 266 268 Leonhard 233 Sebastian 237
KRAUS, George 244 Johannes 279 Peter 281
KRAUSS, Wilhelm 256
KRAUSSE, Daniel Wilhelm 285 Johannes 275
KREBS, Anton 280 Conrad 239 Henry 265 Jean Adam 248 Nicolas 257 259 Philippe 236
KRECKEL, Nicolas 244
KREIN, Christophle 236
KREISSLER, Casimir 268
KREISTHER, Jean Henri 260
KRESS, Henrich 276
KRESSEL, Nicolas 230
KRESSER, Conrad 280
KRESSLER, Gottfried 253
KRETZLER, Frederic 245
KREUZER, Sebastienne 249
KRIEG, Conrad 238 Henry 232 Leonhard 243
KRIM, Frantz 276
KROESER, Christophle 268
KROPF, Johannes 275
KROPFINGER, Jacob 277
KROSSER, Christopphle 265
KRUEL, Conrad 276
KRUG, Daniel 260 Frederich 265 Henry 229 Johann 284
KRULING, Adam 252
KRUM, George 266
KRUMM, George 268
KUCKUMUS, Christian 252
KUEGELER, Johannes 275
KUERSCH, Andreas 279
KUGELER, Georg 285
KUHLMANN, Christophle 263
KUHN, Christoph 244 Conrad 250 Johann 253 Mathias 248
KUKEMUS, 256
KULB, Carl 257
KULONG, Jacques 254
KULUNG, Johann 253
KUMERSHEIM, Friedrich Daniel 279

Index

KUMMERLE, Jacque 262 Jacques 264
KUNCKEL, Frederic 261 Michael 234
KUNCKELL, Frederic 263
KUNES, Etienne 231
KUNGER, Philippe 259
KUNKEL, Henry 231-232
KUNKLER, Jean 259
KUNSITLER, Guillaume 254
KUNSTLER, Guillaume 260
KUNTZE, Andreas 253
KUNTZINGER, Philip Jacob 273
KUNTZLY, Chretien 241
KURTZ, Caspar 266
KURZ, Jacques 260
KUSTNER, Jean Paul 246
KUWATSCH, Jean 254
LACK, Jean 239
LAHR, Jacob 275
LAHRUM, Jacob 272
LANDMAN, Peter 275
LANDOEHR, Jacob 260
LANDSIEDEL, Philipp 284
LANGE, George Henrich 282 Nicolas 244 Philippe 238
LAPP, Jean 239 Johannes 282
LARCH, Jean Henri 261
LASKY, Johan Christian 277
LATZ, Jean 259
LAUBERTH, Gottfried 274
LAUCH, Conrad 257
LAUER, Andre 255 Heinrich 253
LAUNHARD, Henri 268
LEDERER, Michael 257
LEDERSACK, Johann 284
LEHBERG, Henry 233
LEHE, Michael 277
LEHR, Jean 236 Maurice 113 230
LEIB, Wendel 233
LEIBENFEDER, Jean 259
LEIBOLD, Joachim 247
LEICK, Adam 244
LEINROTH, Caspar 279
LEISS, Jacques 246
LELM, Frederic 270
LEMAIRE, Chretien 267-268
LEMPECT, Frederic 246
LEMUNG, Philippe 239
LENTZ, Charles 240 Henry 238 Jean Christophle 232 Johann Christoph 71 John Christoph 110 Lt Col 93 138 152 179 214 224
LENTZE, Friedrich 270
LEONARD, Jacques 247
LEONHARD, Chretien 235

LEOPOLD, Johan Gottfried 284 Samuel Christian 280
LEQUINESE, Commissary 154
LERCH, Henri 262
LESCHHERN, Jean 249
LETH, Adolphe Neuberg 256
LEUBENREDER, Fredric 269
LEUSLER, Caspar 279
LEUTENBACH, Martin 278
LIBERAM, Martin 284
LICHT, Augustin 280
LICHTENWALTER, Michel 270
LIEDELL, Jacques 270
LIEDERER, Michel 259
LIES, Johan Martin 278
LILLER, Jean 231
LINCK, Caspar 232 Etienne 240 Henry 237
LIND, Jean 239 Lt Col 138
LINDAU, Charles 232
LINDEBAUER, Henry 265 Jean 231
LINDNER, Jean 243
LINSS, Guillaume Frederic 241 Jean 241
LIST, Guillaume 246 Pvt 90
LOCHER, Philippe 236
LOCHMANN, Balthasar 248 Guillaume 247
LOEFLER, Peter 279
LOH, Martin 277
LOLTIG, Conrad 252
LOOS, Balthasar 246
LORA, Jean George 246
LOSSBERGER, Jean 248
LOTER, George 244
LOTZ, Andre 246 Conrad 274 Guillaume 239 Jean 233 237 247 Johannes 257 Nicolas 230
LOW, Chretien 254 Christian 253
LOWENSTEIN, Conrad 231
LOWER, Johan Gotfried 275
LUBER, Daniel Jacob 275
LUCI, Volckman Benjamin 278
LUCKARD, Henrich 274
LUCKE, Maj 152
LUDEWIG, Commander 177 Johan Wilhelm 273
LUDWIG, Engelhard 241
LULAY, Jean 269
LUSCHKA, Jacob 273
MACK, Caspar 251 258 Melchior 266
MACLEAN, Francis 27
MADERN, Jean 233
MAEFAI, Lorenz 257
MAHLER, Franciscus 275
MAHLO, Pierre 233

Index

MAHR, George 239 Philippe 239
MAIER, Balthasar 252
MAISCH, Joachim 245
MAJOR, Georg 257
MALCHEBREY, Joseph 272
MANCHE, Conrad 233
MANCKEL, Jean 230
MANGELL, Michael 252
MANIKEL, Henry 235
MARCK, Ernst 273
MAROWFSKY, Antoine 243
MARRECK, Godefroid 254 Gottfried 253
MARTENS, Henry 235 Maj 235
MARTIN, Conrad 281 Gottlieb 278 Guillaume 267 Jean 259 Johan 257
MARTINS, Joachim Gerhard 280
MASER, Matheus 282
MASSOREA, Anthon 252
MATHEUS, Nicolas 267
MATTHEUS, Jean Eberhard 260
MAUCK, Godlieb 263
MAUL, Caspar 239
MAURICE, 141
MAY, Christophle 237
MAYER, Frederic 242 Henry 242 Jean 241
MAYNTZ, Christian 275
MEBIUS, Henri 268 Henry 266
MEBOTT, Jean 233
MEBUS, Johan Friedrich 273
MECHLER, Frantz 279
MEHLMANN, Andreas 275
MEHRLING, Philipp 244
MEIJEN, Daniel 262
MEIJERN, Lt 260
MEIJN, George 262 Jean George 260
MEINONE, Michael 261 Michel 263
MEISSELL, Johan 273
MEISTERLIN, Carl Dietrich 272
MEIXNER, Michel 268
MENCK, Philippe 231
MENGE, Maj 144
MENGES, Georg 256
MENZEL, Johannes 275
MENZELL, Eckart 252
MENZER, Francois Michael 249 Joseph 243
MERCKEL, Reinhard 243
MERCKER, Jean 230
MERGENTHAL, Adam 242
MERSCHEL, Guillaume 236
MERTENS, Johan 275
MERTZ, Henry 236 Jean 250
METHE, Caspar 275
METZE, Johan Conrad 280

METZGER, Charles Christople 241
METZLER, Adam 235 Johan Gottlieb 279 Pierre 247 Sebastian 230 Wilhelm 256
MEUER, Martin 242
MEYER, Anton 276 Dietrich 284 Henrich 273 Herman 272 Jacques 265 265 267 Johan Gottlob 274 Leonhard 250 Mathias 258 Mathieu 259 Theodore 269
MEYSNER, Christian 273
MEZLER, Nicolas 252
MICHAEL, Jacob Anton 279 Johan Henrich 277
MICHAETIS, Frederic 263
MICHEL, Johan Matheus 278
MICHELL, Wendel 278
MICUS, Johannes 282
MIESEL, Philip 283
MOERSCHELL, Jean 246
MOLLER, Andre 259 Conrad 274 Friedrich 272 Henrich 279 Henry 266
MONEY, Capt 194-195 220
MONIN, Capt 48
MONTGOMERY, Gen 28-29 Richard 27
MONTZAMBERE, Mons 72 Monsieur 112
MOOS, Friederich 253
MORGAN, Daniel 30
MORSCH, Casper 273
MORTER, Conrad 239
MOST, Anthon 256 Antoine 262
MOTTER, Henry 235
MOTZ, George Louis 272
MOYER, Theodor 259
MUCH, Theophile 269
MUELLER, Capt 5 Jacob 280
MUHL, George 241
MUHLENHENCK, David 285
MUIRE, Brig 154
MULLER, Adam 229 Andree 249 Balhasar 236 Caspar 236 Chretien 230 241 Conrad 232 254 Friederich 258 George Paul 261 Gottfried 285 Gottlieb 241 Guillaume 254 Guillaume 232 Henrich 280 Henry 246 Jacob 252 Jean 231 246 255 270 Jean Jr 236 242 247 Jean Sr 241 247 Joachim 244 Johan Conrad 280 Johann Christoph 284 Johann Conrad Jr 284 Johann Conrad Sr 285 Johannes 257 Martin 230 Nicolas 248 Paul 263 Philippe 233 Pierre 255 Urban 253 Wilhelm 253 276
MULLNER, Frederic 243
MUNNICH, Frederic 258
MUNRO, Mr 198
MUNTER, Johaannes 257

Index

MUSIC, Philip 274
MUSS, Guillaume 244
NANTZ, Henry 247
NAUHEIMER, George 244
NAUMAN, Friedrich 274 Johannes 273
NEIS, Philip 276
NEIZEL, Johann 257
NENZELL, Conrad 252
NEUBERGER, Auguste 269
NEUBURGER, August 254
NEUMEISTER, Provost 251
NEUMESITER, George 251
NEUNOBEL, Jean 235
NICHTERN, Valentin 269
NICKS, Johannes 256
NIEBERGAL, Georg Peter 280
NIEDERHUBER, Frantz 273
NIEDING, Gebhard 254 Georg 253
NIESTER, Carl 284
NOACH, Bernard 269
NODING, Friedrich 272
NOHE, Leonhard 270
NOHR, Ludwig 257
NOL, Leonhard 259
NOLTE, Friederich 252
NONGESSER, Guillaume 263
NOPPER, Johan Jacob 274
NOX, Dr 167
NUBEL, Henry 243
NUNGESSER, Chretien Guillaume 261
NUT, Lt 74
NUTT, Lt 116
OBRICH, Guillaume 237 Matheus 253
OBRISH, Jean 236
OCHS, Henrich 273
OCHSLEY, Mr 164
OEHM, Johann Peter 284
OESTERLING, Johann Ernst 284
OFERMANN, Jean 261
OHL, Jean 236
OLGEN, Jean 250
ORBACH, Henry 247 Jean 247
ORBEL, Conrad 249
ORBIG, Corp 108
ORT, Johannes 279
ORTH, Conrad 238 Henry 238 Jean 235
ORTNER, Leonhard 251 251
ORTWEIN, Johan Caspar 282 Johannes 274
OTTO, Christian 281 Samuel 243
PAEUSCH, Georg 246
PAHR, George 249
PAMBRUN, Dominique 269
PANNEMULLER, George 267
PAPE, Fraancois 241

PARA, Jean 244
PARNER, Melchior 239
PASSERN, 5 Capt 86-87
PASSNACHT, Jean 263
PASTER, George 267-268
PAUL, Barthel 282 Johannes 280 Michel 247
PAUSCH, Capt 163 169 178 246 Georg 147 246 250
PELZ, Henri 258 Henry 269
PEPLATE, Johan Friedrich 276
PETER, Julius 253-254
PETERS, Frederic 254
PETRI, Johannes 273 Philippe 233 Thome 233
PETZINGER, Jean 247
PEUSCH, Georg 246
PFAFF, Jacques 238
PFANNO, Jacob 273
PFEFFER, Johannes 282
PFEIFFER, Adam 252 Andreas 276 Jacques 241 Johann 252 Peter 277 Pierre 262
PFLUG, Jean 247 Marcus 258
PFORIUS, Frederic 258
PFORRIUS, Fredric 269
PFULFER, Jean David 247
PHILLIPS, Gen 147 203 Maj Gen 134 160 225 William 9 69 101
PICKELL, George 270
PIDDERSON, Lord 164
PILLMANN, Johan Leonhard 256
PINCER, Lt 87
PIRIE, Joseph 265
PITT, William 57
PLANTZKY, Johannes 274
POEHRER, Guillaume 259
POELLNITZ, Capt 110 126 Deputy Adj Gen 204
POHL, Nicolas 240
PORBACH, Jean 245
PORT, Christian 257 David 285
PORTH, Chretien 258 Jean 245
POSDE, Henrich 280
POWELL, Brig 137 141 154 174 194 Henry 74 132
PRAETORIUS, Christian Julius 71 Col 9 Lt Col 71 110 137
PREE, Maj 49
PRELLER, Jean 268
PRESTON, Capt 5
PRINTZ, Wilhelm 280
PROD, Mathias 265
PROSI, George 269
PROSUHN, Johan Henrich 279

Index

PROSY, George 263
PROTH, Mathieu 268
PUB, George 269
PULVER, Henry 233
QUEBEC, Bishop Of 31
QUELMANN, Pierre 248
RAAB, Valentin 247
RABE, Jean 229
RACH, Rudolph 252 Rudolphe 254
RAINSFORD, Charles 4 Col 5
RANSHEIMER, Johan Jost 277
RAPHKA, George 276
RAPP, Henri 259 Henrich 256 Pierre 249
RAPPERT, George 241
RASCH, Henry 244
RATH, Peter 257
RATNAU, Christian Anton 275
RAU, Jean 233 Johan Henrich 272
RAUBENHEIMER, Adam 254
RAUCH, Joachim 239 Johann 253 Louis 232
RAUSCHENBERG, Johan Conrad 273
RAYMONDT, Peter 267
RECK, Jean George 247
REGENBOGEN, Antoine 258 269
REGES, Guillaume 263 Philippe 234
REIBOLD, Georg Friedrich 282
REICHENBACH, Conrad 253-254 Louis 244
REICHHARD, Johannes 278
REICHMANN, Michael 230
REILL, Pierre 254
REINHARD, Johan 280
REINHARDT, Joseph 266
REIS, Conrad 239 Jacob 276
REISCHEL, Frantz 253
REITZ, Caspar 267 Henry 236 John Adam 278
REMSHARD, Jean 249
REMY, Michael 241
RENSCH, Christian Friedrich 277
RESCH, Henry 233 Nicolas 233
REUTER, Christian 283 Thiery 247
REYMONT, Pierre 266
RHEIN, Conrad 262-263 Frederic 263 Jean Frederic 262
RHEINHARD, Joseph 268
RIBERT, Johan Jost 275
RICHTER, Fredric 270 Jean 251 Jean Gottlob 261 Jean Martin 260 Johann 251
RICHTSTEUR, Christian Friedrich 273
RICUS, Johan 278
RIEBECK, Lt 30

RIEDE, Henry 267
RIEDEL, Jean 261
RIEDESAL, 159
RIEDESEL, 115 192 Gen 72 99 111-112 127 129 137 184 190 222 Maj Gen 37 39-40 44-45 48-51 53 67 70 72 100
RIEFEL, Johan Henrich 272
RIEHL, George 269
RIEMENSCHNEIDER, Friedrich 274
RIESCHT, David 283
RINGELER, Cornelius 256
RIPPERT, Johannes 276
RITTER, Bernard 269 Bernhard 263 Johan Friedrich 280
ROBAT, Auguste 243
ROBERTSON, Lt 137
ROBERTSTON, Mr 225
RODIGER, Nicolas 244
ROEDER, Conrad 284
ROEMELI, Johannes 279
ROEMER, Caspar 282
ROERBER, Caspar 248
ROGES, Guillaume 262
ROHRE, Leopold 244
ROLFFS, Conrad 252
ROLFS, Conrad 254
ROMAN, Christoph 275
ROOS, Antoine 257 Johan Friedrich 256
ROOSE, Godefroid 263 Gottefrid 261
ROPPERT, Conrad 253 255 Jean 255 Johann 253
ROPPETER, Philipp 284
ROSCH, Etienne 244
ROSENBERGER, Jean 240
ROSSMANN, Jacob 257 Jacques 258
ROSSMER, Jean 248
ROTH, Anthon 258 Bernhard 278 Conrad 232 Jean 236 262 Jean Thomas 248 Louis 236 Philippe 236 Wilhelm 257
ROTHE, Johan 273 Johan Dietrich 279
ROTTNER, George 244
ROUSSWAU, Commissary 160
RUB, Adam 233 Jean 232
RUDE, Henrich 275
RUEBELING, Samuel 273
RUFFER, Daniel 238
RUHL, Philippe 239
RUL, Caspar 236
RULLMANN, George 236 Jean 245
RUMPF, Matheus 252
RUPERT, Pierre 266
RUPPEL, Conrad 235 Johannes 257
RUPPERT, Michael 285
RUTHARD, Johan Peter 278

Index

RUTSCHER, Frederic 248
RUTZ, Johan Adam 274
SALANS, Baron 198
SALTZMANN, Louis 246
SANDERS, Capt 5
SANDIG, Henrich 276
SANTER, Johann Gottfried 284
SARTORIUS, Carl August 103 Charles Augusta 229 Lt 108
SATLER, Philip Jacob 277
SAUER, Conrad 250 Jean 232
SAUERWEIN, Christoph 249
SAUNDERS, Admiral 8
SAURLAND, Johannes 281
SCCHWAB, Adam 234
SCHACHT, Fredric 269
SCHAD, Caspar 244 Thome 237
SCHADEL, George 239
SCHAEFER, Anton Chretien 261 Conrad 268 Gotthard 270 Jacques 255 Johan 272 Johannes 280 Joseph 278 Nicolas 268 Peter 280 Philip 272 Wilhelm 279
SCHAEFFER, Gregor 249 Jacob 253 Johan Dietrich 275 Johannes 276 Thomas 253
SCHAFFER, Conrad 267 Frederich 265 George 267 Jacques 240 Michael 266
SCHALL, Joseph 277
SCHALLER, Francois 269
SCHAMBACH, Johannes 277
SCHAPER, Wilhelm Christoph 279
SCHATTACK, Pierre 254
SCHAUBERGER, Jean 239
SCHAUER, Theophile 243
SCHAUM, Jean 263
SCHAUS, Caspar 280
SCHAWACK, Pierre 269
SCHEEFER, Frederic 248
SCHEEL, Capt 93 108 113 Carl August 62 88 Charles Auguste 229
SCHEERMESSER, Andreas 279
SCHEFER, Balthasar 237 Chretien 231 Conrad 240 Jean Jr 235 Martin 231 Paul Guillaume 229 Philippe 238
SCHEFFER, Pierre 247
SCHEID, Valentin 260 262
SCHEIMAR, Frantz 281
SCHELLENBERG, George Frederic 232
SCHELLHAAS, Lorentz 277 Martin 277
SCHENCK, Henri 267 Henry 269 Jean 232
SCHENTZELL, Gottlieb 271
SCHERER, Henry 236
SCHERRING, Johan George 278
SCHEURER, George 265

SCHILLING, Guillaume 262 269 Henry Jr 233 Henry Sr 233
SCHILT, Johan Jacob 276
SCHILTHEIS, Jacob 281
SCHIMMING, Conrad 241
SCHINDLING, Jacob 274
SCHITTER, Guillaume 243
SCHLATTERER, Christian 252
SCHLAUG, Joseph 257
SCHLAUSH, Paul 236
SCHLERETH, Adam 257
SCHLERETT, Adam 258
SCHLINGLUST, Conrad 240
SCHLUCHTERLEIN, Philip 267
SCHMID, Andre 261 Chretien 269 George 250 Heinrich Wilhelm 285 Henry 245 Jean 269 Jean Philipp 261 Johan Friedrich 277 Johan Henrich 275 Johannes 276 280 Joseph 275 Ludewig 274 Mathias 272
SCHMIDT, Chretien 265 Gerhard 242 Heinrich 253 Jacque 266 Jean 229-230 Jean Sr 230 Leonhardt 249 Michel 248 Nicolas 232
SCHMIETT, Conrad 246
SCHMITH, Andre 263 Guillaume 259 Jacob 258 Jacques 259 Philippe 263 Valentin 263
SCHMITT, Caspar 235 Conrad 236 George 237 Jacques 240 Jean Med 230 Johann 253 Melchior 231 240 Nicolas 239 Wilhelm 257
SCHMITZ, George 283
SCHMOLL, Christoph 245
SCHMORR, Benjamin 262-263
SCHNABEL, Caspar 258 Conrad 266
SCHNABELL, Conrad 268
SCHNEIDER, Daniel 282 Elias 260 264 Friedrich 273 George Wilhelm 273 Guillaume 255 Henry 245 Jean 259 Martin 272 Michael 267 Peter 285 Phillipe 246 Pierre 262 Thoma 242 Wilhelm 252
SCHNETTER, Nicolas 245
SCHOBERT, Joseph 278
SCHOELL, 106 Capt 88 Frederic Louis 235
SCHOENAUER, Peter Wilhelm 284
SCHOENEWOLTZ, Johann Heinrich 285
SCHOEPNER, 267
SCHONBURGER, Pierre 231
SCHONER, Jean 238
SCHOPNER, Henry 265
SCHOTT, Charles 232

Index

SCHRADER, Justus 275
SCHRAMM, Johann George 284
SCHRANCK, Johannes 281
SCHREIBER, Conrad 285 George 235
  Henri 262-263 Ulrich 246
SCHREINER, Conrad 234
SCHRODER, Jean 247 Johan Conrad 276
SCHROEDER, Chretien 261 Pierre 233
SCHROTH, Henri 255
SCHUBERT, Jean 270
SCHUBERTH, Johan Adam 274
SCHUCH, Caspar 245
SCHUCHEN, Johann Sebastian 284
SCHUCKARD, Paul 266 268
SCHULER, Jean 236
SCHULTZ, Carl Wilhelm 281 Conrad 266 268
SCHUMAN, Benedictus 281
SCHUMM, Henry 230
SCHUSMMER, George 254
SCHUSTER, August 257 259 Caspar 280
  Johan Theis 273
SCHWAB, Henry 236 Jean George 247
  Pierre 233
SCHWALM, Chretien 244 270
SCHWART, Christian Langen 273
SCHWARTZBICH, Peter 277
SCHWARZ, Johann 284 Wilhelm 252
SCHWARZHAUPT, Henry 236
SCHWEINSBERGER, Hieronime 238
SCHWIMMER, Louis 265
SCHWIND, Jean 234
SCHWINGHAMER, Nicolas 277
SCMID, Francois 230
SEE, Jean 234
SEEBACH, Conrad 243
SEELANDER, Chretien 267
SEELICH, Jean 231
SEIBERT, Balthasar 267-268 Friedrich 111
  Philippe 230
SEIBT, Jean Gottefrid 261
SEIDEL, Jean 270
SEIFFERT, Lt 114 133 144 154 157 165 179
SEILER, Jean 236
SEINIMGEN, Christophle 263
SELTZER, George 247 Jean 239
SEMMINGEN, Christophle 260
SENTNER, Jacob 253
SENTZELL, Nicolas 248 Pierre 247
SENZEL, Jean 235
SERENY, Jacques 268 270
SESTMAN, Henrichen 277
SEYDIL, Johannes 258

SEYN, Johannes 275
SICKENBERGER, Jean Weil 239
SIEBELITZ, Wilhelm 276
SIEBENHAAR, Francois 259 Franz 257
SIEBERT, Ensign 90 117 135 141 149 157
  George 243 Heinrich 82 Henry 229
  Jean George 248 Lt 165 172 184 188
  194 196 208 216 221
SIEFFERT, Lt 86 107
SIEGEL, George 236
SIGMUND, Johan Ulrich 276
SILBERLING, Conrad 266
SIMON, Adam 260 Conrad 236 Martin 251
  Michael 249
SINGER, Frederic 260 Guillaume 263
SINTZ, Peter 282
SIRY, Wolfgang 259
SKEEN, William 195
SKENE, Col 156 Gov 164
SOHL, Charles Frederic 242
SOHN, Adam Johan Jacob 280
SOMER, Johan Georg 274
SOMMERLADE, Conrad 239
SONDEMAN, Johan Martin 275
SOUTHERLAND, Nicholaus 144
SPAETH, Col 9
SPAHN, Adam 266 Caspar 248 253 Conrad
  231 Jean 249
SPALT, Johan Elias 283
SPANGENBERG, George Dittmar 246
SPANGERBERG, Henry 265
SPANIER, Anselme 244
SPATZ, Gottlieb 252 254
SPECHT, 199 Brig 74 135 141 162 169 180
  200-201 Brig Gen 33 Friedrich 116
  Henrich 273
SPENGLER, George 241
SPETH, Ernst 135 Lt Col 187
SPIELMANN, Conrad 242 Pierre 265
SPRIESTERBACH, Henrich 282
SPRIZERSBACH, Johan Wilhelm 278
SSCHENGER, Bernhard 249
STAASY, Henry 232
STADERMANN, Jean 270
STAHL, Jean 269
STAHRENFENGER, Henry 266
STAM, Johan Georg 276
STAMIN, Martin 263
STAMM, George 230 Martin 263
STANG, Johan George 273
STARCK, Caspar 230 Philippe 267 Phillip 257
STAUBER, Jean 270
STAUBERAND, Chretien 260

301

Index

STAUDINGER, Ernst 251
STEGER, Louis 262 Michel 259
STEIN, Conrad 241 Frederic 238 George 237 Gottefrid 261 Heinrich 257 Henri 259 Jost 266 Pierre 239
STEINBACH, Michael 260
STEINBEGER, Michael 258
STEINHAUER, Frantz Anton 274 Johannes 273
STEINHOFF, Johannes 275
STEINMACHER, Valentin 261
STEINWEG, Johannes 281
STEMMETZ, Chretien 259
STENZELL, Sammuel 268 Samuel 266
STEPHAN, Adam 257
STERN, Georg 252
STERNBRING, Daniel 252
STHL, Valentin 257
STICKEL, Henry 233 Phillip 256
STIER, Gottlieb 245
STILL, Christophle 233
STILLING, Georg 258 George 259
STIRNER, Jean 268-269
STOBAND, Johannes 283
STOCK, Michael 231 Valentin 244
STOLL, Henry 245
STOPEL, Nicolaus 108
STOPNELL, George 278
STOPPEL, Nicolas 235
STORCK, David 273 Siegmont 251
STORR, Frederic 262
STRAUS, Jacob 277
STREBE, Johan Henrich 277
STREBEL, Friederich 252
STREICH, Friederich 252
STREITEL, Babtiste 266
STROH, Henry Paul 247 Martin 250 Pierre 231
STROTH, Jean 266
STRUETER, John Martin 278
STUBENHAUER, Jean 255
STUBINGER, George 270
STUMPH, Jacob 273
STURM, Ernst 266
SULGER, Jean 244
SUSS, George 270
SUSSEBACH, Johannes 284
SUSSNER, George 268
SUTHERLAND, Lt Col 214 222
TACK, Jacques 239 Philippe Charles 230
TANNEBERG, Johan Friedrich Wilhelm 279
TELLER, Lorentz 253
TEMPELL, George 246

THEER, Henrich 278
THEILHEIMER, Georg 257 George 258
THENELL, Charles 269
THEOBALD, Erneste 229
THIEL, Conrad 282 Joseph 277
THIELEMAN, Wilhelm 280
THIENELL, Charles 259
THIEREDOTT, Conrad 273
THISER, Martin 263
THOENE, Herrnrich 252
THOMA, Philip Martin 281
THOMAS, Daniel 263 Jean Daniel 261 Johan Paul 275
TOPFER, George 243
TRABAND, Conrad 236 Jean 236 250
TRABANDL, Jean 241
TRAEGER, Ephraim 274
TRAMM, Christian 253
TRAU, Philippe 235
TRAUT, Christophle 231 Conrad 238 Jean 230 Philippe 230
TREULIEB, Guillaume 230
TROBER, Ludwig 257
TROSTLER, Joseph 257 259
TROTT, Carl W 272
TRUMPER, George 254 Michael 252
TURCK, Henri 261
TWISS, Lt 134
UFFELMANN, Michel 247
UFFER, Henry 247
UFFERMANN, Nicolas Jr 233 Nicolas Sr 233
UHL, Adam 242
UHRLEDIG, Henry 232
ULLIUS, Johann Wilhelm 284
ULLRICH, Jean Conrad 260 Pierre 271
ULM, Joseph 277
UMM, Wendel 261
UMPFENBACH, Jean George 261
UMSTATTER, Heinrich 257
UNGAR, Andre Jr 236 Andre Sr 235
UNGER, Eberhard 249 George Charles 239
UNSCHUCK, Conrad 250
URBACH, Adam 229
UTZ, Friedrich 257
VALENTINE, Capt 151 Quartermaster Gen 174
VANDERHOOPE, 4
VAUPEL, Corp 108 Samuel 238 Sr Corp 91
VEHLER, Jean George 262
VEHS, George 267
VEITH, Francois 259 269 Guillaumes 243
VELTEN, Augustin 230
VEMPEL, George 238

Index

VETTON, Adam 236
VICARIO, Jean 244
VINPUCKLER, Lt Count 117
VOELCKER, Hans Claus 273
VOELP, Jean 265
VOGD, Frantz Joseph 276 Stephan 276 Wilhelm 280
VOGELER, Philip 277
VOIGT, Hartman 266 Hartmann 268
VOLCKER, Johannes 277
VOLMERT, Nicolas 250
VOLTZ, Conrad 233 Henry 232 Marten 236 Martin 93 Musketeer 115
VOMENT, Johan Henrich 272
VONBARNER, Ferdinand Albrecht 95 Maj 63 205
VONBISCHHAUSEN, Lt 115 152 165 189 213 215
VONBISCHHHAUSEN, Lt 186
VONBUTTLAR, Lt 81-82 89 106 113 115 135 142 156 167-168 181 185 188 194 197 207 222 Maurice 81
VONDENVELDEN, Wilhelm 251
VONDERWEYD, Conrad 281
VONEHRENKROOK, Johann Gustav 73 104 Maj 161
VONESCHWEGE, Christian 81 Lt 91-92 119 138 141-142 148 187-188 206 208 215-216
VONFOERSTNER, Standard Bearer 61
VONFORSTNER, Flag-bearer 87
VONGALL, 149 Brig 39 66 74-75 82 86 89 92 94 103-104 106 108 116-117 125 129 132-133 138 180 185 187 187 196 207 219 Brig Gen 33 48-49 62 88 193 204 Col 9 11 Court Marshal 2 Wilhelm Rudolph 33 81
VONGEREN, Capt 217
VONGERMANN, Friedrich 117
VONGEYLING, 1st Lt 88 2nd Lt 88 Ensign 179 181 185 194 197 202 222 222 Friedrich 62 85 Lt 92 111 113 129 148-149 161 166 178-179 185 190 194 196 213-214 216
VONHEERWAGON, Ensign 88
VONHILLE, Flag Bearer 61
VONHOHORST, 2nd Lt 88 Ensign 88
VONHOHORT, 2nd Lt 106
VONHORST, Ludwig 62 80
VONLANDAU, Lt 130
VONLINDAU, Lt 93 111 113 150 163 168 172 184 197 208 213 216 224
VONLUCKE, Maj 149 210 225
VONMENGE, Maj 167 181
VONPASSERN, Capt 62 81-82 84-85 Ludwig Wilhelm 88 Maj 62 88 150 174 185 213 221
VONPINCIER, Christian Theodor 61
VONPOELLNITS, Brig Maj 45
VONPOELLNITZ, Adj Gen 138 Brig Maj 47 52 Capt 61 71 Deputy Adj Gen 62 73 Julius Ludwig August 38
VONPOELNITZ, Capt 88
VONPUCKLER, Count 135 Lt 90 Lt Count 82 141 144 154 156 168 188 190 201 210 221 225
VONRANTZOW, Count 61 87
VONRHRENKROOK, Maj 184
VONRICHTERLEBEN, Ensign 85 146
VONRICHTERSLEBEN, Ensign 79 82 91 112 125
VONRIEDEEL, Gen 52
VONRIEDESEL, Frierdrich Adolph 87 Gen 52 67 72 126-127 138 142 180 182 184 190-191 193 204-205 209 222 L S 42 Maj 171 Maj Gen 38 50 52 61 63 67-68 70 72 87 95 100 124-125 132 153 158 160-162 164-165 167 169-170 174 185 190 199
VONSCHACHTEN, Capt 135 144 144 149 152 206 210 214
VONSCHOELL, Capt 88 106-107 146 Friedrich Ludwig 84
VONSIEFFERT, Lt 94
VONSPECHT, Brig 133 Johann Friedrich 33
VONSPETH, Lt Col 163
VONTROTT, Lt 89 105 113 115 132-133 135 138 144 148 157-158 172 181 203 213 215 225
VONWEYHERS, Ensign 94 114-115 131 144 152 165 178 187 189-190 195 201 208 213 224 Ernst 86
WACHS, Conrad 243
WACHTELL, Bernhard 275
WACHTERSHAUSER, Jean 231
WAGEMANN, Laurent 263 Lorentz 251
WAGENER, Johann 257 Ludwig 257
WAGNER, Frederic 259 Fredric 269 George 261 Jean 259 268 Nicolas 266 268 Philipp 253 Philippe 255
WALDSCHMID, Hartman 273
WALL, Conrad 246
WALLER, Daniel Jr 235 Pierre 247
WALLISSER, Feorge 266
WALT, Philippe 238
WALTER, Jean George 247
WALTHER, Philip 280

Index

WALTZMULLER, George 280
WALZER, Johan Gabriel 274
WAMBACH, Johan Jacob 274
WANDROCK, David 284
WANGENHEIM, Adam Jules 284
WEBER, Andre 244 Caspar 244 Chrretien 249 Conrad 270 276 Jean 232 Johann 253 Pierre 238 269
WECTZELL, Nicolas 248
WEGENER, Conrad 271
WEGMANN, Pierre 248
WEIBELL, Frederic 268 George 266
WEIBLING, Charles 232
WEIDNER, Michel 253
WEIGAND, Jean 233 Nicolas 266-267 Oswald 266 268 Pierre 233
WEIL, Hartmann 234 Thomas 247
WEIMAR, Adam 244 Auguste 237
WEINEM, Leonhard 267-268
WEINGARTNER, Frederic 238
WEININER, Frederic 268
WEINLEIN, Christian 251
WEINRICH, Henri Auguste 260
WEISMAN, Johan Conrad 276
WEISMAURER, Johan Peter 276
WEISS, Frederic 262 Jean George 260 Surgeon's Mate 85-86
WEISSENSTEIN, Charles 255 Johann 252 Pierre 233
WEIZEL, Jean 239
WELAN, Capt 129
WELTOR, Caspar 239
WEMZEL, Jacques 243
WENDERICH, Chretien 255 Johann 253
WERHEIM, Conrad 231 Laurent 237
WERLING, Jean 241
WERNER, Carl Henrich 279 Chretien Freericv 241 Christoph 257 Jacob 282 Jacques 245 267 269 Jean 266 Johan J 272 Laurent 236 Nicolas 231 Philippe 245
WERTHS, Paul 274
WESTPHAL, Godefroid 230 Henry 232
WETZLER, Johan Jacob 282
WEYD, Jean 237
WEYDEMAN, Philip 277
WEYHERS, Ensign 93-94 210 Ernest 238
WIDERAM, Christople 241
WIEDMAN, Johan Georg 276
WIEGAND, Balthasar 276 Matheus 276
WIESELL, Conrad 270
WIESENECKER, Johan Peter 257
WIESNER, Chretien 254

WIESSENER, Christian 252
WILCKENS, Jean Philipp 262
WILD, Alexander Joseph 274
WILHELM, Diedrich 285 Jean 245
WILHELME, Ernst 256
WILKINSON, Lt 225
WILL, Jean 231
WILLE, George 265
WILLMANN, Michel 247
WIMMER, Fredrich 265
WINCKLER, Johan Herman 256
WINTER, Christoph 279 Johan 256
WIRSING, Christian 275 278
WISKERMAN, Christophle 238
WISSENBACH, Drummer 80 Jean Philippe 230 Joseph Philipp 79
WITHSACK, Sammuel 268
WITTGENSTEIN, Capt 260 262
WITTMANN, Carl 256 Henri Charles 270 Johann 253
WITTSACK, Samuel 266
WOCHLER, Jean Frederic 246
WOLF, Caspar 261 Henri 261
WOLFE, James 8
WOLFF, Guillaume 259 269
WOLLENDORF, Daniel 271
WUEST, Balthasar 278
WURTZ, Michel 251
WUST, Johannes 257
WUTH, Carl 256
YORKE, Joseph 5
ZAUN, Gerlack 274
ZEH, Caspar 243
ZEHNER, Adolph 241 Nicolas 232 Pierre 233
ZEILLMANN, Louis 270
ZELLMANN, Daniel 261 264
ZETH, Ulric 231
ZEUL, Conrad 231
ZICKLAMM, Jean George 248
ZIEGENHAIN, Pierre 262
ZIEGENHAYN, Jean Pierre 260
ZIEGLER, George 239
ZIEWE, Conrad 241
ZIMMERMAN, Carl Joseph 273 Heinrich 257
ZIMMERMANN, Jean 238
ZINCK, Jean 244
ZINCKHAN, Jean 233 Martin 242
ZIPF, Adam 230 Charles Frederic 241 Louis 266
ZIPSY, Adam 236
ZISCHLER, George 249

Index

ZOHN, Henry 247
ZORBACH, Charles 234 David 247 George
    247
ZORN, Jean 258
ZUMBE, Wilhelm Matheus 279
ZURCKER, Chretien 255
ZWHNER, Adolf 108

THE AUTHOR

Bruce E. Burgoyne was born 25 October 1924 in Benton Harbor, Michigan, and is married with three grown sons. His wife Marie, a Doctor of Education from the University of Southern California, is a helpful research companion and source of encouragement. Mr. Burgoyne's education includes a Master of Arts in Social Science (History, Economics, and Government) from Trinity University in San Antonio, Texas, plus course work at half a dozen other colleges and universities in America and overseas. He has also completed numerous military courses in such subjects as German language, Counterintelligence, and Public Information.

His employment, in addition to recently teaching a seminar course on the Hessians at Delaware State University, has included twenty years of military service in the Navy, Army, and Air Force, and six years as a civilian intelligence officer with the Army. During his military and civilian service he lived six years in Germany during which time he attended German language school in Oberammergau and two months of in-depth study, living in German households and undergoing Berlitz-type training. His daily duties required interviewing and interrogating in German, which further developed his knowledge of the language.

His forty years of research on the role of the Hessians in the American Revolutionary War have taken him and his wife to archives in England and Holland, as well as those in Germany and the United States, and resulted in the translation of more than 35 major Hessian documents.

Other Heritage Books by Bruce E. Burgoyne:

A Hessian Officer's Diary of the American Revolution Translated from an Anonymous Ansbach-Bayreuth Diary and the Prechtel Diary

Canada During the American Revolutionary War: Lieutenant Friedrich Julius von Papet's Journal of the Sea Voyage to North America and the Campaign Conducted There

CD: A Hessian Diary of the American Revolution

CD: A Hessian Officer's Diary of the American Revolution

CD: A Hessian Report on the People, the Land, the War of Eighteenth Century America, as Noted in the Diary of Chaplain Philipp Waldeck, 1776-1780

CD: Ansbach-Bayreuth Diaries from the Revolutionary War

CD: Canada During the America Revolutionary War

CD: Diaries of Two Ansbach Jaegers

CD: The Hessian Collection, Volume 1: Revolutionary War Era

CD: They Also Served: Women with the Hessian Auxiliaries

CD: Waldeck Soldiers of the American Revolutionary War

Defeat, Disaster, and Dedication

Diaries of Two Ansbach Jaegers

Eighteenth Century America (A Hessian Report on the People, the Land, the War) as Noted in the Diary of Chaplain Philipp Waldeck (1776-1780)

Enemy Views: The American Revolutionary War as Recorded by the Hessian Participants

Georg Pausch's Journal and Reports of the Campaign in America, as Translated from the German Manuscript in the Lidgerwood Collection in the Morristown Historical Park Archives, Morristown, N.J.

Hessian Chaplains: Their Diaries and Duties

Hessian Letters and Journals and a Memoir

Journal of a Hessian Grenadier Battalion

Journal of the Hesse-Cassel Jaeger Corps

Most Illustrious Hereditary Prince: Letters to Their Prince from Members of Hesse-Hanau Military Contingent in the Service of England During the American Revolution

Notes from a British Museum

Order Book of the Hesse-Cassel von Mirbach Regiment

Revolutionary War Letters Written by Hessian Officers: Generals Wilhelm von Knyphausen, Carl Wilhelm Von Hachenberg, Friedrich Wilhelm von Lossberg, Johann Friedrich Cochenhausen, Friedrich Von Riedesel and Major Carl Leopold von Baurmeister
Bruce E. Burgoyne and Dr. Marie E. Burgoyne

The Diary of Lieutenant von Bardeleben and Other von Donop Regiment

The Hesse-Cassel Mirbach Regiment in the American Revolution

The Third English-Waldeck Regiment in the American Revolutionary War

The Trenton Commanders: Johann Gottlieb Rall and George Washington, as Noted in Hessian Diaries

Waldeck Soldiers of the American Revolutionary War

www.ingramcontent.com/pod-product-compliance
Lightning Source LLC
Chambersburg PA
CBHW052053230426
43671CB00011B/1890